SHOPPING AND TRAVELING IN EXOTIC HONG KONG

Impact Guides available through your local
bookseller or directly from Impact Publications:

Shopping and Traveling in Exotic Asia: Hong Kong, Thailand, Malaysia, Singapore, and Indonesia

Shopping and Traveling the Exotic Caribbean: The Bahamas, Bermuda, Barbados, Dominican Republic, Haiti, Jamaica, St. Martin/Sint Maarten, St. Thomas, and Puerto Rico

Shopping and Traveling in Exotic Hong Kong

Shopping and Traveling in Exotic Indonesia

Shopping and Traveling the Exotic Philippines

Shopping and Traveling in Exotic Singapore and Malaysia

Shopping and Traveling in Exotic Thailand

Shopping in Exciting Australia and Papua New Guinea

Shopping in Exotic Places: Hong Kong, Korea, Thailand, Indonesia, and Singapore

Shopping the Exotic South Pacific: Australia, New Zealand, Papua New Guinea, Fiji, and Tahiti

Available in 1992:

Shopping and Traveling in Exotic India

Shopping and Traveling in Exotic Morocco

SHOPPING AND TRAVELING IN EXOTIC HONG KONG
Your Passport to Asia's Most Incredible Shopping Bazaar

Second Edition

Jo Reimer
Ronald L. Krannich
Caryl Rae Krannich

IMPACT PUBLICATIONS
Woodbridge, VA

**SHOPPING AND TRAVELING IN EXOTIC HONG KONG
Your Passport to Asia's Most Incredible Shopping Bazaar**

Second Edition

Copyright © 1989, 1991 by Jo Reimer, Ronald L. Krannich, and Caryl Rae Krannich

All rights reserved. Printed in the United States of America. No part of this book may be used or reproduced in any manner whatsoever without written permission of the publisher: IMPACT PUBLICATIONS, 4580 Sunshine Court, Woodbridge, VA 22192, Tel. 703/361-7300.

Library of Congress Cataloging-in-Publication Data

Reimer, Jo, 1940-
 Shopping and traveling in exotic Hong Kong : your passport to Asia's most incredible shopping bazaar / Jo Reimer, Ronald L. Krannich, Caryl Rae Krannich.—2nd ed.
  p. cm.
 Rev. ed. of: Shopping in exotic Hong Kong. c1989
 Includes index.
 ISBN 0-942710-43-6
 I. Shopping—Hong Kong—Guide-books. 2. Shopping—Macao—Guidebooks. 3. Shopping—China—Guide-books. 4. Hong Kong—Description and travel—Guide-books. I. Krannich, Ronald L. II. Krannich, Caryl Rae. III. Reimer, Jo. 1940- Shopping in exotic Hong Kong. IV. Title
TX337.H85R44 1991
380.1'45'000255125—dc20   91-20419
                                                              CIP

Cover designed by ABS Graphics, 8564 Custer Court, Manassas, VA 22111, Tel. 703/361-7415.

For information on distribution or quantity discounts, call 703/361-7300 or write to: Sales Department, IMPACT PUBLICATIONS, 4580 Sunshine Court, Woodbridge, VA 22192. Distributed to the trade by National Book Network, 4720 Boston Way, Suite A, Lanham, MD 20706, 301/459-8696.

CONTENTS

Preface xi

PART I
WELCOME TO HONG KONG

CHAPTER ONE
Welcome To Exotic Hong Kong 1
   Shop 'Til You Drop 1
   Happy Capitalists Playing For Time 2
   Prepare For Hong Kong's Pleasures and Pitfalls 3
   Be a Quality Shopper 5
   Approach Hong Kong Right 6
   Do It On Your Own 8
   Join Inexpensive and Convenient Tours 8
   Beware of Recommended Shops 8

CHAPTER TWO
The World According To Hong Kong 11
   A City On the Go 11
   Asia's Economic Powerhouse 12
   A City With Character 13
   A Shopper's Heaven 13
   Paradise On the Harbor 14
   Discover Diversity, Value, and Quality 15

CHAPTER THREE
Know Before You Go 17
   Location and Area 17
   Climate, Seasons, and When To Go 18
   Getting There 19

Documents You Need 20
Recommended Reading 21
Hong Kong Tourist Association 23
Professional Shopping Services 25
Useful Associations 27
Newspapers and Television 28

PART II
TRAVELING SMART

CHAPTER FOUR
Prepare For a Unique Travel and Shopping Adventure 31
Develop An Action Plan 31
Welcome Serendipity and Good Luck 32
Conduct Research and Network For Information 32
Check Customs Regulations 35
Manage Your Money Well 35
Use Credit Cards Wisely 37
Secure Your Valuables 38
Take All Necessary Shopping Information 39
Do Comparative Shopping 40
Keep Track of Receipts 41
Pack Right For Hong Kong 43
Keep It Light 44
Take Comfortable Shoes 44
Choose the Right Clothing 45
Men's Clothing 46
Essential Clothes For Women 46
Throw In a Calculator 49
Carry Business Cards 49
Review Your Packing Checklist 50

CHAPTER FIVE
Arriving and Surviving Hong Kong 53
Arrival 53
Immigration Lines 54
Baggage Retrieval 54

Customs Procedures 55
Departure Tax 55
Airport Security 55
Airport Tourist Services 56
Airport To Hotel Transportation 57
Currency and Exchange Rates 58
Water 59
Electricity 59
Business Hours 60
Transportation 60
Tours and Travel Agents 64
Language 64
Tipping and Service Charges 65
Safety and Security 66
Photography and Film 66
Keeping Fit 66

CHAPTER SIX
Experiencing Conveniences and Inconveniences 68
A Nine-Star City 68
Massive Crowds 69
Questionable Service 70
Touts and Cheating 70
Surprising Restrooms 71
Irritating Smokers 72
Adapt To the Situation 73

CHAPTER SEVEN
Discovering Fine Hotels and Restaurants 74
A Gastronomic Delight 74
Fine Chinese Food and Restaurants 75
Favorite Dining Spots 78
Selecting Accommodations 79
Outstanding Hotels 80

PART III
SHOPPING WELL

CHAPTER EIGHT
Conquering the Streets of Hong Kong 83
　Do Your Homework 83
　Orient Yourself To Key Areas 86
　Map the City 87
　Plan Your Attack 88
　Get a Good Overview of the City 88
　Balance Your Schedule 89
　Locate Quality Shops 89
　Network For Information 90
　Go For Quality 91
　Communicate Your Needs With Clarity 92
　Custom Tailoring—Myths and Realities 93
　Homemade Shoes 95
　Delivery Arrangements 96
　Follow the Rules 96

CHAPTER NINE
Planning, Bargaining, and Procuring Quality Products in the Local Shopping Culture 98
　Bargain For Bargains 98
　Plan and Compare Prices 99
　Treat Stated Prices As Starting Prices 100
　Determine Fair Local Market Values 100
　Prepare For Price Uncertainty 101
　Establish Value and Price 102
　Get the Best Deal Possible 104
　Practice the 12 Rules of Bargaining 105
　Bargain For Needs, Not Greed 112
　Examine Your Goods Carefully 112
　Beware of Scams 112

PART IV
DISCOVERING HONG KONG'S SHOPPING SECRETS

CHAPTER TEN

What To Buy **117**

Exports and Imports 118
Best Bargains 118
Arts and Antiques 119
Handicrafts 122
Carpets and Rugs 123
Furniture 124
Home Furnishings and Accessories 126
China, Porcelain, Crystal, and Glassware 126
Gems and Jewelry 127
Watches 129
Furs 129
Leathergoods 131
Silks and Other Fabrics 131
Tailor-Made Clothing 132
Ready-to-Wear Clothing 133
Shoes 134
Optical Goods 135
Cosmetics and Perfumes 136
Stereo, Hi-Fi, and Video Equipment 136
Televisions, Cameras, and Accessories 136
Computer Hardware and Software 137
Tea 139
More Discoveries 139

CHAPTER ELEVEN

Where To Shop **140**

Shopping Areas 140
Kowloon 141
Hong Kong Island 143
Shopping Centers 147
Hotel Shopping Arcades 149
Department Stores 150
Chinese Emporiums 151

Factory Outlets 153
Markets, Bazaars, and Lanes 155
Shopping On Limited Time 157
Fastest Transportation Between Shopping Areas 160

CHAPTER TWELVE
Packing, Shipping, and Returning Home With Ease 162
Shipping With Ease 163
Packing Right 163
Surveying Your Alternatives 164
Doing Your Own Shipping 165
Arranging Shipments Through Shops 165
Choosing a Local Shipper 166
Deciding on Unaccompanied Baggage 167
Making Arrangements 168
Selecting Services 168
Returning Home and Facing Customs 169

CHAPTER THIRTEEN
Enjoying Greater Hong Kong, Macau, and China 172
Favorite Hong Kong Pleasures 172
Discovering Macau 173
Journeying Into China 177
Returning To Paradise 180

PART V
APPENDICES

A
Custom Tailoring 183
Choices Galore 183
Plan Your Tailoring Needs 184
Men's Tailoring Concerns 184
Women's Tailoring Issues 184
Beware of Ultrasuede 186
Tailoring Skills and Customer Satisfaction 186

Contents ix

    Choosing a Tailor Shop 187
    Finding Appropriate Fabrics 189
    Specifying the Right Style 191
    Communicating With Tailors 193
    Avoid Haste 194
    Expected Costs 194
    Getting a Good Fit 195
    Custom-Made Shirts 198

B
The Shops 199
    Arts and Antiques 199
    Cameras 202
    Carpets and Rugs 202
    China and Porcelain 203
    Computerware 203
    Fabric, Yarn, and Sewing Notions 204
    Furniture 204
    Furs 205
    Gems and Jewelry 205
    Handicrafts 207
    Jade 208
    Leathergoods 209
    Optical Goods 209
    Pearls 210
    Ready-to-Wear Clothing 210
    Shirt-makers 213
    Silver 214
    Tailored Clothing 214
    Shoes and Boots 215
    Watches 216

C
Hotels 217
    Kowloon 218
    Hong Kong Island 219

Index 221

PREFACE

Exotic Hong Kong offers wonderful traveling and shopping opportunities for those who know what to look for, where to go, and how to shop it properly.

Since we first visited Hong Kong over 20 years ago, Hong Kong has lured us back again and again. It's a wonderful city. Fascinating and fast paced Hong Kong is Asia's most incredible shopping bazaar. We return home from each trip with wonderful purchases to enhance our homes and wardrobes—including clothing, jewelry, carpets, ceramics, art, embroideries, leathergoods, and furniture. For us Hong Kong is one giant shopping high, complete with great hotels, outstanding cuisine, and exotic sights and sounds. Hong Kong is both convenient and comfortable. If approached properly, it may well become one of your favorite travel and shopping destinations.

The chapters that follow represent a particular perspective on shopping in Hong Kong. Based on several years experience in shopping Hong Kong's many streets, as well as leading shopping groups to Hong Kong, we purposefully decided to write more than just another travel guide with a few pages on shopping. Moreover, the book had to go beyond other shopping books that primarily concentrate on the *"whats"* and *"wheres"* of shopping. Our experience convinces us that there is a need for a book that carefully explains the *"how-tos"* of shopping in Hong Kong along with the *"whats"* and *"wheres."* Such a book would both educate and guide you through the shopping maze of Hong Kong. This book, as do other volumes in the

"Impact Guide" series, focuses on the shopping **process** as well as provides you with the necessary details for making excellent shopping **choices** in specific shopping areas, arcades, centers, department stores, markets, and shops.

Rather than just describe the *"what"* and *"where"* of travel and shopping, we include the critical *"how"*—what to do before you depart on your trip as well as while you are in Hong Kong. We believe you and others are best served with a book which leads to both **understanding and action**. Therefore, you'll find little in these pages about the history, culture, economics, and politics of Hong Kong; these topics are covered well in other types of travel books. Instead, our focus is on the whole shopping process in reference to alternative shopping choices in Hong Kong.

The perspective we develop throughout this book is based on our belief that traveling should be more than just another adventure in eating, sleeping, sightseeing, and taking pictures of unfamiliar places. Whenever possible, we attempt to bring to life the fact that Hong Kong has real people and interesting products that you, the visitor, will find exciting. This is a city of talented designers, craftspeople, traders, and entrepreneurs who offer you some wonderful opportunities to participate in their society through their shopping process. When you leave Hong Kong, you will take with you not only some unique experiences and memories but also quality products that you will certainly appreciate for years to come.

Our focus on **the shopping process** is important for several reasons. The most important one is the fact that few non-Asians are prepared for Asian shopping cultures. Shops may be filled with familiar looking goods, but when there are no price tags on items, the process of acquiring them can be difficult if you do not understand such basic processes as bargaining, communicating, and shipping. What, for example, will you do if you want a suit made but you have never worked with a tailor? What type of fabric, cut, lining, lapel, pockets, buttons, and stitching do you want? Can you explain in detail exactly what you want? What should you do when you find a lovely piece of jewelry but no price tag is displayed? How do you know you are paying a *"fair"* price? More important, how do you know you are getting exactly what you bargained for in terms of quality and authenticity? And if you buy large items, how will you get them back home? These *"how"* questions go beyond the basic *"what"* and *"where"* of shopping and the answers will be very important to ensuring that you will have a successful trip to Hong Kong.

We have not hesitated to make qualitative judgments about shopping in Hong Kong. If we just presented you with shopping information, we would do you a disservice by not sharing our discoveries, both good and bad. While we know that our judgments may not be valid for everyone, we offer them as **reference points** from which you can make your own decisions. Our major emphasis is on quality shopping. We look for shops which offer excellent quality and styles which we think are appropriate for western wardrobes and homes. If you share our concern for quality shopping, you will find many of our recommendations useful to your own shopping.

Buying items of quality does not mean you must spend a great deal of money on shopping. It means that you have taste, you are selective, you buy what fits into your wardrobe and home. If you shop in the right places, you will find quality products. If you understand the shopping process, you will get good value for your money. Shopping for quality may not be cheap but neither need it be expensive. But most important, shopping for quality in Hong Kong is fun and it results in lovely items which can be enjoyed for years to come!

Throughout this book we have included *"tried and tested"* shopping information. We make judgments based upon our experience—not on judgments or sales pitches from others. Our research was quite simple: we did a great deal of shopping and we looked for quality products. We acquired some fabulous items, and gained valuable knowledge in the process. However, we could not make purchases in every shop nor do we have any guarantee that your experiences will be the same as ours. Shops close, ownership or management changes, and the shop you visit may not be the same as the one we shopped. So use this as a start, but ask questions and make your own judgments before you buy.

Special thanks goes to the Hong Kong Tourist Association for assisting us with this project. Their commitment to providing the very best services for visitors is exceptional and clearly reflected in the many maps, brochures, and tourist guides they produce as well as the tours and information services offered visitors. Be sure to take advantage of the many services available through this fine organization.

We also wish to thank Omni The Hong Kong Hotel (Tsimshatsui, Kowloon) and the Marriott Hotel (Central/Wanchai, Hong Kong) for their hospitality. Both are excellent hotels, centrally located for shopping tourists, and offering fine accommodations, restaurants, and related services. We highly recommend them as your *"home away from home"* when visiting Hong Kong.

We wish you well in your travel and shopping adventure in Hong Kong. The book is designed to be used on the streets of Hong Kong. If you **plan** your journey according to the first seven chapters, **handle the shopping process** according to the next two chapters, and **navigate** the streets of Hong Kong based on the final chapters and appendices, you should have a marvelous time. You'll discover some exciting places, acquire some choice items, and return home with fond memories. If you put this book to use, it will become your passport to shopping in exotic Hong Kong!

PART I
WELCOME TO HONG KONG

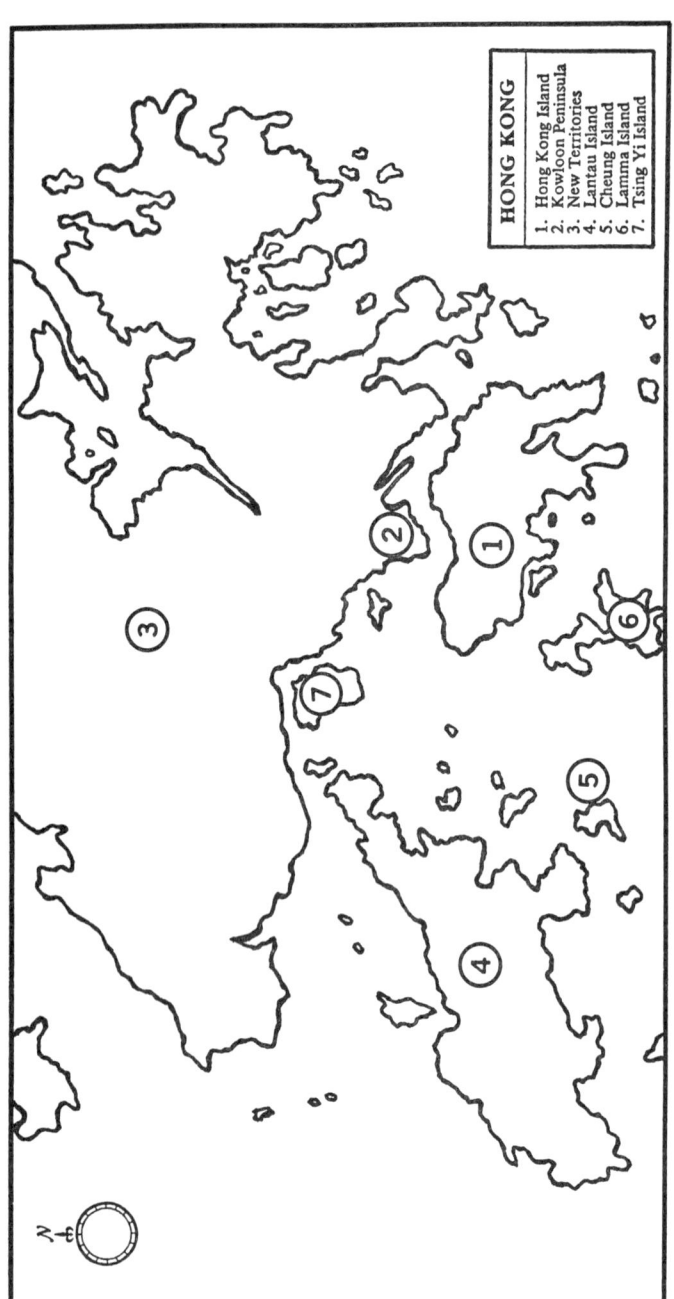

1 WELCOME TO EXOTIC HONG KONG

Welcome to the world's most exciting shopping bazaar! If you love to shop, see exotic sights, and pamper yourself with outstanding food and accommodations, then Hong Kong may well become your favorite shopping and travel destination. You are about to experience one of the world's most unique and fascinating travel adventures—all in the comfort and convenience of a grand city!

Here is one of the world's great cities. Nestled on a spectacular harbor and clinging to majestic hills, Hong Kong is a vibrant city of exciting people, places, and things. It's a big, crowded city populated by millions of hard working people in the import, export, and re-export businesses who have transformed this British colony into one of the world's great economic miracles. A surprisingly easy city to navigate, Hong Kong offers a kaleidoscope of varied pleasures that beckon first-time visitors to return again and again to indulge their shopping and travel fancies.

SHOP 'TIL YOU DROP

Hong Kong is one of the world's most fascinating cities. The beauty of the Hong Kong harbor viewed from Victoria Peak and the always scenic ride on the Star Ferry between Kowloon Peninsula and Hong Kong Island are the two most noteworthy pauses from what is otherwise the primary tourist goal in Hong Kong—shopping. The overflow of consumer goods crammed into the dazzling array of small row shops, shopping malls, hotel shopping arcades, department stores, chic boutiques, emporiums, and colorful open-air markets totally assault the Hong Kong visitor like no other city in the world. Window shopping does not last long as one becomes quickly immersed in an orgy of buying.

Hong Kong is where you can literally *"shop 'til you drop"* and then wake up in anticipation of more to come. Intoxicating and addictive, shopping in Hong Kong is like gambling in Las Vegas—impersonal, sometimes sleazy, capitalism run amuck. It's a city that is likely to liberate you from the ordinary constraints of living and working back home. Like a kid in a candy store, you may want to taste everything. In Hong Kong you may do things you never thought of doing back home—and feel great in having been so adventuresome!

Faced with an incredible number of choices, many uninitiated visitors become completely overwhelmed by this city. Some have difficulty making decisions among so many competing alternatives. Others—perhaps feeling they have died and gone to shoppers' heaven—lose all control of their shopping senses and go on a shopping binge! Once home, their local shopping centers look pathetic in comparison to their Hong Kong experience. But more important, they return home with a wonderful collection of memories and stories about a truly exotic place called Hong Kong.

HAPPY CAPITALISTS PLAYING FOR TIME

Hong Kong is all about money—the pursuit of money, the pleasures of spending money, and the uncertain future for money. The business of Hong Kong is business, be it manufacturing, trade, commerce, finance, or tourism. Despite China's treaty to acquire this city and territory in 1997, Hong Kong remains a very pragmatic and capitalistic city. Playing many roles, above all it teaches China and the world how to do better business. At least until 1997, tomorrow is now. As one writer, Richard Hughes, so eloquently captured Hong Kong's character, this is a *"borrowed place living on borrowed time."*

Hong Kong also is an exciting place living an economic dream come true. Political winds may blow in Beijing and London, but Hong Kong remains one of the world's most unique happenings. For history buffs, it's a fascinating story of success against all odds—of pirates, missionaries, mercenaries, traders, bankers, entrepreneurs, adventurers, refugees, *taipans,* and *tai tais.* It's the Orient at its most inscrutable, audacious, and aggressive self. It's where the East met the West and decided the two could work quite well together, thank you. It's where the Chinese and expatriates worked together in teaching the British a lesson in successful capitalism while British officials played their classic games of bureaucrat, soldier, politician, and keeper of a once glorious colonial empire. This is where the sun finally sets on the British Empire but continuously rises for Hong Kong's expatriate Americans, British, Japanese, and Australians, and its hard working, entrepreneurial Chinese—the ones who really run the place.

You must experience Hong Kong to understand what this is all about. You must walk its streets; poke around its lanes; climb its hills; ride its ferries and trams; tour its roads; visit its factories, stores, shopping complexes, hotels, towns, villages, and islands; and watch its *tai tais* parade their class and wealth at tea time in the Peninsula Hotel lobby. If you are not careful, you just may *"shop 'til you drop"* in what undoubtedly is one of the world's most fabulous cities for merchants, traders, tourists, and seasoned shoppers. If you don't learn to love this magnetic place, something may be wrong with you. Indeed, it isn't difficult to spend several days shopping in Hong Kong and still wish you had more time to further explore its many shopping and travel pleasures!

PREPARE FOR HONG KONG'S PLEASURES AND PITFALLS

Traveling to Hong Kong can be both a rewarding and a punishing experience. Many people come here for business purposes. Others stop over on their way to other Asian destinations. And still others specifically come to Hong Kong to engage in a shopping spree. Whatever your reason for visiting Hong Kong, you will undoubtedly find unique shopping opportunities as you engage in an extremely rewarding travel adventure.

Hong Kong rewards travelers who seek new experiences, set specific goals, plan well, remain flexible, are open to serendipity, and have good luck. The rewards are found in enjoying the travel process itself, acquiring new experiences, and returning home with a storehouse of wonderful memories recorded on film, savored in funny anecdotes, and remembered by exciting Hong Kong purchases.

Yet, travel is not all pleasure. At times it is hard work and can be a punishing experience. The best laid plans can go awry. Canceled flights, crowded airports, missing luggage, long lines, shoddy service, illness, overpricing, misrepresentation, unhealthy environments, and disastrous weather can spoil what was otherwise planned as this year's dream vacation. Despite such trials and tribulations, we continue to seek new and enjoyable travel experiences because we love the adventure of discovering unique and exotic places.

Above all, we love to travel and shop at the same time. And as we get older and wiser from trial and error learning, we have become much more discriminating travelers. We seek to minimize the pain and maximize the pleasure of travel and shopping abroad by constantly upgrading the quality of our accommodations, food, transportation, and service and thereby minimize many of the hassles—especially wasted time—attendant with a great deal of budget travel.

This is not to say that we travel primarily to shop, spend a great deal of money, and encourage others to do so. Indeed not. Rather, we enjoy traveling, budget according to our means, know how to get a good deal on what's important to us, and find shopping to be one of the great rewards in our varied itinerary of visiting historical sites and museums, enjoying good hotels and restaurants, sampling fine cuisines, meeting new people, and immersing ourselves in different cultures.

We love to shop while we travel, because we discover wonderful items—many which we couldn't find back home—get good bargains, and enjoy the challenge and serendipity of the shopping process. Finding beautiful antiques and furniture, locating unique home decorative items, discovering exquisite jewelry and accessories, acquiring some of the finest tailored clothes in the world, and designing our own handmade rugs are only a few of the many wonderful shopping rewards from our many sojourns to exotic Hong Kong.

BE A QUALITY SHOPPER

We assume you are a quality shopper—you seek good quality goods and services at the best price possible. If you are like us, you want to return home with unique items that complement your home and wardrobe, make nice gifts, generate fond memories of a wonderful trip to Hong Kong, and can be admired for years to come.

It's best to visit Hong Kong with a discriminating eye for quality. For Hong Kong offers quality at both ends of the spectrum—from ordinary and mediocre goods dominating night markets to the finest quality products accenting the many glamorous boutiques and shops found in deluxe hotels and arcades.

It isn't easy for everyone to discriminate quality in Hong Kong. We gradually learned to do so only after many years of living, working, studying, shopping, and traveling abroad. We discovered the secrets of successful shopping in exotic places by trial and error. Indeed, we've made more than our share of mistakes when shopping abroad. We encountered the *"have I got a deal for you"* hawkers in Kowloon; rashly bought a lovely silk blouse at an unbeatable price only to discover the sleeves were set in backwards; and smugly purchased a copy brand-name watch which only worked for two days. We've berated ourselves for being poorly prepared and bemoaned the absence of a no-nonsense book which would assist novice international travelers by identifying the practical how-tos of shopping in Hong Kong and other exotic countries. We wish we had known many years ago what we now know about shopping in exotic places. We hope our hard lessons will be your gain as you explore the remainder of this book.

Most important, we've learned what and where **not** to buy, along with **what** best to buy, **where** best to buy, and **how** best to buy. In short, we've learned how to become discriminating international shoppers by being able to sort the good from the bad. By learning to go beyond the touts and tourist shops and local tour leaders, we've discovered that Hong Kong does indeed offer a wonderful world of quality shopping for those who know the what, where, and how of shopping its many streets, lanes, shopping centers, hotel shopping arcades, and factory outlets.

If you seek quality, as we do, shopping becomes extremely rewarding work. You become very selective, seeking reputable shops which have the type of products you desire. You learn to buy fewer things as you select quality items which you will appreciate for years to come. You avoid the typical tourist knickknack shops and primarily look for items which enhance your home and wardrobe as well as make nice gifts for friends and relatives. Since Hong Kong possesses her own particular set of shopping strengths and weaknesses, you learn to organize yourself to benefit from the **strengths**. To be able to distinguish good quality from poor; to know what fits well into your environment back home; to know the what, where, and how-to of buying in Hong Kong; and to get everything at a reasonable price and shipped home in good condition requires specific knowledge and skills not normally found in the typical travel book nor through a tour.

It is this knowledge and ability to shop well and enjoy shopping in exotic Hong Kong that we wish to share with you, the discriminating reader. While we include many of the general what's, where's, and how's of shopping found in other travel guides, we do so with one major difference: we assume you wish to avoid the tacky, buy quality at the lowest price, and experience the least amount of hassle in the process. Based on this assumption and our latest research and experience, the following chapters outline what we've found to be the secrets of shopping for quality, price, and convenience in Hong Kong. Each chapter is designed to lead you through the shopping process as painlessly as possible and leave you time to enjoy Hong Kong's many other pleasures. Most important, the book should enhance your travel experience with wonderful and rewarding shopping experiences which will be remembered and relived for many years to come.

APPROACH HONG KONG RIGHT

Shopping and Traveling in Exotic Hong Kong is designed to provide you with the necessary **knowledge and skills** to become an effective shopper in relation to your particular goals. The next chapter in this section, *"The World According to Hong Kong,"* develops a perspective on Hong Kong by examining its character with particular reference to its economic roles. Chapter Three presents basic facts on Hong Kong's geography, climate, entry requirements, and useful information sources for planning your adventure.

The four chapters in Part II, *"Traveling Smart,"* provide practical information on how to prepare for as well as enjoy your Hong Kong shopping adventure with a minimum amount of hassle, from packing and arriving at the airport to enjoying great hotels and restaurants. First-time visitors to Hong Kong should find these chapters especially useful.

The two chapters in Part III, *"Shopping Well,"* are designed to provide you with the most effective methods and strategies for shopping in Hong Kong. Emphasizing the shopping process, these chapters outline the local shopping culture, appropriate shopping strategies, and effective bargaining principles for achieving your specific shopping goals.

The four chapters in Part IV, *"Discovering Hong Kong's Shopping Secrets,"* address the critical *"what"* and *"where"* questions of shopping in Hong Kong. Our focus here is on locating quality products at the best possible price and with the fewest hassles. This section also includes information on enjoying your stay in Hong Kong as well as visiting additional shopping areas in neighboring Macau and China.

The three appendices in Part IV provide you with useful information on tailoring, shops, and hotels. Appendix A, *"Custom Tailoring,"* outlines how to select a good tailor, choose quality fabrics, and communicate your design preferences to Hong Kong tailors. Appendix B, *"The Shops,"* includes the names and addresses of shops offering different types of products; this is your directory to some of Hong Kong's best shops. Appendix C, *"Hotels,"* provides information on Hong Kong's best hotels.

Three maps appear in this book to provide you with a basic orientation to Hong Kong's major shopping areas. These are overview maps—not definitive maps to be used in navigating the many streets and small lanes of Hong Kong. As soon as you arrive in Hong Kong be sure to pick up a more detailed map of the city which is in both English and Chinese. These maps are provided free of charge by the HKTA and are available at the airport and at the Hong Kong Tourist Association (HKTA) Information and Gift Centres.

When examining the *"what"* of shopping (Chapter Ten and Appendix A), we devote a great deal of space to purchasing clothes, accessories, and tailoring services. We do so because what should be a major Hong Kong shopping strength often becomes a major shopper's weakness. Indeed, time and again we find many shoppers making mistakes in these areas. Most shoppers who are used to purchasing ready-made clothes in stores with fixed prices and return privileges are unfamiliar with how to bargain for the best price (Chapter

Nine), select fabrics and styles, and communicate effectively with tailors (Appendix A), especially those who speak little English or are unfamiliar with your preferences in styles. In addition, regardless of how specific you think you have been in communicating your preferences to a tailor, the results are often not what you expected. And you cannot return your custom-made clothes! Encountering such problems is unfortunate, because one of the great shopping bargains and enjoyments in Hong Kong is having your clothes tailor-made. It is neither a bargain nor fun if you get stuck with clothes that are not right for you.

DO IT ON YOUR OWN

The book is designed to be self-directed or can be used in conjunction with local shopping services and with organized tours. Our experience in traveling and shopping alone in Hong Kong has been very positive. Never fear. While Hong Kong may be exotic and far from home, you will not get lost and disappear for very long. If you go out on your own and take normal sensible precautions, your chances of getting robbed or mugged are probably much less in Hong Kong than in major American or European cities. It is easy to organize your own itinerary and make the trip on you own, perhaps including other Asian countries in your itinerary.

JOIN INEXPENSIVE AND CONVENIENT TOURS

At the same time, this book can be easily used in conjunction with organized shopping tours. Numerous 7 to 20-day shopping tours to Hong Kong and other parts of Asia are available for anyone wishing to choose this alternative. The tours have several advantages over independent trips. The major advantages are price and convenience. It is usually cheaper to take a shopping tour to Hong Kong than to arrange your own flights, hotel, and guides. Several companies offer a 6 to 10 day all inclusive shopping tour to Hong Kong for under $1600. Try matching that price on your own, especially given the escalating price of accommodations in Hong Kong! Groups also provide convenience; they save you time and spare you the hassles of arranging transportation, accommodations, and local tours.

Welcome to Exotic Hong Kong

BEWARE OF RECOMMENDED SHOPS

One word of caution before you read further. Throughout this book we concentrate on providing you with the necessary **knowledge and skills** to become an effective shopper in Hong Kong. Unlike other shopping books, we avoid including extensive lists of *"recommended"* shops. We have done this purposefully, because we believe it is much more important for you to **know how to shop** than to be told where to shop. If, for example, you understand how to set your own shopping goals, organize a shopping plan, locate quality shops, and bargain and communicate effectively with shopkeepers, you will be much more effective in discovering your own *"best shopping"* than someone who is only armed with names and addresses of someone else's recommended shops.

The real secret to effective shopping in Hong Kong is knowing the *"how"* along with the *"what"* and *"where."* However, because so many of our readers do want specific shops suggested, in Chapters Ten and Eleven, we do mention certain shops by name and address as well as include a directory of shops in Appendix B. Such names and addresses will not make you a more effective shopper, although such contact information should put you into shops that offer the type of quality and service we expect when shopping in Hong Kong. While we prefer not recommending and listing specific shops and services, we also recognize your need for useful details for beginning your shopping adventure.

Please be cautious whenever specific names and addresses appear in this book. Even though we have attempted to be as objective as possible in identifying quality shops, we are reluctant to recommend that you shop where we do. First, we have no guarantee that the shops we have worked with effectively will treat you the same. After all, you are a stranger who does not have a personal relationship with the shopowner. And personal relationships are **very** important in Hong Kong to ensure quality, appropriate pricing, honesty, and reliability. Furthermore, shops often change ownership, management, merchandising policy, and the quality of stock. Despite assurances from China to the contrary, the next decade may usher in an entirely new set of business practices, and at a faster pace than expected.

Second, the shopping scene in Hong Kong is very fluid. New shops and shopping centers seem to spring up everywhere; many of the new shops are branches of shops found in other shopping areas.

A shop which did excellent work and gave good service six months ago or in another shopping area may be out of business or have changed personnel by the time this book is off press. There is no guarantee the quality and service will remain consistent over a period of time. Given this situation, it is best for you to know how to *"read"* shops, discriminate quality, and communicate effectively with shopkeepers than to take someone's recommendation on faith.

Third, the Hong Kong Tourist Association (HKTA), an organization designed to promote tourism and business, sets standards for its member businesses as well as publishes a list of recommended shops. Such recommendations are worth considering, because the HKTA establishes a standard of performance, polices its members, and promises assistance should you have any problems with your purchases—even after you return home. We know this association takes its job seriously and can be helpful. But their recommendations should not be viewed as definitive. You must be discriminating, with a healthy sense of skepticism.

When we list specific shops we do so only as reference points from which to start your own shopping. We cannot guarantee the quality of products and service. In many cases our recommended shops offer exceptional quality products, honesty, and service. While we believe you should have the advantage of this information, we also caution you to always evaluate a business by asking the necessary questions to determine if it's right for you. Should you encounter any problem with these recommendations, we would appreciate hearing about it. While we cannot solve your problems, future editions of this book will reflect the experiences—both positive and negative—of our readers.

2 THE WORLD ACCORDING TO HONG KONG

Hong Kong is unlike any other city in the world. Perched on a mountainous southeast corner of China and capturing one of the world's finest harbors, Hong Kong is a visually spectacular picture-postcard city. Hundreds of high-rise commercial and residential buildings, many of architectural renown, accent its dramatic skyline, bustling harbor, and energetic streets. Still a British colony benevolently ruled by an appointed governor from London, Hong Kong remains a political mystery for many observers. Serving as China's most important window to the world, Hong Kong plays a strategic economic role throughout the region as well as the world. Above all, this city is a mecca for millions of shoppers from around the world who become dazzled by Hong Kong's delightful commercialism on the harbor.

A CITY ON THE GO

Hong Kong may not have heart, but it has lots of character, and a keen sense of where it is going. Everything about this city shouts *"unique"* and *"exotic."* Known as the *"Queen of Exotic Cities," "The Pearl of the Orient,"* and *"The Fragrant Harbour,"* Hong Kong functions as the financial, commercial, manufacturing, retail, wholesale, transportation, and communication crossroads of Asia. Despite its geographic location, ethnically and culturally Hong Kong is more East Asian than Southeast Asian. Commanding an influential Asian international role once reserved solely for Shanghai, Hong Kong is Asia's major center for banking and commerce, and a world center for diamonds and other precious stones.

ASIA'S ECONOMIC POWERHOUSE

Hong Kong ranks as one of the world's major banking, trading, and manufacturing powerhouses. One of four newly industrialized countries in Asia (along with Singapore, South Korea, and Taiwan), it is Asia's first financial capital and the world's:

- Third most important financial and banking center—after London and New York City.

- Largest exporter of garments, toys, watches, and radios.

- Third busiest container port and air cargo operation.

- Third busiest gold market and center for diamonds.

Its booming economy regularly achieves annual growth rates in excess of 10 percent. In 1988 alone, for example, Hong Kong's re-exports increased by a phenomenal 47 percent over the previous year! Even during the recessionary years of 1990 and 1991, Hong Kong's economic growth rate continued to out-pace that of most countries.

As a central transportation and communication hub for all of Asia, Hong Kong serves as an important transit point for millions of people and billions of products and dollars. Most tours to China, for example, enter and exit at Hong Kong. Major airlines fly into Hong Kong and then proceed to other cities in Asia, Europe, and North America. Hong Kong is a port of call for major cruise ships, freighters, and container ships in Asia.

A CITY WITH CHARACTER

Hong Kong has a great deal of character. It is the ultimate greed-city. Here the seemingly mysterious and colorful East mixes well with the commercial, high-tech West. You'll love it before you hate it. And if you ever come to hate it, you'll still want to come back for more. It's an intoxicating and addictive city where one easily gets high on shopping, food, people, and breathtaking views. Its numerous high-rise office buildings, shopping centers, hotels, and condominiums continue to sprout as if there were no tomorrow. Its hectic and beautiful harbor is filled with bloated ships, timeless junks, lumbering ferries, and aquaplaning jetfoils. And its crowded streets, sidewalks, and shops beckon shoppers to buy, buy, buy, and buy.

Hong Kong visually assaults you like no other city in the world. Here's a city that transforms itself every two to three years with an incredible mix of architecturally adventuresome skyscrapers alongside dull and aging commercial buildings. Viewed from Victoria Peak on a clear night, it is one of the world's most beautiful and romantic cities. Yet, Hong Kong has pockets of ugliness, a city of hectic strip development and flashing neon signs which quickly disorient many newcomers. It's Las Vegas without the gambling. But step into a shop and watch your money disappear on oh-so-glorious shopping. If Las Vegas is the gambler's heaven, then Hong Kong is the shopper's heaven.

A SHOPPER'S HEAVEN

You are about to shop in the fast lane and live in what China alternatively views as decadent and dynamic capitalism—both running amuck. It's not a cheap city, but it need not be expensive. The best way to prepare for this city is to take lots of money—preferably cold cash, but plastic will do just fine, thank you—just in case you need it. For you are about to contribute to its life blood—money, money, money. If you are just a casual shopper, you are about to lose your innocence. If you love shopping, Hong Kong is the closest you will ever get to a shopper's paradise!

One of the world's most exciting cities, Hong Kong invites you to indulge your shopping, gastronomic, sightseeing, and recreational fancies. It is an exotic, colorful, intense, and glamorous city, but one that is also well organized, sophisticated, cosmopolitan, familiar, convenient, and comfortable for visitors. If you only have time for one Asian city, spend a week in Hong Kong. While it is not representative of Asia, Hong Kong definitely hints at what pleasures may lie ahead in other equally fascinating Asian destinations.

If you plan to visit other Asian cities, make Hong Kong your gateway city. It will not disappoint you. Hong Kong will more than meet your expectations of a shopping paradise. A week will enable you to only scratch the surface of this city as you both shop and take in various city tours. As you leave you will look forward to coming back some day to further explore this ever-changing city. At the very least, Hong Kong will test your hidden shopping skills as well as challenge your concepts of shopping, leisure, wealth, money, capitalism, greed—and the future of communism for both China and Hong Kong.

PARADISE ON THE HARBOR

Once a small fishing village and pirates' lair, and since 1941 a British Crown Colony, today Hong Kong is a vibrant metropolis commanding one of the world's great harbors and dominating a significant portion of the world's trade and commerce. Moving from piracy to opium to manufacturing to services over a 150-year span, Hong Kong remains an anachronistic and fading British colony—programmed to become China's property in 1997—and faring far better economically than its colonial homeland.

The city bulges with people and things. Its streets are crowded with people in search of shops and market places offering some of the world's great treasures and temptations. Whatever you want to buy is available here, and the prices often boggle your mind. A city of sophisticated traders, merchants, and assorted entrepreneurs, Hong Kong has learned well the fine art of capitalism. In Hong Kong the game is to give a little, take a little, and, above all, make a profit and support your family.

Hong Kong's industrious Chinese and expatriates have created a shopper's paradise centering around a large volume of imported, exported, and re-exported goods flowing in and out of Hong Kong. It's a shopper's paradise for many reasons. First, cheap labor, linked to an outstanding financial, transportation, and communication infrastructure, has attracted many manufacturing companies—especially the garment, plastics, and electronic industries—from the United States, Europe, and Australia to Hong Kong. Factories produce an over-abundance of garments, toys, and radios for unpredictable world markets. As a result, tons of factory overruns, rejected seconds, and knock-offs find their way into the local marketplace to yield abundant treasures for avid shoppers from all over the world.

Second, Hong Kong is a duty-free port. It does not impose the ubiquitous yet hidden European Value Added Tax (VAT) nor does it levy import-export taxes, duties, or tariffs. As a result, most goods manufactured and sold in Hong Kong cost approximately one-third less than they would in North America, Europe, or Australia. Some imported goods are even less expensive in Hong Kong than in their country of origin. Indeed, Hong Kong is one of Japan's favorite dumping grounds for electronic goods and photo equipment. Many Japanese tourists are amazed to discover how much cheaper they can purchase Japanese goods in Hong Kong than in stores back home!

As the largest exporter of clothing in the world, Hong Kong's clothing industry employs 44 percent of the total industrial workforce and exports over $7 billion worth of garments each year. The surpluses, the overruns, the seconds, and the goods manufactured just for the local market are sold in over 40,000 retail outlets to locals and visitors from all over the world. Some factories have their own factory outlets, while others sell to shops which make it their business to buy and sell ex-factory goods at prices rivaling those at the best sales you can find back home.

DISCOVER DIVERSITY, VALUE, AND QUALITY

Bargains are found everywhere in Hong Kong if you know the *"what"* and *"where"* of shopping here. A dress, for example, retailing for $100 in the United States costs $14-15 to manufacture in Hong Kong and then retails in local shops for $50. It's even cheaper during the sales—and a real steal if it's sold as a second.

Hong Kong is one big sewing workroom. To discover what's going on, ride up an elevator, wander down a hallway, or visit a manufacturing company at random. You'll find many women sitting at their sewing machines or workbenches turning out piecework for $16-a-day wages. Tailoring workrooms are abuzz with sewing machines, steam irons, and noisy chatter as tailors ply their trade. While few tailors attempt to make a 24-hour suit, they do produce some of the world's best tailored garments in three or four days. Each person has a specific job skill with one man working on the hems and zippers while another cuts, and still another does the pad stitching for lapels and collars. In Hong Kong, most workers in the garment factories are women; all tailors are men.

Hong Kong is one big wholesale market with an astounding variety of goods. The shopping is fabulous with bargains galore for those who are willing to hunt. Like all cities, the downtown areas have the highest rents and thus shops there charge the highest prices. They also offer the best quality goods, house the designer boutiques, and often display fixed prices. But just around the corner, or up a few flights of stairs, you will find wonderful little cluttered rooms full of goodies awaiting the true bargain hunter. Even the designer boutiques offer goods at bargain prices compared to what you would pay in New York City or San Francisco—a 25 to 35 percent savings.

Beyond a question, Hong Kong is a shopper's paradise for diversity, value, and quality of merchandise. Shop and browse in air-conditioned malls, elbow your way through the crowds of local people in the night markets, explore streets lined with shops, boutiques, and stalls selling everything from high fashion and leather goods to powdered sea horses and live snakes. Discover streets devoted to footwear, and other streets selling mainly furniture. The streets of Hong Kong are astonishing. Factory outlets on both sides of the harbor will tempt you by offering the latest fashion trends at bargain prices. Hong Kong is just the place to pick up that special treasure in porcelain, jade, or gold.

Plan to spend some time in this unique city—a minimum of four days. Do some planning on the *"what"* and *"where"* of Hong Kong, but don't overdo it. Hong Kong may overwhelm you at first, but it will quickly grow on you if you position yourself to go with its remarkable flow.

3 KNOW BEFORE YOU GO

If you are a first-time visitor to Hong Kong, you should be aware of certain basic facts about this place before you arrive. This information will help you better plan how, when, and where you will arrive.

LOCATION AND AREA

Hong Kong is located on the southeast tip of China, 110 miles downstream from Guangchou (Canton), at the mouth of the muddy Pearl River. Boasting a strikingly beautiful harbor surrounded by towering hills and mountains and a majestic skyline of giant soaring buildings, Hong Kong is home to 5.8 million people who receive over 4 million visitors each year.

The major gateway city to all of East and Southeast Asia, Hong Kong is conveniently located on major international air and sea routes. By air, it is approximately 17 hours from New York, 12 hours from San Francisco and Seattle, 13 hours from London, 4 hours from Seoul, 3 hours from Beijing, Singapore and Jakarta, and 2 hours from Bangkok.

Consisting of a peninsula and 236 islands, Hong Kong is divided into four major sections: Hong Kong Island, Kowloon Peninsula, New

Territories, and the outlying islands. **Hong Kong Island** was originally ceded to Britain in 1841. Today, it occupies an area of 32 square miles. It houses Hong Kong's major financial district, shopping centers, hotels, resorts, recreational areas, and colorful coastal towns.

Kowloon Peninsula, ceded to Britain in 1860, is another major commercial, shopping, hotel, and residential area. Part of the mainland, it is connected to Hong Kong Island by ferry, tunnel, and subway. Occupying 3.5 square miles, Kowloon Peninsula is situated at the tip of the **New Territories**, an area of nearly 365 square miles. Leased to Britain in 1898 for 99 years, the New Territories consist of nearly 700 villages and towns and house Hong Kong's major manufacturing plants and housing estates. When the lease expires on June 30, 1997, the New Territories and the rest of Hong Kong will once again become part of China.

The 235 **outlying islands** are sparsely populated. In addition to Hong Kong Island, the four largest and most densely inhabited islands are Lantau, Lamma, Cheung Chau, and Peng Chau. Lantau is actually the largest of all the islands; its 55 square miles are occupied by a population of only 17,000.

At present all of Hong Kong consists of 413 square miles (1,070 square kilometers), but its land mass continues to grow as more and more land is reclaimed from Hong Kong harbor each year.

CLIMATE, SEASONS, AND WHEN TO GO

Since much of your stay in Hong Kong will be confined indoors to air-conditioned hotels, shopping arcades, and malls, Hong Kong can be enjoyed year-round. To best enjoy your stay, you should plan your trip according to two different types of seasons: climate and sales.

Hong Kong generally has two unpredictable **climatic seasons:** hot/wet and cool/dry. The hot/wet season occurs between March and September (Spring/Summer) and is best characterized as a combination of hot, humid, and rainy weather. This is the period of the wet Southwest Monsoon. Tropical cyclones and typhoons often occur between May and September.

The cool/dry season is between October and February (Fall/Winter). This is the period of the dry Northeast Monsoon. The season begins with warm days, clear skies, and cool nights, and ends with cool days, cold winds, gray skies, mist, and an occasional frost in the mountains.

You will encounter the best weather in Hong Kong during the months of October and November. The temperature ranges from 60F to 80F, humidity is relatively low, and skies are sunny and bright. However, like March and April, these are **high season** months for tourists, and prices for transportation and hotels escalate accordingly. If you plan to combine a trip to China with a stop in Hong Kong, the end of September to the first of October is the best time to visit both places.

The best rule of thumb for dress is to plan as if you were traveling to the southern parts of Louisiana, Alabama, Mississippi, or Georgia. In the spring and summer—Hong Kong's March through September— average temperatures are from 60F to 80F and humidity is in the 83-85 percent range. Take lightweight clothes and an umbrella in anticipation of hot and humid days. During the March through May period you may need a jacket. In the winter—Hong Kong's January to February with average temperature at 59F and humidity at 75 percent—take a sweater and a warm jacket or overcoat.

Hong Kong's best climatic seasons unfortunately do not coincide with its best **sale seasons**. The best times to shop in Hong Kong are during the fabulous semi-annual sales at the end of December and the end of June. The end-of-June sales occur during one of the most oppressive months for heat and humidity. In addition, the June sales occasionally become *"Typhoon Sales"* as an unpredictable typhoon shuts down Hong Kong for a few days. The end-of-December sales take place just before the Chinese New Year during one of the coldest and most dank months of the year. If you decide to travel to Hong Kong during these two sale months, plan to spend most of your time shopping in the arcades and malls rather than the street markets and lanes. The weather seldom cooperates to give you good opportunities for sightseeing and outdoor recreation.

GETTING THERE

Most visitors arrive in Hong Kong by air at Hong Kong International Airport. Hong Kong also is serviced by major passenger ships and freighters. Assuming your choice is air, connections into Hong Kong are frequent and convenient. Thirty airlines have regularly scheduled flights to Hong Kong, and several charter airlines also service Hong Kong.

Airfares to Hong Kong from the United States, Canada, or Europe are some of the best airfare bargains in the world. If you shop around, you can fly round-trip from the U.S. West Coast to Hong Kong for as little as $709 (hotel not included). Round-trip airfare from New York City or Washington, DC to Hong Kong can be as little as $849. Comparable inexpensive tickets are available in Europe, especially among London's *"bucket shops."*

For most tourists from America and Europe, the flight to Hong Kong is a long one. Thus, you may wish to upgrade your ticket to *"Business Class"* for more room and comfort. You will pay more for this upgrade but the increased comfort may be well worth it.

You should consider a package tour to Hong Kong regardless of whether you are a first-time visitor or a seasoned traveler to Hong Kong. Many of the organized shopping tours as well as the airfare/hotel combinations are very good buys—around $1200 for 7 days in Hong Kong. Some tours concentrate on Hong Kong while others include two or more cities as well as supplementary packages to add-on cities of your choice. Most of these tours include round-trip air transportation (coach class), transfers to hotels, accommodations in deluxe and first-class hotels, Western style buffet breakfast, a city tour, and guided shopping tours to various shopping centers, factory outlets, markets, and shops. It is very difficult to beat these prices by arranging your own flights and hotels. Paying the rack rate alone at a first-class Hong Kong hotel can equal the total price of the special shopping tour package. And if you have already done the extras which are included in the package, you can gracefully bow out and go off to do your own thing. Consult your travel agent and survey the travel sections of the Sunday *New York Times, Washington Post, Los Angeles Times,* and other major city newspapers for special airfares and packages to Hong Kong. You may be pleasantly surprised at what you find.

DOCUMENTS YOU NEED

Hong Kong requires few documents for entry and exit. Most visitors only need a valid passport and an on-going ticket. If you look like an itinerant, immigration officials may ask for evidence that you have sufficient funds to support your stay.

Know Before You Go 21

Visa requirements vary depending upon one's nationality. Citizens of Commonwealth countries face the fewest restrictions while those from socialist and communist countries must spend some time getting visas.

Citizens from most countries can stay in Hong Kong from one to three months without a visa. U.S. citizens need only present a valid passport for a one-month stay. Visa extensions are relatively easy to arrange in Hong Kong.

Hong Kong does not require health documents. Should you be coming from an infected smallpox or cholera area within 14 days prior to arriving in Hong Kong, you will be required to show evidence of appropriate vaccinations.

RECOMMENDED READING

A great deal of resources are available on Hong Kong to help prepare you for this city's many travel, shopping, and cultural delights. If you would enjoy a literary introduction to get a feel for Hong Kong's setting and character, read Richard Hughes' ***Borrowed Place, Borrowed Time*** (mainly available in Hong Kong); James Clavell's ***Taipan*** or ***Noble House***; John Le Carre's ***The Honourable Schoolboy***; Robert Ludlum's ***The Bourne Supremacy***; and Jan Morris' ***Hong Kong***.

One of the best ways to orient yourself to Hong Kong is to read the beautifully illustrated ***APA Insight Guide: Hong Kong*** prior to your arrival. This book provides an excellent overview of the history, people, places, culture, and travel to Hong Kong and Macau. Since the book is big and bulky to pack, read it before you go. The final section, entitled *"Guide in Brief,"* provides detailed information on the practical aspects of traveling to Hong Kong.

Harmony Books publishes a useful illustrated shopping map of Hong Kong: ***Shopwalks Hong Kong*** by Corby Kummer. It is available in many major bookstores in the United States.

Fodor's two books, ***Hong Kong*** and ***Southeast Asia***, also are excellent guides to the standard aspects of travel to Hong Kong. The ***Hong Kong*** guide is a handy reference with detailed sections on accommodations, food entertainment, arts, shopping, and sightseeing. Baedeker's ***Hong Kong*** is also a useful guide to sights although the map needs updating.

Budget travelers should examine the Lonely Planet volume, ***Hong Kong, Macau, and Canton***. The bookstore at the YMCA on Salisbury Road in Hong Kong (Kowloon side) also has one of the best collections of budget books on Hong Kong as well as other Asian countries.

The Hong Kong Tourist Association publishes a monthly guide book, ***The Official Hong Kong Guide***, and a detailed map of the city, ***The Hong Kong Guide Map***. The guide includes a section on shopping in Hong Kong as well as ads from numerous HKTA-approved shops. You should also pick up a copy of HKTA's ***The Official Guide to Shopping, Eating Out, and Services in Hong Kong***. This directory lists the names, addresses, and telephone numbers of shops approved by HKTA. Such establishments display the red junk logo on the front door of their shops. Since the names are in both English and Chinese, this directory—along with HKTA's map—will help you communicate with taxi drivers. To get copies of these free publications before arriving in Hong Kong, write or call the HKTA office nearest you. Once arriving in Hong Kong, you can pick up this literature at the HKTA desk in the Buffer Hall of Kai Tak International Airport or at any of the HKTA Information and Gift Centres: Shop G2, Royal Garden Hotel, 69 Mody Road, Tsimshatsui East, Kowloon; Star Ferry Concourse, Kowloon; and 35th floor, Connaught Center, Central, Hong Kong Island. The helpful HKTA personnel will also answer any of your questions and provide advice on where, when, and how to make your stay in Hong Kong most rewarding.

If you plan to visit factory outlet stores, you should purchase Dana Goetz's ***The Complete Guide to Hong Kong Factory Bargains***. This handy little guide provides detailed maps, names, addresses, telephone numbers, annotated descriptions of shops, hours, sizes, price ranges, and payment methods. It includes directions in Chinese for taxi drivers. This book is widely available in bookstores and hotels in Hong Kong. If you are at the Star Ferry, Hong Kong side, go next door to the **SCMP Book Shop**. This store has Goetz's book as well as other useful guides on Hong Kong. HKTA also publishes a small booklet—***Factory Outlets in Hong Kong***—to assist visitors in locating factory outlets selling clothes and jewelry.

Susan Thomas' ***Born to Shop: Hong Kong*** (Bantam) is widely available in major bookstores in the United States. A chatty book written from an American perspective, it provides useful advice on shopping in Hong Kong and outlines the *"where"* and *"what"* of shopping for particular items.

The best resource guide we have found for purchasing gems and jewelry is written by experienced professionals who know the trade: Joan Reid Ahrens' and Ruth Lor Malloy's *Hong Kong Gems & Jewelry* (HK$49). The book is primarily available in Hong Kong bookstores or can be ordered directly from the publisher by sending a bank draft for U.S. $9.50, made payable to Delta Dragon Publications, Ltd., to: Delta Dragon Books, 6th Floor, Sun Pin Ind. Bldg., 916 Cheung Sha Wan Road, Kowloon, Hong Kong. Look for other useful guides published by this same company, such as *The Complete Guide to Hong Kong Factory Bargains, The Hong Kong Shopping Manual—A Tactical Brief,* and *Cheap, But Great, Restaurants in Hong Kong.*

If you are interested in arts and antiques, be sure to get a copy of Drummond's *Hongkong Guide to Art & Antique Dealers.* Published by one of Hong Kong's leading art and antique dealers—Altfield Enterprises—this useful book identifies the best of Hong Kong's dealers by name and address as well as includes brief descriptions and maps. The book is available in Hong Kong bookstores (HK$39.50 or US$5) and some art and antique dealers. It also can be ordered directly from Altfield's: Altfield Enterprises, 31 Lyndhurst Terrace, Central, Hong Kong. If you order from abroad, send a check made payable to Altfield Enterprises for US$7.50 to cover the cost of both the book and international postage.

HONG KONG TOURIST ASSOCIATION

The **Hong Kong Tourist Association (HKTA)** is the official government-sponsored body representing the entire tourism industry in Hong Kong. HKTA is organized to assist you while you are in Hong Kong. Their Ordinary Member shops prominently display the HKTA sign, a red junk surrounded by a red border. Bona fide members agree to provide reliable and polite service, give good value for money, accurately represent products sold, and promptly rectify justified complaints. Contact their Telephone Information Service by dialing 801-7177, 8am to 6pm daily. HKTA Information and Gift Centres are found at the Buffer Hall in the airport (accessible only to arriving passengers); Star Ferry Concourse, Kowloon; Royal Garden Hotel, Shop G2, 69 Mody Road, Tsimshatsui East, Kowloon; and 35th Floor, Connaught Centre, Central, Hong Kong Island (main office).

HKTA publishes a great deal of free literature for tourists which is available at the airport, HKTA offices, and in hotels. Be sure to pick up one of their excellent maps. The street names are in both Chinese and English and detail the major shopping areas; the maps are particularly useful in communicating with taxi drivers. HKTA also publishes a weekly newspaper for visitors—*Hong Kong*—and a series of useful pamphlets: *Places of Interest by Public Transportation; Hotel Guide; Culture; Museums and Arts and Crafts; The Official Guide to Shopping, Eating Out, and Services in Hong Kong; Shopping Guide to Video Equipment; Hong Kong Discovery Guide; The MTR/KCR Tourist Guide; Factory Outlets; Come Horseracing; Outlying Islands*. Be sure to pick up the current issues of HKTA's monthlies: *Shopping Guide to Hong Kong* and *The Official Hong Kong Guide*. Check HKTA's display for others useful publications. All are designed to enable travelers to easily find their way around Hong Kong on their own.

Before leaving for Hong Kong, you should contact the nearest Hong Kong Tourist Association offices for information. In the United States you can write or call:

>Hong Kong Tourist Association
>10940 Wilshire Blvd., Suite 1220
>Los Angeles, CA 90024
>Tel. 213/208-4582

>Hong Kong Tourist Association
>360 Post Street, Suite 404
>San Francisco, CA 94108
>Tel. 415-781-4582

>Hong Kong Tourist Association
>333 N. Michigan Avenue, Suite 2323
>Chicago, IL 60601-3966
>Tel. 312/782-3872

>Hong Kong Tourist Association
>590 Fifth Avenue
>New York, NY 10036
>Tel. 212/869-5008

PROFESSIONAL SHOPPING SERVICES

If you have limited time and find the notion of shopping with a local resident of Hong Kong to be appealing, consider contacting one of the local professional shopping services. Each of the services with which we are most familiar is knowledgeable, reputable, well organized, and efficient. They customize shopping trips and services in response to individual or group needs, pre-negotiate prices, refuse commissions from shop owners, and pass the savings on to the client. Either service can provide speakers, set up Hospitality Desks for conventions, and provide unique local tours.

Using a shopping service can be a wise investment for some people and need not be an extravagance since the service will most likely save a shopper more money than the fee. And it's fun to shop with a resident. Whether you are a first-time visitor, a business person with a critical time-shortage, or are first-name familiar with Hong Kong, now, more than ever before, this service can be a wise investment. Political and business situations cause more shops to move or close daily, and only someone who makes it her business to stay on top of the latest changes is qualified to provide professional shopping services.

By providing the shopping service with detailed information prior to your trip you will ensure that actual shopping time is spent efficiently. Send a listing of your shopping priorities, and if you have any physical disability at all be sure to reveal the nature of your needs before your shopping day so they can make appropriate arrangements for you. Payments can be made by personal check, cash, or travelers checks.

You can arrange you shopping itinerary—as well as any additional tour services—before arriving in Hong Kong by contacting the following professional shopping services.

Asian Cajun provides numerous shopping services for visitors to Hong Kong. You can contact them as follows:

ASIAN CAJUN
Helen Giss, Managing Director
12 Scenic Villa Drive 4/F
Pokfulam, Hong Kong
Tel. 566-9010, 817-3687
Fax 855-9571

Since Asian Cajun arranges for visitors to buy from reliable vendors at pre-negotiated prices, this service helps you get the best value for your shopping dollars. Asian Cajun charges US$55 per hour (three hour minimum) and the fee can be shared between friends. Using public transportation to get around Hong Kong is encouraged, primarily because it is fast and convenient. They hire cars when needed for a particular excursion or because the client requires it, the cost of which is passed on to the client.

The first objective of a shopping day with Asian Cajun is to find your priority items. Then you'll learn about other good buys and visit favorite vendors, with tidbits about local history and customs thrown in for the fun of it. Your shopping day will concentrate on special shops which provide the unusual bargain for quality or value. Then you'll receive recommendations about local shopping spots which are worth your time and effort another day.

Most of Asian Cajun's expatriate shoppers speak one or more language other than English and can be paired with non-English-speaking visitors.

Other Asian Cajun services include Package Tracking, local sightseeing, House and Garden Tours, and assisting buyers for boutiques who are in search of unusual items.

Temptations Asia also provides shopping services for visitors. You can contact them as follows:

TEMPTATIONS ASIA
Valentina Gillies
GPO Box 10935
Hong Kong
Tel. (852) 541-6929, 541-6685
Fax (852) 541-7411

or

Stella Martin
1231 Jefferson Terrace
Macon, Georgia 31201 USA
Tel: 912/742-2425
Fax: 912/742-2489

Temptations' goal is to provide savings which far exceed the cost of their service—and do so in style, using reputable sources which are ordinarily unavailable. Shopping excursions are tailored to finding specific items on a client's shopping list. Clients are charged only for the actual shopping time, not for advance research. Rates range from US$80/per hour for the minimum four hour shopping tour, depending upon the number of people in the party and includes a chauffeur-driven limousine with an American Shopping Consultant, and lunch.

Prior to arrival in Hong Kong the client is sent a shopping questionnaire. A follow-up phone call helps to match clients with the best guide and most appropriate shops. They can usually find what you want, but if an item cannot be located the client will be notified with alternate options. *"It's like shopping with a friend who lives in Hong Kong,"* says Temptations Asia. Clients are assured that they can buy with confidence and eliminate the hassles of searching for the best price and quality. Tourists commonly pay top dollar, but Temptations negotiates discounts in advance, which are passed on directly to the client.

A third group, **Victoria Treasures**, provides similar escorted shopping services. When using public transportation, they charge one or two people HK$180 for three hours. Mercedes-Benz and Rolls-Royce services are also available at additional charges—HK$280 for three hours in a Mercedes-Benz or HK$730 for four hours in a Rolls-Royce. You can contact Victoria Treasures by phone (852/525-6125) or fax (852/810-6277).

The longer the shopping list the more sense it makes to use a shopping service, for their advance footwork ensures that none of your valuable time will be wasted. And even if you have little to shop for, it's a good way to get out of the hotel to do some special sightseeing and perhaps have tea.

Check the morning newspaper, *South China Morning Post,* the tourist weeklies, and the Yellow Pages of the telephone book for other shopping services.

USEFUL ASSOCIATIONS

The **American Women's Association of Hong Kong** prints a list of recommended shops for its members and others. You can request a copy of *Factory List* after you arrive in Hong Kong by contacting:

American Women's Association of Hong Kong
48 Kennedy Road, Flat C7, Monticello
Hong Kong
Tel. 527-2961

Other organizations, including airline associations, also publish recommended listings of shops.

Several other organizations in Hong Kong can assist you in dealing with various aspects of your shopping adventure:

Diamond Information Centre
10F Malaysia Building
Wanchai, Hong Kong Island
Tel. 823-0117

The Gemological Association of Hong Kong
P. O. Box 97711
Tsimshatsui, Kowloon
Tel. 366-6006

American Chamber of Commerce
1030 Swire House
Central, Hong Kong Island
Tel. 526-0165

NEWSPAPERS AND TELEVISION

Hong Kong has an ample supply of English language newspapers, magazines, and books. You will find four English newspapers: *The South China Morning Post, The Hong Kong Standard, The Asian Wall Street Journal,* and *The International Herald Tribune.* Two television channels broadcast in English from mid-afternoon to late evening.

PART II

TRAVELING SMART

4 PREPARE FOR A UNIQUE TRAVEL AND SHOPPING ADVENTURE

Preparation is the key to experiencing a successful and enjoyable shopping adventure. But it involves much more than just examining maps, reading travel literature, and making airline and hotel reservations. Preparation, at the very least, is a process of minimizing uncertainty by learning how to develop a shopping plan, manage your money, determine the value of products, handle customs, and pack for the occasion. It involves knowing what products are good deals to buy in Hong Kong in comparison to similar items back home. **Preparation helps organize all the aspects of your trip.**

DEVELOP AN ACTION PLAN

Time is money when traveling abroad. The better you plan and use your time, the more time you will have to enjoy your trip. If you want to use your time wisely and literally hit the ground running, you should plan a detailed, yet tentative, schedule for each day. **List** in order of priority the 10 things you most hope to accomplish in the time you have. Next, using a separate sheet of paper, **divide** each day into four 3-hour time segments. For each 3-hour segment, plan a short period of rest, especially if all you are doing is shopping. Assign to each day a set of objectives, or things you wish to accomplish, over a 12-hour time frame. Within each 3-hour time segment **identify** where you plan to be and what you plan to do. At the end of each day **summarize** what you actually accomplished in relation to your 10 priorities. Your tentative plan might follow the form on page 33.

Make enough copies of this form for each day of your trip. Such a detailed plan not only helps you get organized and directed toward your goals as soon as you arrive in Hong Kong, it also serves as your daily diary for future reference.

WELCOME SERENDIPITY AND GOOD LUCK

Planning is fine but it will not ensure a successful trip. People who engage in excessive planning often overdo it and thus ruin their trip by accumulating a list of unfulfilled expectations. Planning needs to be adapted to good luck. You should be open to unexpected events which may well become the major highlights of your travel and shopping experiences.

If you want to have good luck, then plan to be in many different places to take advantage of new opportunities. Expect to alter your initial plans once you begin discovering new and unexpected realities. Serendipity—those chance occurrences that often evolve into memorable and rewarding experiences—frequently interferes with the best-laid travel and shopping plans. Welcome serendipity by altering your plans to accommodate the unexpected. You can do this by revising your plans each day as you go. A good time to summarize the day's events and accomplishments and plan tomorrow's schedule is just before you go to bed each night.

Keep in mind that your plan should be a means to an end— experiencing exciting travel and shopping—and not the end itself. If you plan well, you will surely experience good luck on the road to a successful trip!

CONDUCT RESEARCH AND NETWORK FOR INFORMATION

Do as much research as possible before you depart on your Hong Kong adventure. A good starting place is the periodical section of your

DAILY PLANNING AND SCHEDULING FORM

Date: _____ City: _____

Desired accomplishments (prioritize):

1. _____ 6. _____
2. _____ 7. _____
3. _____ 8. _____
4. _____ 9. _____
5. _____ 10. _____

	Where I will be	What I hope to accomplish
9am—12 noon		
12—3pm		
3pm—6pm		
6pm—9pm		

Summary of today's accomplishments
in reference to my 10 priorities:

local library. Here you will find numerous magazine and newspaper articles on travel and shopping in Hong Kong. Indeed, Hong Kong is one of the most popular subjects for travel writers. When you find references to shops, add these names to your growing list of places to visit.

You should also **network for information and advice**. You'll find many people, including relatives, friends, and acquaintances, who have traveled to Hong Kong. Many of these people are eager to talk about their trip as well as share their particular Hong Kong shopping secrets with you. They may direct you to some great shops where they found cashmere, pearls, or jade of good quality or at exceptional prices. Ask basic who, what, where, why, and how questions:

- What shops did you particularly like?
- What do they sell?
- How much discount could I expect?
- Whom should I ask for?
- Where is the shop located?
- How do I get what I want?
- Is bargaining expected?
- When were you there?

This final question is particularly significant. Not only do shops change ownership or go out of business in Hong Kong as they do anywhere, but prices have been increasing there and significant changes have taken place during the past few years. Information gleaned from people's experiences over the past 2-3 years will be most relevant.

Many people collect business cards from favorite shops, and they will be happy to share them with you. Be sure **to record all the information that you receive in an orderly manner**. Use, for example, an ordinary address book to list the names, addresses, telephone numbers, and products of shops; list them alphabetically by types of merchandise.

Don't neglect to contact the Hong Kong Tourist Association office nearest you. Ask for a map and any information on travel and shopping in Hong Kong that would assist you in planning your trip. This is a free service. The United States offices are listed in Chapter Three.

Prepare For a Unique Travel and Shopping Adventure

CHECK CUSTOMS REGULATIONS

It's always good to know Customs regulations before you leave home. If you are a U.S. citizen planning to return to the U.S. from Hong Kong, the United Customs Service provides several helpful publications which are available free of charge from your nearest U.S. Customs Office, or write P.O. Box 7407, Washington, DC 20044.

Know Before You Go (Publication #512) outlines facts about your basic exemptions, mailing gifts, duty-free articles, and prohibited and restricted articles.

Trademark Information For Travelers (Publication #508) deals with unauthorized importation of trademarked goods. Since you will find many copies of trademarked items in Hong Kong—the ubiquitous "knock-offs"—this publication will alert you to potential problems with custom inspectors prior to returning home.

International Mail Imports answers many travelers' questions regarding mailing items from foreign countries back to the U.S. The U.S. Postal Service sends all packages to Customs for examination and assessment of duty before it is delivered to the addressee. Some items are free of duty and some are dutiable. The rules have recently changed on mail imports, so do check on this before you leave the U.S.

GSP and the Traveler itemizes goods from particular countries that can enter the United States duty-free. GSP regulations, which are designed to promote the economic development of certain Third World countries, permit many products, especially arts and handicrafts, to enter the United States duty-free. Since Hong Kong is now classified as a Newly Industrialized Country, it no longer enjoys GSP status. Therefore, it is unlikely that items you purchase in Hong Kong will be exempted from duty. Antiques, defined by U.S. Customs as over 100 years old, are free of duty. Be sure this is noted on your sales receipt.

If you are in Hong Kong and uncertain about U.S. duties on particular items, phone 523-9011 for local U.S. Customs assistance.

MANAGE YOUR MONEY WELL

It's best to carry traveler's checks, two or more major credit cards with sufficient credit limits, U.S. dollars, and a few personal checks. Our basic money rule is to take enough money and sufficient credit limits so you don't run short. How much you take is entirely up to you, but it's better to have too much than not enough when you're shopping in Hong Kong.

We increasingly find **credit cards** to be very convenient for managing our money in Hong Kong. We prefer using credit cards to pay for major purchases such as jewelry or electronic equipment as well as for those unanticipated expenses incurred when shopping. Most major hotels and stores honor MasterCard, Visa, American Express, and Diner's cards—and in that order of preference. It's a good idea to take one or two bank cards and an American Express card.

Take plenty of **traveler's checks** in U.S. denominations of $50 and $100. Smaller denominations are often more trouble than they are worth, but you may want a few. On occasion the smaller traveler's checks come in handy, especially when you really need local currency but the local exchange rate is poor. In Hong Kong you will usually receive a better exchange rate with traveler's checks than with cash. Most major banks, hotels, restaurants, and shops will also take traveler's checks, although some do add a small service charge for accepting them. Banks and money changers will give you the best exchange rates, but at times you'll find hotels to be more convenient because of their close proximity and better hours.

Personal checks can be used to obtain traveler's checks with an American Express card or to pay for goods to be shipped later—after your check has cleared your bank. Some shops will also accept personal checks. Remember to keep one personal check aside to pay customs should you have dutiable goods when you return home.

Use you own judgment concerning how much **cash** you should carry with you. Contrary to some fearful ads, cash is awfully nice to have in moderate amounts to supplement your traveler's checks and credit cards. Several US$1 bills are handy for tips when you first arrive. But of course you must be very careful where and how you carry cash. Consider carrying an *"emergency cash reserve"* primarily in $50 and $100 denominations, but also a few $20's. Cash can be used instead of your larger denomination traveler's checks when you want to change a small amount of money to local currency.

Prepare For a Unique Travel and Shopping Adventure 37

USE CREDIT CARDS WISELY

Credit cards can be a shopper's blessing. They are your tickets to serendipity, convenience, good exchange rates, and a useful form of insurance. Widely accepted throughout Asia, they enable you to draw on credit reserves for purchasing many wonderful items you did not anticipate finding when you initially planned your adventure. In addition to being convenient, you usually will get good exchange rates once the local currency amount appearing on your credit slip is converted by the bank at the official rate into your home currency. Credit cards also allow you to float your expenses into the following month or two without paying interest charges. Most important, should you have a problem with a purchase—such as buying a piece of jewelry which you later discover was misrepresented or has fake stones, or electronic goods which are incompatible with your systems back home—your credit card company may assist you in recovering your money and returning the goods. Once you discover your problem, contact the credit card company with your complaint and refuse to pay the amount while the matter is in dispute. Businesses accepting these cards must maintain a certain standard of honesty and integrity. In this sense, credit cards may be an excellent and inexpensive form of insurance against possible fraud and damaged goods when shopping abroad. If you rely only on cash or traveler's checks, you have no such institutional recourse for assistance recovering your money.

The down-side to using credit cards is that many businesses in Hong Kong will charge you a *"commission"* for using your card, or simply not go as low in the bargaining process as they would for cash or traveler's checks. Commissions will range from 2 to 6 percent. This practice is discouraged by credit card companies; nonetheless, shops do this because they must pay a 4-5 percent commission to the credit card companies. They merely pass this charge on to you. When bargaining, keep in mind that shopkeepers usually consider a final bargained price to be a *"cash only"* price. If you wish to use your credit card at this point, you will probably be assessed the additional 2 to 6 percent to cover the credit card commission or lose your bargained price altogether. Frequently in the bargaining process, when you near the seller's low price, you will be asked whether you intend to pay cash. It is at this point that cash and traveler's checks come in handy to avoid a slightly higher price. However, **don't be *"penny wise but***

pound foolish." You may still want to use your credit card if you suspect you might have any problems with your purchase.

A few other tips on the use and abuse of credit cards may be useful in planning your trip. **Use your credit cards for the things that will cost you the same amount no matter how you pay,** such as lodging and meals in the better hotels and restaurants or purchases in most department stores. Consider requesting a higher credit limit on your bank cards if you think you may wish to charge more than your current limit allows.

Be extremely careful with your credit cards. Be sure merchants write the correct amount and indicate clearly whether this is U.S. dollars or Hong Kong dollars on the credit card slip you sign. It is always a good practice to write the local currency symbol before the total amount so that additional figures cannot be added or the amount mistaken for your own currency. For example, 780 Hong Kong dollars is approximately equivalent to 100 U.S. dollars. It should appear as *"HK$780"* on your credit slip. And keep a good record of all charges in local currency—and at official exchange rates—so you don't have any surprises once you return home!

SECURE YOUR VALUABLES

Be sure to keep your traveler's checks, credit cards, and cash in a safe place along with your travel documents and other valuables. Consider wearing a money belt or a similar safety cache. While the money belt may be the safest approach, the typical 4" x 8" nylon belts can be uncomfortable in hot and humid weather. Women may want to make a money pouch which can fasten inside their clothing. If you choose not to use a money belt or pouch, another approach for women is to carry money and documents in a leather shoulder bag which should be kept with you at all times, however inconvenient, even when passing through buffet lines. Choose a purse with a strap long enough to sling around your neck bandolier style. Secure the purse with a strong grip and always keep it between you and the person accompanying you. Purse snatchers can quickly ruin your vacation if you are not careful.

For men, keep your money and credit cards in your wallet, but always carry your wallet in a front pocket. If you keep it in a rear pocket, as you may do at home, you invite pickpockets to demonstrate their varied talents in relieving you of your money, and possibly venting your trousers in the process. If your front pocket is an uncomfortable location, you probably need to clean out your wallet so it will fit better.

You may also want to use the free hotel safety deposit boxes for your cash and other valuables. If one is not provided in your room, ask the cashier to assign you a private box in their vault. Under no circumstances should you leave your money and valuables unattended in your hotel room, at restaurant tables, or in dressing rooms. Remember, there are many talented and highly motivated thieves who prey upon what they see as unsuspecting rich tourists. You may want to leave your expensive jewelry at home so as not to be as likely a target of theft. If you get robbed, chances are it will be in part your own fault, because you invited someone to take advantage of your weaknesses by not being more cautious in securing your valuables. In our many years of traveling we have not been robbed. But we try to be careful not to encourage someone to take advantage of us. We know people who have had problems, but invariably they were easy and predictable targets, because they failed to take elementary precautions against thieves.

TAKE ALL NECESSARY SHOPPING INFORMATION

Depending on what you plan to buy, you should take all the necessary information you need to make those important shopping decisions. Put this information in a separate envelope. If you are looking for home furnishings, along with your *"wish list"* you should include room measurements to help you determine if particular items will fit into your home. You might take photographs with you of particular rooms you hope to furnish. Be sure to include measurements of dining tables and beds since you can find wonderful table linens and bedspreads in Hong Kong.

If you plan to shop for clothes, your homework should include taking an inventory of your closets and identifying particular colors, fabrics, and designs you wish to acquire to complement and enlarge your present wardrobe. If you have been color-charted, be sure to take your chart with you. Since Hong Kong tailors are particularly talented at copying designs from pictures or models, we strongly recommend that you assemble a file of pictures with styles you wish to have copied. If you have a favorite blouse or suit you wish to have copied, take the actual article with you. It is not necessary to take patterns, because Hong Kong tailors do not use these devices for measuring, cutting, and assembling clothes. All they need is to take your measurements and have a clear idea of your style and fit preferences.

DO COMPARATIVE SHOPPING

An equally important bit of homework is to go comparison shopping. Once you arrive in Hong Kong the only comparisons you can make are between various shops within the city, and contrary to what you've heard, the prices just might be higher and the quality lower than they are back home! You'll never know unless you have done your homework.

Your shopping goal should be this: **to buy what you need at a price that is so low that even after adding duties and shipping charges (if applicable), the item will still cost less than you would pay at home.** But unless you know what the value is at home you won't recognize a bargain when it stares you in the face.

Know comparative prices before you travel. The first step is to determine what you want and need. Make lists. As you compile your list spend some time *"window"* shopping in the local stores, examining catalogs, and telephoning for information.

If, for example, your list includes electronic equipment or cameras, you should compile a list of prices for comparable items found in stores and discount houses back home. In the United States, for example, call the toll-free numbers of reliable mail-order discount houses in New York City for phone quotes on cameras, film, computers, and electronic equipment: Bi-Rite (800/223-1970), 47st Photo (800/221-7774), Focus (800/331-0828), Executive (800/223-7323), and Olden Computer (800/223-1444). The Sunday and Wednesday editions of *The New York Times* include ads from these highly competitive firms. You will quickly discover their prices may be 10-30 percent cheaper than the best price you can find in your local discount houses. Some of these New York firms will even bargain over the phone when you inform them of a competitor's better price! You will also discover that most imported camera and electronic equipment purchased through these mail-order sources may be 20 to 40 percent cheaper than in Hong Kong. So be sure to do your pricing research

before you buy such items in Hong Kong. There's nothing worse to deflate your shopping enthusiasm than to return home with what appeared to be a terrific Hong Kong bargain and then discover you could have gotten the same item for less at home.

Jewelry is another item you need to price as well as learn more about if you are not an expert. Read about determining quality in jewelry; your local library should have several useful books for this purpose. After reading, visit jewelry stores at home to learn how to identify quality and compare prices. Ask salespeople questions, especially about craftsmanship, settings, quality, and discounts.

You can get terrific buys on jewelry in Hong Kong **If** you know what you are doing. Most people, however, are simply overwhelmed by the choices confronting them. Novices shopping for jewelry in Hong Kong often end up with much less than they had bargained for. Many think they are getting a *"steal"* and then later discover it was the shop that got the real steal!

A comparative shopping form like the one on page 42 will make this task easier. List each item you want down the left side of a sheet of paper with some specific information such as size, length, pattern, etc. Draw 3-6 columns to the right for prices.

Set aside a day or two and go shopping. Before you go make up a form similar to this comparative shopping form and price each of the items which you want in a department store, in a specialty store, and in a discount/off-price store, if available. If you don't have access to these stores, at least price from catalogs, keeping in mind that you can't always judge quality from catalogs. A day-long pricing excursion to the big city will pay in the long run. Leave the last two or three columns blank for some comparison shopping in Hong Kong. Prices vary there, too.

KEEP TRACK OF RECEIPTS

It's important to keep track of all of your purchases in order to make an accurate Customs declaration. Since it's so easy to misplace receipts, we've devised the following system which really works. Staple a sheet of notebook or accountant's paper to the front of a large manila envelope and number down the left side of the page. Draw one or two vertical columns down the right side (If you intend some really

COMPARATIVE SHOPPING FORM

	STORE				
ITEM	A	B	C	D	E
30" 6mm pink pearl necklace					
4 x 6 handwoven area rug					
Watercolor—24" x 36"					
Cloisonne lamp—24"/12"					
Geo. Jensen silver tea service (5 pieces)					
Anne Klein II silk blouse					

serious shopping you may need several pages!). Each evening we sort through that day's purchases, write a description including style and color of the purchase on the accompanying receipt, and enter that item on our receipt record. The item number is recorded on the receipt so that later we'll know exactly which item belongs to the receipt. The receipts all go into the manila envelope and the purchases are packed away. If you didn't receive a receipt for some reason, make a note of it beside the appropriate entry.

CUSTOMS DECLARATION RECORD FORM

RECEIPT #	ITEM	PRICE (HK$)	PRICE (US$)
1	white sweater	HK$350	
2			
3			
4			

PACK RIGHT FOR HONG KONG

Packing is one of the great travel challenges for many people. Trying to get everything you think you need into one or two bags can be frustrating, especially if you are visiting two or more countries which have different climates. You'll either take too much, and carry more than is necessary, or you'll take too little, thinking you'll buy what you need there, only to find that just the right items are ever so elusive.

We've learned over the years to err on the side of taking too little. If we start with less, we'll have room for more. Our ultimate goal is to make do with three changes of very versatile outfits, loosely packed into the lightest and largest carry-on the airlines will allow. Good hotels provide efficient laundry and drycleaning services, and you can always hand wash your *"undies"* yourself if you choose. Since extremely inexpensive luggage is so readily available, there's really no need to take any extra luggage for purchases you may make along the way. However, if you know you're going to buy a lot, you might decide to take a second empty suitcase with you. We have done this by nesting one inside the other with our trip clothing packed in the inside piece of luggage as well as by stuffing a second piece of luggage with the bubble wrap and other packing materials we will need later to protect our purchase. While softsided luggage is lighter weight, it will not provide the protection of a good hardsided piece for either your clothing or your shopping treasures.

Your goal is to avoid lugging an extensive wardrobe, cosmetics, library, and household goods around the world! Why not adopt our guiding principle for packing: *"When in doubt, leave it out."*

Above all, you want to return home loaded down with wonderful new purchases without paying extra weight charges. Hence, pack for the future rather than load yourself down with the past.

KEEP IT LIGHT

You should initially pack as lightly as possible. To do this you'll need to wisely select the proper mix of colors, fabrics, styles, and accessories. You'll want to wear some of your new acquisitions, too. Choose fabrics which are light in weight, and styles which don't have lots of extra fullness or weight, styles which mix with all the other garments you're taking.

But do take comfortable shoes, specific medication, and makeup you will need on the trip. This is not the place to save luggage room. These items may be difficult to find in the quality, brands, and price ranges you require. Take a double supply of necessary prescription drugs with you, divided and carried in two physically separate places, so if you lose one you'll still have the medicines you need. Transfer your cosmetics to small plastic containers and take only as much as you'll need.

TAKE COMFORTABLE SHOES

Hong Kong is definitely a walking city which requires good walking shoes to navigate many miles of very hard concrete sidewalks. Please don't buy new shoes for your trip unless you have several weeks to break them in. We prefer to clean up and polish two very comfortable pair of shoes which we've worn for a year or more.

We recommend taking at least one pair of comfortable walking shoes and one pair of dress shoes. Several major manufacturers of sport shoes now make attractive shoes which are engineered just for walking. Take only essential shoes which will coordinate with all of your outfits. Should your shoes become damaged, they can be repaired inexpensively and quickly in Hong Kong.

Don't worry about the appearance of your shoes. Our guiding principle for travel shoes: *"Be concerned about your overall visual appearance from the knees up; consider your comfort to be most important from the knees down—even if this means wearing sneakers with a skirt!"* In a crowded city few people will see or notice your feet.

CHOOSE THE CLOTHING TO TAKE

Color makes such a difference. Good color choices can make your travel wardrobe functional, versatile, and appealing. Choose a color scheme based on one basic color, either a versatile neutral such as black, grey, cream, brown, tan or navy, or one versatile medium tone such as blue or red which can serve as a neutral. The color you choose depends upon your taste and current wardrobe. We usually choose shoes first and then select clothing colors which will go with the shoes.

Your choice of travel clothes can make a difference in your self-confidence and comfort level. Be very selective in the clothing you take, and remember that you can buy inexpensive, comfortable, and attractive clothes along the way.

When planning your Hong Kong wardrobe, begin by visualizing the appropriate type of clothes for each day's activities. You will be shopping and traveling in a cosmopolitan city, so don't dress too casually. Search your closet for suitable items, hang them on a rod, and then start paring them down to the bare essentials. Select lightweight wool, cotton, or other natural fibers, perhaps mixed with a bit of polyester for wrinkle resistance, and choose with an eye to the season. Avoid wool from April through October, opting instead for light cottons and blends. Knits work very well because they resist wrinkles and require little or no pressing. A word of caution here, though: don't trust your knits to the hot water and hotter clothes dryers of the hotel laundry. Instead, send your knits to the dry cleaners, even though it may cost a bit more.

Don't count on shopping for ready-made men's or women's slacks in Hong Kong. We seldom find any which fit. Bring a pair or two and have some custom-made. Nor do you need to take cold weather clothes. Hong Kong is blessed with lots of sunshine and warm days. And even during the cool winter months you'll be quite comfortable dressed in layers: a long sleeved shirt or blouse, a sweater, and a windbreaker or raincoat will keep you warm and dry.

If you enjoy dressing well when you travel, you can easily do so without loading down your luggage by coordinating styles and color for different types of situations.

MEN'S CLOTHING

Men seem to have an easier time putting together a flexible wardrobe than women. Two or three pair of slacks—navy and tan and gray, three or four color coordinated sport shirts and one dress shirt plus a navy blazer will serve you well. You can pick up an inexpensive silk tie from one of the street stalls, and you are set for a week of sightseeing, shopping, and dining.

The most versatile sport shirt is one which includes at least two slacks colors in it: red with tan and navy, or yellow with gray and navy, for example. You can opt for solid colors, of course, but they are more apt to show soil.

Be sure to pack sufficient underwear. Men's cotton briefs and undershirts can be hand laundered but may take two days to dry. Throw in whatever you need for exercise: your swimsuit and running shorts and running shoes. Hong Kong has many interesting places to run and many hotels have pools or exercise facilities. In Hong Kong shorts are inappropriate as daytime wear in public.

ESSENTIAL CLOTHES FOR WOMEN

The choices for women are a bit more difficult, especially for those who set high standards for their appearance.

One of our basic guidelines for dressing, whether at home or abroad, is to start the day looking the best we can no matter where we are or how limited our wardrobe. Take time to complete your outfit and to feel good about yourself. Coordinate the colors, add a well-chosen accessory, light makeup, and a pretty but easy hair style. The extra few minutes it takes will do wonders for your self-esteem. If you plan well, a minimum number of items will get you through a two week trip, and you will look and feel terrific about your appearance at all times.

Prepare For a Unique Travel and Shopping Adventure 47

Packing a concise wardrobe involves carefully selecting easily interchangeable clothes. There are three basic rules for doing this:

- Choose **colors** which look attractive on you. Colors must coordinate.

- Choose **styles** which are comfortable, roomy, and appropriate for your destination. Items must be interchangeable.

- Choose **fabrics** which have a high natural fiber content (cotton, linen, wool). Cotton is best, especially if it is treated to resist wrinkles or contains small amounts of polyester. Cotton knits are great—packable, comfortable, and wrinkle resistant. Linen is cool and comfortable but wrinkles so badly that it's not recommended for travel. Very light-weight wool jersey (knit) and crepe are great for Hong Kong in the winter. 100% man-made fibers, such as polyester, are easy to care for but have the disadvantage of not breathing; they are very uncomfortable on hot and humid days.

A basic and adequate wardrobe consists of bottoms, tops, a jacket or sweater and a few accessories. Consider taking two skirts, one pair of slacks, a jacket which coordinates with the skirts and slacks, four to five tops to provide variety and which coordinate with every skirt and slacks. And include a few neck accessories which coordinate colorwise with your skirts and slacks. These could include necklaces, scarves, or pins, one item which matches the color of each bottom piece. Wearing a neck accessory which matches the skirt with a blouse of another color visually brings the skirt color up and balances the outfit. Scarves are great: lightweight and versatile, but you may not want the extra layer during warm, humid weather. One blouse should be dressy enough to put with one of the skirts for a fancy dinner. Your jacket should coordinate with this outfit, too. Remember those super cool air-conditioners you may encounter. A good selection of basic clothes and accessories might include:

Skirt/slacks:
- cream skirt
- tan/camel slacks
- black or navy skirt

Tops:	• cream/red check blouse • black/tan/cream print blouse • cream short sleeve sweater • blue blouse • black or navy camisole
Jacket:	• black or navy blazer
Accessories:	• beads: wooden, ivory, onyx • belts: red, cream, black, blue • scarves to coordinate

It's possible to travel fashionably with even fewer clothes if you start with a simple base. A base is either a classic one-piece dress or a matching bottom and blouse/sweater. By adding several sets of colorful accessories to this base, you can appear well dressed, and different, every day.

Focus around two or three of your own favorite colors and you'll have enough combinations to wear a different outfit nearly every day of your trip and look great. Leave most of your expensive jewelry at home, especially any jewelry that would focus unwanted attention on you. Wear a simple wedding band and a pair of pretty earrings which will go with everything. After all, if you are shopping for bargains, don't impress upon shopkeepers or muggers that you are loaded!

Choose a purse and a couple of belts to match your color scheme. One daytime purse, preferably with shoulder strap, is plenty. You might want to carry a large, lightweight nylon tote bag with a top zipper and outside pockets. This has room for purchases, map, notebook, and pen. Change for public transportation is in one of the outside pockets, and serious shopping money and credit cards are in your money stash—a carefully carried purse or hidden under your clothes. You might pack a small flat clutch for evening dress-up or purchase an inexpensive beaded evening bag in Hong Kong. Add a belt or two to match your basics and perhaps one more for a splash of color.

Pack sufficient underwear and sleepwear. And don't forget your swimsuit if your hotel has a pool.

If you follow this advice, you will be dressed well for all occasions, feel good about your appearance, and be able to carry all your clothes in one carry-on.

THROW IN A CALCULATOR

Since you will be doing a great deal of shopping, take a small battery operated calculator for adding your purchases and converting currency equivalents. Using a calculator when bargaining also impresses upon shopkeepers that you are a serious shopper who seems to know what you are doing. Solar calculators may be convenient to carry, but you may have difficulty operating them in dimly lit shops. There are several brands of *"conversion calculators"* now available, usually at your local luggage shop. These have the advantages of retaining memory even after they are turned off, so once you enter the conversion factors for the foreign currency its easier to calculate the equivalents. These conversion calculators also aid you in converting meters to yards and celsius to fahrenheit.

A currency conversion chart also can be a time-saver for figuring currency equivalents. You can make your own by listing the equivalent amounts for several standard US$ amounts ($5, $25, $60) on a small piece of heavy paper or on a business card; keep a copy in your pocket for quick reference.

CARRY BUSINESS CARDS

Asians, especially Chinese and Japanese, generously distribute, and expect to receive, business cards. For these very status conscious people, such cards are the ultimate sign of one's status and legitimacy. Asians appreciate receiving these cards, because they help alleviate the anxiety of having to figure out another's status for determining appropriate behavior toward one another. But more important, many Asians are afflicted by the *"big shot"* syndrome. You need to be aware of this syndrome and associated behaviors if you wish to benefit from it. Whether you like it or not, you will be participating in a relatively sophisticated social system where the buying and selling culture has many nuances; they determine how well you will come away with a good bargain.

When you present a business card to shopkeepers, many may think you are important enough to deserve a special price and that you may *"spread the word"* to your employees and business associates and encourage them to visit their shop. Many shops collect and proudly display the cards they have collected, especially cards from "big shots."

Knowing about this game, you may want to play, too. The easiest way to impress upon shopkeepers that you, too, are an important person who expects the very best price and service is to introduce yourself with your business card. Of course, you won't use your card everywhere. It's not appropriate or necessary in factory outlets, markets, China products stores, or with street vendors; but it often works wonders in a jewelry shop or with tailors. When you enter a shop where you intend to do serious business, approach a sales clerk, hand him or her your card, and say something like, *"I'm looking for a nice string of pearls"* or *"I need to have some garments tailored."* If you haven't played the business card game before, you'll be pleasantly surprised with the response.

If you don't carry a business card, consider having some printed at a local print shop. Of course, the more impressive your title, the greater the impression the card will create. The down side is that while an impressive title may get you better service, it may also mean a high price. At the very least a business card is an easy way to leave shipping information for items too large to carry with you. A business card can be especially useful in getting corporate discounts at hotels.

REVIEW YOUR PACKING CHECKLIST

Before you close your suitcases and bags, check to see if you have packed everything you need by reviewing this checklist:

Packing

- Included only the essentials for the trip
- Kept total weight to a minimum

Luggage

- Two suitcases
- One carry-on with one change of clothes, toiletries, cosmetics, and documents
- One or more collapsible bags
- Small nylon backpack (for camera and maps)

- Can carry all baggage by myself without the assistance of a porter or a pushcart

Purse and Wallet

- Leather shoulder bag with outside pocket (women)
- Clutch purse (women)
- Wallet, purse, and clutch includes only essential items needed for this trip

Packing Materials

- Plastic bubble-wrap for wrapping delicate items
- Scissors and/or pocket knife (packed in check-through luggage)
- Wrapping cord and strapping tape
- Carrying strap

Film/Camera

- Camera and accessories for purse and/or backpack
- Sufficient film
- Film protectors for X-ray machines

Electrical Appliances

- Hairdryer (converts to 220-volt)
- Curling iron (220-volt or butane)—can purchase in Hong Kong
- Plug adaptors
- Voltage converter
- Shaver (converts to 220-volt)

Clothes

- Coordinated wardrobe
- Swim suit

Shoes

- One or two pair of comfortable walking shoes
- One pair of dress shoes (comfortable too!)
- Slippers or shower thongs

Accessories

- Watch
- Neck pieces or necktie
- Ring

Security

- Flashlight
- Burglar/firm alarm

Reading Materials

- Paperback book(s)
- Travel guides
- Envelope with travel information

Odds and Ends

- Travel alarm clock
- Aspirin, cold remedies, medicated ointment for cuts
- Medication for diarrhea
- Prescription drugs
- Prescription for eyeglasses
- Sunglasses
- Band-aids
- Notepad, pens, paper clips, rubber bands
- Sewing kit and safety pins
- Ziplock bags
- Shampoo
- Manila envelopes
- Collapsible umbrella
- Calculator
- Suntan lotion with sunscreen/Solarcaine
- Deodorant
- Cosmetics
- Small mirror
- Moist towlettes
- Handi-wipes
- BenGay
- Nail clippers, file, and emery board
- Retractable tape measure
- Laundry soap
- Skirt hangers

5 ARRIVING AND SURVIVING HONG KONG

You should now be well prepared to begin your shopping adventure in earnest as soon as you arrive in Hong Kong. Assuming you will arrive and depart Hong Kong by air, it's useful to examine how to best orient yourself to the arrival and departure processes so that you can truly enjoy Hong Kong from the very moment you arrive.

ARRIVAL

Your flight into Hong Kong International Airport will be one of the most interesting and memorable landings anywhere in the world. On a clear day the approach view to Hong Kong is breathtaking. But you may or may not want to view all of this rather exciting landing. It may, indeed, take away your breath as you experience your first great Hong Kong adventure!

On the typical arrival, within 20 minutes of landing, you begin seeing the South China coast and numerous islands dotting the coastal area. Located just off the congested Kowloon section, Hong Kong International Airport offers pilots a true challenge complete with turbulence and quick maneuvers. Seasoned pilots still marvel at this configuration. The landing approach is one of the world's most unusual as pilots must carefully guide their planes into *"Typhoon Alley."* Approaching the final 15 miles at 750 feet above sea level, with visibility often near zero and turbulence high, the pilot banks the plane to avoid the hills and high rise housing estates hugging the harbor of Hong Kong Island. As the screaming turbines glide over the numerous junks, sampans, water-taxis, cargo ships, patrol boats, and ferries plying the choppy silver-and-green harbor waters, tall buildings seem to poke at the belly of the plane. Suddenly in the final approach apartments, hotels, and office buildings appear beside the plane as you peer into their windows. The alert pilot levels the plane's wings at 200 feet and gently touches down on the 8,000-foot-long concrete runway that thrusts into Kowloon Bay on reclaimed land. This is just the first of many exhilarating experiences awaiting you in Hong Kong!

IMMIGRATION LINES

After deplaning, you quickly proceed to the Immigration desks. Unfortunately, Hong Kong's reputation for organization and efficiency is not always well served in its Immigration lines, especially when more than one plane of passengers arrives for processing. While Immigration officials now use computers to check passport names and numbers against their records, processing can be slow. Non-English speaking tourists—many who failed to complete their Immigration forms while on the plane—further back up the lines as they try to communicate with Immigration officials. Two useful suggestions at this point. First, pick up some of the complimentary tourist literature which is conveniently located near Immigration as you move into the long lines and do some reading on *"what's up this week"* while you wait your turn. Second, try to choose a line with English-speaking western tourists. Such a line will be processed much faster than lines with non-English speaking people.

BAGGAGE RETRIEVAL

After Immigration, you will proceed to the nearby baggage claim area where you retrieve your luggage for your final stop at the Customs section. As you leave Immigration look straight ahead for a sign that tells you which carousel has your bags. You may also want to receive

Arrive and Survive Hong Kong 55

a plastic bag filled with tourist literature offered to you by airport employees waiting to greet you as you leave the Immigration counter.

Be prepared to carry your own luggage since this section of the airport seems to be short on pushcarts and few porters are available. Look for signs marked *"Non-Residents"* which are suspended from the ceiling over the Customs booths; queue in front of one of the booths.

CUSTOMS PROCEDURES

Customs is relatively efficient. However, if you get into a line of Asian travelers, you may have a long wait. Hong Kong Customs officials tend to spend more time probing the luggage of fellow Asians than the bags of North Americans, Europeans, and Australians. They are looking for drugs. Fellow Asians, especially frequent travelers, seem to be more likely candidates for such checks.

Hong Kong Customs permits you to bring in duty-free 200 cigarettes or 50 cigars or 60 grams of tobacco and one liter of alcohol. Be forewarned that Hong Kong has very strict laws against importation of firearms, ammunition, drugs, and mace. You will need a special license for firearms and ammunition; your mace will be confiscated; and you go directly to jail for illegal drugs.

DEPARTURE TAX

When you leave Hong Kong by air, you will be charged an airport departure tax. At present it is HK$100 (US$12.82) for adults and HK$50 (US$6.41) for children between the ages of 2 and 11. Be sure to set aside enough local currency to pay this exit fee. We stash our HK$100 inside our passport so we will be sure not to spend it.

AIRPORT SECURITY

Hong Kong has one of the most thorough airport security systems in the world. Not only do they X-ray all luggage, they sometimes hand check carry-on pieces and do body scans. Since the security check system can take a great deal of time, allot yourself enough time to pass through this system when departing.

If you carry an aerosol can of mosquito repellent, be sure to pack it in your check-through luggage when leaving Hong Kong. If it is in your carry-on luggage, it will be confiscated. The X-ray machines always detect these aerosol cans. Indeed, the airport has a backroom with hundreds of such confiscated aerosol mosquito repellent cans, along with aerosol cans of spray paint and lysol! The only aerosol cans permitted in carry-on luggage are hairspray and deodorant.

AIRPORT TOURIST SERVICES

After Customs you will enter the **Airport Buffer Hall** and from there you are free to leave the airport. But before exiting to the street for a hotel limo, bus, or taxi, you should consider making two or three more airport stops. The first thing you will see in the Airport Buffer Hall are money-changers. Be wary here. While you will need some local currency to get to your hotel, don't change much money here. If you are with a tour group, avoid changing any of your money now. The airport exchange rates are some of the worst in the world. Since money-changing is not regulated in Hong Kong, these places are free to set any exchange rates they feel they can get away with, and indeed they do! Expect to lose anywhere from 4 to 8 percent on your money changed at the airport exchange windows. Since most taxi rides should not cost more than US$5, you don't need to exchange a great deal more than that. Your hotel will give you a better rate, and it is only 20 minutes away. The airport money-changers may try to persuade you to change more money by saying they give the same exchange rates as the banks, but this has not been our experience.

Also in the Airport Buffer Hall and near the money-changers are two desks worth visiting. The **Hong Kong Tourist Association (HKTA)** desk will provide you with tourist literature, including excellent maps, self-guided tour brochures, and a shopping and dining guide. The friendly personnel are very helpful and can answer most of your questions.

Another nearby desk is operated by the **Hong Kong Hotel Association (HKHA),** but you can easily miss it since it is located off to the far right side from the other desks. If you do not have hotel reservations, this desk will help you. Do not phone hotels to make your own reservations since you will be wasting your time and money and the experience will be frustrating. Use the HKHA service. The personnel specialize in making hotel reservations, it costs you nothing, and it is by far the best airport hotel reservation service we have ever encountered. The service represents most hotels in Hong Kong and is not biased toward deluxe and first-class accommodations. You can even make reservations here for the relatively inexpensive and superbly located YMCA. Just tell the person at this desk what type of accommodations you wish in terms of price, services, and location. The person then opens a loose-leaf book with pictures and listings of rates and services for each hotel in reference to a map. You will be told how convenient or inconvenient each option is in terms of public transportation and proximity to shopping areas. Once you decide on a particular hotel, the person will call the hotel to see if there is a vacancy in your price and service range. If you ask for a discount, the person will make this inquiry for you.

AIRPORT TO HOTEL TRANSPORTATION

Once you have a confirmed hotel reservation in hand, the personnel at the HKHA desk will also arrange your hotel transportation through one of the airport coaches, hotel buses, or hotel cars which are conveniently located just outside the adjacent exit door.

An air-conditioned Airbus service, departing the airport every 15 minutes, takes passengers to most major hotels in Hong Kong. Route A1, for example, operates from 7am to 11:30pm and stops at 15 hotels in Tsimshatsui district of Kowloon. The fare is HK$5. Route A2 operates from 6:50am to 11:20pm and stops at seven hotels in Central and Wanchai districts on Hong Kong Island. The fare on this route is HK$7. Route A3 operates from 6:55am to 11:25pm and stops at three hotels in Causeway Bay, Hong Kong Island. The fare on this route is also HK$7.

Many hotels have a bus or car parked beneath a signboard just outside the Buffer Hall, behind the HKTA desk. The signboards are in English and in alphabetical order. At times this area becomes very disorganized as Rolls Royces, Mercedes-Benz, and BMWs complete for curb space. If it appears confusing to you, just ask some of the many hotel personnel working in this area—most carry clipboards and walkie-talkies—for information on your hotel representative.

Should you wish to take a taxi instead, walk to the left of the hotel transportation area and proceed around the corner until you come to the taxi queues. This area is also the front entrance to the large arrival hall. If you do this, ask the Hong Kong Hotel Association representative to give you a hotel brochure or write the name and address of the hotel in Chinese so you can give it to a taxi driver who may not speak or understand English.

Exiting the airport through the main exit area can be a disorienting experience. If you don't need to stop at the service desks in the Buffer Hall, stay to your left as you leave Customs and you will enter a large arrival hall. This area is normally crammed with people waiting for their friends and relatives. This is a typical Asian airport scene. Asians tend to bring whole families to airport departure and arrival areas and thereby overload these facilities. The crowds should not be interpreted as an indication of overpopulation—only familial bonds. At this point push your way through the crowds to the taxi queue just outside the front door. The queues are well organized and taxis are frequent. You should not have to wait long for transportation, although at peak landing times there may be a wait. The taxis are metered, air-conditioned, inexpensive, and comfortable. Take a taxi whenever you can during your stay in Hong Kong.

CURRENCY AND EXCHANGE RATES

Each Hong Kong dollar is roughly equivalent to US$.13 or HK$7.80 for each US$1. The Hong Kong dollar is divided into 100 cents, and coins are issued in 5¢, 10¢, 20¢, 50¢, HK$1, HK$2, and HK$5 denominations. Notes are printed in HK$10, HK$50, HK$100, HK$500, and HK$1,000 multi-colored bills.

If you don't use a pocket calculator, the easy ways to convert the local currency into a close approximation of the U.S. dollar value is to divide quoted prices by eight or type up a simple pocket-sized conversion table which shows at a glance the common equivalents. Since the Hong Kong currency is relatively stable against the U.S. dollar, such approximations and tables are fairly accurate.

You will receive the best exchange rates at banks and among the licensed money-changers in the business and shopping districts, some of which give better rates than the banks. Traveler's checks receive a better exchange rate than currency. Airport money-changers and hotels give the worst exchange rates. Other than at the airport, the licensed money-changers offer good exchange rates, but they do

Arrive and Survive Hong Kong 59

charge commissions. These vendors often advertise *"no commission,"* but this is confusing and somewhat misleading. The so-called *"no commission"* applies only when you *"sell"* your Hong Kong dollars to the vendor for a foreign currency; you pay a commission when you *"buy"* Hong Kong dollars with a foreign currency. In other words, you must pay a commission when you exchange your foreign currency for Hong Kong dollars. Welcome to Hong Kong entrepreneurship!

You may choose to pay your hotel and restaurant bills with credit cards since you will receive the official bank exchange rate when the charge is processed through the banking system.

If you use foreign currency or traveler's checks when shopping, be sure you receive the bank exchange rate. The current bank exchange rate is published each day in Hong Kong's major English newspaper, the *South China Morning Post*.

WATER

Use your own judgment as to whether or not to drink the local tap water. We still prefer bottled water. All water from Government mains, which covers most of Hong Kong, supposedly meets United Nations World Health Organization standards and is deemed safe to drink. Water in parts of the New Territories and Outlying Islands is still drawn from wells and is not safe to drink. Many of the new and recently renovated hotels will have a built-in faucet in your bathroom for purified water. Others provide a thermos pitcher of pure water. And still others supply your room refrigerator with bottled water. The water which is served in tourist-type restaurants is safe to drink. Outside these locations it is best to drink bottled soft drinks and fruit juices; skip the ice since it may be made from impure tap water. You'll find a wide selection of carbonated beverages, such as Coke, Pepsi, 7-Up, and Sprite as well as numerous fruit juices which make wonderful drinks and can be easily carried in your bag. Local beers are good, rivaling the best of the European beers. Coffee and tea are always available.

ELECTRICITY

While electricity in Hong Kong is supplied at 220 volts and 50 cycles, Hong Kong has one of the world's strangest electrical outlet configurations. If you take electrical appliances, you will need a voltage convertor and a special 3-prong adaptor. Buy the convertor and adaptor at luggage shops or other travel-related stores at home. These adaptors can also be purchased in an electrical appliance shop in Hong Kong or your hotel should supply you with one upon request. In addition, you may have difficulty inserting your appliance into the outlet, because many outlets have safety-lock features which require you to insert a stick in the outlet to unlock the other prongs. When in doubt as to how to use the local electricity, call housekeeping for a demonstration.

BUSINESS HOURS

Hong Kong business hours vary depending on the particular type of business. **Offices** are normally open between 9am and 5pm. **Banks** are generally open from 9:30am to 4pm Monday through Friday and from 9:30am to 12 noon on Saturdays. Most licensed **money-changers** stay open until 5pm, but many also stay open until late evening in busy shopping areas.

Hours for **shops** differ from one shopping district to another. In the Central District (Hong Kong side), shops are open from 10am to 6pm. In Causeway Bay (Hong Kong side), and Tsimshatsui (Kowloon side), most stores are open from 10am to 10pm; many are open by 9:30am. Most shops are open seven days a week and on all holidays, except the first few days of the Chinese New Year. However, there are exceptions, especially among the antique shops along Hollywood Road on Hong Kong Island; many are closed on Sundays. Before venturing far from your hotel for Sunday shopping, check with your hotel or the Hong Kong Tourist Association concerning shopping hours.

TRANSPORTATION

Hong Kong is an easy city to get around in, although your first foray into the crowded streets may be confusing. Above all, this is a compact walking city with ample forms of excellent and inexpensive public transportation. The major requirement for successful shopping is a good pair of walking shoes and a great deal of perseverance and persistence. You need not hire a private car and driver, unless you want to pamper yourself with the elegant privacy of an expensive Rolls Royce or Mercedes-Benz. Within each shopping district you can easily walk from one shop to another. In going from one shopping area to another, you can take trams, taxis, ferries, double-decker buses or the subways. There are lots of mini-buses buzzing around the city but the routing and destinations are obscure and the English destination is difficult to read. To go between Kowloon Peninsula and Hong Kong Island you can take the ever charming Star Ferry, subway, or taxi. However, if you take a taxi be aware that you will pay the tunnel toll charge **both ways**, since taxis are licensed to operate only on one side of the harbor and you have to pay for his return trip. If you plan to travel to the New Territories, your choices are train, bus, or taxi. Trips around Hong Kong Island are most fun by double-decker bus.

If you are not used to taking public transportation, Hong Kong is an excellent place to learn quickly and enjoy the experience. We normally start our stay with a first-class, 10¢ ride on the **Star Ferry** which connects Kowloon Peninsula with Hong Kong Island. It's a wonderful way to get a feel of the city as you view the skyline of tall buildings and mountains and watch the water traffic of bobbing junks, water taxis, ferries, and freighters plying the colorful Victoria Harbour.

The **subway**, an underground railway system known in Hong Kong as the MTR (Mass Transit Railway), is fast, efficient, clean, convenient, safe, and easy to understand. It operates along the north shore of Hong Kong Island between Sheun Wan and Chi Wan, goes under the harbor to Kowloon, and extends northwest to Tsuen Wan and east to Kwun Tong. Each station has several entrances, which are identified by the MTR sign which looks like a six-legged spider. Panels inside the station and in the subway cars show the routing and give clear directions for paying and boarding. Spend as much time as you need to figure out the system. There are helpful information booths at the upper level of each station, and you can get a free copy of *The MTR Tourist Guide* here. You will need exact fare in $1, $2, and 50¢ coins. Change machines are available. The cheapest way to use the MTR is with a HK$15 MTR Tourist Ticket which you can purchase at the HKTA offices, MTR offices, or Hang Seng Banks at the major MTR stations. You'll need to show your passport to prove your tourist status.

The MTR is an ideal method of travel between Nathan Road in Kowloon and Central or Causeway Bay on Hong Kong Island—your major shopping destinations. However, the system gets very crowded during rush hour. Use MTR especially when you are in a hurry to return to your hotel and have few items to carry.

Riding the double-decker **buses** is a wonderful means for touring Hong Kong Island, especially for traveling to Stanley and Aberdeen and for other long distance rides. In Kowloon the red and cream buses operated by the Kowloon Motor bus Company (KMB) can be boarded at the Star Ferry terminal. On Hong Kong Island the blue and white buses operated by the China Motor Bus Company (CMB) are conveniently located near the Connaught Centre, Star Ferry, and the Admiralty MTR Station. Contact the Hong Kong Tourist Association office (Star Ferry, Kowloon or Connaught Centre, Hong Kong) for a detailed leaflet on the major bus routes. Buses operate from 6am to midnight. Since buses do not give change, take plenty of coins—80¢ to $5—for exact change.

Trams, or double-decker electric street cars, run on tracks along the north shore of Hong Kong Island for about 10 miles connecting North Point, Wanchai, Central and Kennedy Town districts. Seating yourself on the top deck, this is a great form of transportation for viewing the main streets of these districts and is one of the best and cheapest tours in all of Hong Kong.

Minibuses carry approximately 14 people and are conveniently located throughout Kowloon Peninsula and Hong Kong Island. An inexpensive form of transportation preferred by locals, these red and yellow minivans have destinations printed in large Chinese characters followed by small English letters. Minibuses are convenient ways to travel the length of Nathan Road, from Central to Wanchai, and to Causeway Bay and North Point. Depending on the distance traveled, fares range from HK$2 to HK$6. Just shout when you want to get off and pay as you exit.

Maxicabs are similar to minibuses. These green and yellow vehicles are numbered and make regular stops, although some drivers stop whenever they feel like it. Fares range from HK$1 to HK$4 depending on the distance traveled. Carry HK$1 coins and try to give exact change. A useful maxicab to remember is No. 1. This maxicab leaves the Star Ferry Kowloon every five minutes for Tsimshatsui East—one of the easiest and least expensive ways to travel to this major shopping destination.

We normally use **taxis** when we are in a hurry, are hot and tired, want private air-conditioned transportation, or have several packages to transport back to our hotel. In short, we use taxis a lot. Taxis in

Hong Kong are metered, comfortable, and inexpensive. They are red and silver and available on both sides of the harbor. The current fare is HK$5 for the first two kilometers (1.2 miles) and 70¢ for each additional ¼ kilometer—quite a bargain since a ride is seldom longer than 2½ kilometers. If you take a taxi between Kowloon and Hong Kong Island, you must pay an additional HK$10 for the Harbour Tunnel toll. It is cheaper to cross the harbor by ferry or subway. In many areas you must queue for taxis which at times may involve long lines. But use them whenever you can. Make sure you have an English-Chinese map to point out where you want to go since most taxi drivers do not speak English.

In addition to the Star Ferry, one of the most memorable rides is the **Peak Tram** to Victoria Peak on Hong Kong Island. It runs 1305 feet, stops twice on the way up, and provides a spectacular view of Hong Kong Harbour and Kowloon Peninsula. At the top you will find shops, restaurants, and some pleasant walks. Board the Peak Tram from its lower terminal at the St. John's Building entrance, a 10 minute walk from the Star Ferry. A free shuttle bus operates daily from 9:10am to 6:50pm from the Star Ferry. Look for a green bus stop sign and the double-decker green bus which runs at 20 minute intervals. You should take the tram at least once. Better still, take it twice—once during the day and once at night. You will see two different Hong Kongs—both breathtaking, one romantic.

Rickshaws are available for tourists who wish to confirm their worst stereotypes of the Orient. Located near the Star Ferry at Connaught Centre on Hong Kong Island, several emaciated-looking old men wait to prey on unsuspecting tourists. They will pose for pictures or give short rides to those who are willing to pay. Contrary to what you might think, these are not necessarily nice old men, although they appear very friendly—at first. Many are rip-off artists who entrap you into paying high prices (HK$15-$25, or more if they can get it from you) for what you may think is a cute idea. If you wish to indulge in this rather pathetic form of tourist entertainment, make sure you agree on prices before taking a picture or climbing into their red cages of human bondage. By refusing to patronize these people, you can help hasten their demise before China does so in 1997!

TOURS AND TRAVEL AGENTS

The Hong Kong Tourist Association (HKTA) provides excellent maps and brochures to assist you in planning your own shopping and sightseeing activities or joining organized tours of the New Territories, Kowloon Peninsula, Hong Kong Island, and the surrounding islands. If you prefer the comfort and convenience of organized tours, you can arrange these through your hotel or contact the tour operators directly. The Hong Kong Tourist Association has compiled a useful booklet entitled **Sightseeing** which outlines most of the tours offered by these companies. You can visit the HKTA offices or call their inquiry service at 801-7177 for this information. Several tour companies and agencies provide two to three-hour guided tours of Hong Kong by coach or private car. These are excellent ways to get a good overview of Hong Kong. The HKTA provides information on these tours.

Hong Kong is the best place in Asia for arranging flights to other countries and for purchasing discounted air tickets. Contact a travel agent to make such arrangements. If you are planning to visit China, make the China Travel Service one of your first stops. They handle all travel into China. You should be able to quickly arrange to join one of their many one to three day tours into China—mainly to Guangzhou (Canton)—operated by several tour companies in Hong Kong. You also can arrange tours to Macau through the Macau Tourist Information Bureau (Room 305, Shun Tak Centre, 200 Connaught Road, Central, Tel 540-8180).

LANGUAGE

English is spoken in most places you will frequent in Hong Kong. Within the commercial districts, most signs and menus are in both English and Chinese. The owners and managers of most businesses know English quite well since they do business daily with Australians, Britons, and Americans. Should someone answer the telephone in Chinese, just tell the person what you want in English. Most of the time the person will quickly switch to English or call someone else to the phone who can communicate with you. English language newspapers, magazines, and telephone books are widely available.

One language problem you may encounter relates to taxi drivers. Few seem to speak or even try to understand English. Moreover, except for the magic words *"Star Ferry,"* close enough does not count with most taxi drivers; they seem to have difficulty comprehending names approximating the actual Chinese pronunciation. You either get the name right, or you don't get it at all. Thus, it is best to have an English-Chinese map ready as well as addresses written in Chinese before you enter a taxi. Hotel personnel as well as shopkeepers will be happy to write in Chinese the information you need to communicate to your taxi driver. It is always a good idea to take a hotel card with you so you can easily communicate to taxi drivers where you want to return. Also, collect business cards from stores and shops you may wish to return to so you can easily direct a taxi driver back to the location. Always check to be sure the taxi meter has been reset and is running.

Other language problems can occur when you wander off the beaten path. If you travel to the non-tourist areas of Hong Kong, especially in the New Territories, you may find few people during the day who speak English. In these situations you will have to do your best with a combination of sign language and a good sense of humor. Don't worry; you will not get lost for long, and half the fun are the amusing encounters you will have with non-English speaking people as both you and they attempt to find you a way back. Often young students who are studying English can assist you—if they are not too shy and run away from you!

TIPPING AND SERVICE CHARGES

While most Hong Kong hotels and restaurants are not noted for fabulous service, they nonetheless charge you for service. In addition, their personnel hope to receive tips. Since Hong Kong's tipping culture is not well defined, you can use your own judgment as to whether a service deserves a tip.

Ten percent is the general tipping rule in Hong Kong for most services. Since most hotels and restaurants add a 10 percent service charge to your bill, we do not encourage you to leave tips when you are already paying a service charge. Do so only when a service is exceptional. Compared to other Asian countries, Hong Kong service is fair to good but seldom exceptional; at times it is surly. But waiters and others do appreciate an additional tip; loose change, rather than a percentage tip, is acceptable. Taxi drivers do not expect a percentage tip, but they do welcome rounding-up their meter fares to the next Hong Kong dollar. If you need special assistance, a few up-front dollars will normally get you what you want; money does talk in Hong Kong. In situations where prices for services are unclear, such as rickshaw pullers and porters, agree to the price in advance.

SAFETY AND SECURITY

Hong Kong is a relatively safe city. However, like any big city, it has its share of pickpockets, thieves, and thugs. When traveling abroad, it's always best to err by being overly cautious than not cautious enough.

Always close your hotel room door behind you as you come into the room. Never leave it ajar. Always check through the peephole before opening the door to anyone. If someone has offered to bring merchandise to your room, take the precaution to have someone else in the room with you. Be very careful whom you invite into your room.

On the street, women should keep their shopping bag and purse next to their body; men should keep their wallet in their front pocket. When waiting to cross the street, stand a few feet back from the curb and keep bags close in front of you.

PHOTOGRAPHY AND FILM

You'll enjoy having your favorite camera as you tour and shop Hong Kong. Fast film and/or a flash is needed for indoor shots, and a wide angle and mini zoom is handy for street shots. You may quickly discover that some people dislike having you take their picture, so do ask first or shoot fast. Processing is quick, reliable, and inexpensive at the many one-hour labs which are scattered throughout the city.

KEEPING FIT

Hong Kong is a wonderful city for aerobic walking and running. Indeed, some of the hotels now issue running maps showing several running/walking areas which avoid heavy foot and car traffic. And many of the better hotels offer exercise facilities within the complex, such as swimming pools, weight equipment, and fitness rooms.

On Kowloon you can exercise on the top deck of Ocean Terminal, around the terminal and the connecting hotels and shopping complexes at street level, and along the harbour side of the Regent and Shangri-La hotels. Join the locals at one of the area parks early in the morning for Tai Chi exercises.

On Hong Kong Island you will find several exercise areas. However, they may be more challenging given the steep vertical incline of the city. You will find several large parks as well as many stadiums with running tracks.

6 EXPERIENCING CONVENIENCES AND INCONVENIENCES

Hong Kong is a very convenient city to visit. You will easily find everything you need here. However, like any other city, Hong Kong does have its inconveniences and irritants that can make an otherwise wonderful trip less than satisfactory. The more you are aware of the inconveniences, the better prepared you should be to adjust to the situation and enjoy your stay.

A NINE-STAR CITY

On a scale of 1 to 10, Hong Kong is a 9-star city. It leaves little to the imagination. It is the ultimate city for traveling comfort and convenience as well as a nice transition from the familiar comforts of home to the exotic experiences of Asia. Indeed, many travel agents wisely book their clients into Hong Kong for a few days at both ends of their Oriental adventures.

Hong Kong has many things going for it as an attractive travel and shopping destination. Arrival at the airport is relatively efficient; the

Hong Kong Tourist Association provides a great deal of self-directed information and assistance; the transportation alternatives are numerous and inexpensive; many tours are available; English is widely spoken; and fine hotels and restaurants are plentiful.

This is a relatively hassle-free city, organized to make your visit most rewarding for both you and the local economy. The streets may initially be disorienting, but once you walk around a few hotels, restaurants, and shopping complexes, you will adjust quite well to this city.

For a price, you can get just about anything you want in Hong Kong. Hairdressers and barbers are plentiful; the postal system is excellent; telephones work well; and cables, telexes, and international telephone calls and faxs can be made easily. The compactness of Hong Kong means that most of your shopping, restaurants, services, and entertainment are located within walking distance or only a short taxi ride from your hotel. In Hong Kong you can purchase inexpensive air tickets to other parts of the world as well as arrange last-minute trips to the nearby gambler's paradise of Macau, into China, over to Taiwan, up to Seoul and Tokyo, and down to Bangkok, Singapore, Jakarta, and Manila. This convenience factor is one of the major reasons that shopping in Hong Kong is such a pleasure. With a little effort, hassle-free Hong Kong becomes a wonderful travel and shopping experience.

But Hong Kong also has its downsides which can irritate visitors who are not prepared to deal with what may become problems for them. Among Hong Kong's inconveniences and irritants are massive crowds, questionable service, touts and cheats, restrooms, and smokers.

MASSIVE CROWDS

A very crowded and congested city, Hong Kong bothers many westerners who are used to having greater personal space and privacy. You will indeed experience the teeming masses wherever you go in Hong Kong. The crowds are both visually and physically exhausting for many tourists.

Hong Kong is very crowded and congested, with waves of humanity pushing and shoving in many shopping areas and especially during rush hour and on weekends as if one were at Times Square during Christmas and New Years! To best enjoy your shopping experience, don't spend long hours in these crowds. Occasionally retreat to you hotel room or an uncongested restaurant to experience an hour or so of personal space.

Weekends are a good time to avoid shopping arcades. On Saturdays and Sundays the sidewalks and shopping arcades in Hong Kong tend to be very crowded with children and office workers who have the weekend off. If you decide to tour outside the city, avoid visiting Macau on the weekend when thousands of Hong Kong residents flock to this gambling paradise.

QUESTIONABLE SERVICE

Service varies greatly in Hong Kong. You will encounter some of the world's most outstanding service in such deluxe hotels as the Mandarin, Regent, and Peninsula as well as in many restaurants and shops. However, service in many other hotels, shops, and restaurants may leave much to be desired. Sometimes you will be overwhelmed with sales people who follow you around watching your every move in their shop. As salespeople hover around, you may feel uneasy browsing in the shop. In other places salespeople may neglect you altogether as they sit around eating or talking to friends. And service in other places may simply be surly, or you may feel you are dealing with pushy con artists.

As noted earlier, many hotels and restaurants automatically add a 10 percent service charge to your bill. Given the varied levels of service found in Hong Kong, do not feel obligated to give additional tips just because tipping may be a local custom or an expectation. Tip only for special or exceptional service. Many visitors, especially Americans, have a habit of over-tipping as well as tipping for questionable service.

TOUTS AND CHEATING

Sooner or later you will encounter the Hong Kong tout who preys on tourists. These are the "10 percent men"—you are potentially worth 10 percent to them if you buy where they take you. They approach you ostensibly to help you get a good deal on anything from buying jewelry

Experience Conveniences and Inconveniences 71

to satisfying your sexual fantasies. They stand on street corners and hang around hotels frequented by tourists. Avoid these people. They only take you to places which give them a commission. You'll pay 20 to 50 percent more than you could have on your own without their assistance.

When approached by such people, do not start a conversation since you will merely encourage them to further pester you. Keep walking and firmly say *"No, not interested today."* End the conversation there.

You should also beware of tour guides and taxi drivers who want to end your journey by giving you one *"extra"*—an unscheduled trip to a local factory or shop where they will give you a *"very special deal."* The so-called *"special"* is most likely you getting ripped-off and the guide getting a 10-20 percent commission on any of your purchases. If and when this *"extra"* is offered to you, insist that you be returned immediately to your hotel since you do not want to take advantage of this deal. It's okay to be adamant at this point, and insist on your right to be returned to your hotel. The pattern is always the same. If you are being taken to a special shop, you are indeed being *"taken."* If you like the looks of the shop, return on your own without the local tour guide.

You may occasionally encounter some form of cheating, mostly petty. This cheating will range from misrepresentation of goods, such as fake watches and jewelry, to giving you the wrong change or overcharging you for hotels, meals, and transportation. Big cheating is found with jewelry, antiques, and electronic goods in the small shops of Hong Kong; most of these shops are not sanctioned by the HKTA. The major problem is *"bait and switch."* While purchasing an item, the clerk may go to the back room to get you one in a box. But later you discover the item in the box is not the one you purchased; it's either a completely different model or an outdated item. You can avoid such a problem by opening the box and carefully checking your purchase before you pay and leave the store.

SURPRISING RESTROOMS

Should you find yourself in need of a restroom while you are out shopping, head for the nearest tourist hotel. Public facilities are generally located in the lobby or on the first floor. Restrooms are often available, though not always conveniently located, in major shopping arcades and in restaurants. If you are shopping outside the central districts of the city, be prepared for the Asian toilet experience. The waterseal toilet is the standard fixture found outside most western hotels and restaurants. Built of porcelain and nearly level with the floor, it requires squatting skills which most westerners find discomforting. Be prepared to encounter a few of these in your travels.

Toilet paper is usually absent in such places. Be advised to always travel with an emergency supply of paper or tissues. You may also encounter restrooms which seem dirty and smelly, but you generally won't find people using the sidewalks as they do in parts of Europe.

IRRITATING SMOKERS

If you are a non-smoker and have a low tolerance for smokers who pollute your air, many Asians may bother you with their public smoking behavior. Asians tend to be heavy smokers, and they tend to disregard the presence of non-smokers as well as ignore *"no smoking"* signs. If you are a non-smoker and encounter problems, it is best to take preventive action or nicely complain. In public waiting areas, such as the airport which does not set aside *"no smoking"* areas, try to seat yourself as far away from crowds as possible or near a ventilated door or window. Use a hand fan. If the smoke gets too oppressive, which it often does, ask personnel in charge for assistance in getting relief.

In restaurants without *"no smoking"* sections, ask to be seated by a window or near a ventilated area. If you are in the middle of your meal and smoke begins to bother you—ask to be moved to another table and nicely complain that *"the smoke is terrible in your restaurant."* The restaurant will usually accommodate. In fact, if more people made such requests, maybe more restaurants would have the good sense to set aside *"no smoking"* areas. Many of the restaurants in major hotels have already taken the initiative to reserve *"no smoking"* sections. If you have been given a hotel room which was recently and obviously vacated by a smoker, ask to be assigned to another room. The usual remedy, a heavy spray of room deodorizer, isn't very effective.

If you are sitting in a *"no smoking"* section on an airplane and someone lights up, by all means nicely point out this fact to the airline personnel who will then ask the person to either extinguish their cigarette or move to the *"smoking"* section. Do this rather than complain directly to the violator. Asian passengers, while equally disturbed by smoking, usually do not take such initiative. Therefore, it may be up to you to point out the problem.

ADAPT TO THE SITUATION

You need to be prepared to respond to potential problems as well as avoid certain situations which inevitably lead to disappointments. Remember, Hong Kong is not home; you may or may not have it as good or better than home, depending on how you position yourself in Hong Kong. Since complaining and confrontation will not help you much in getting your way, you are always better off practicing a certain degree of *"avoidance behavior"* to most enjoy your trip. Like many Asians, you must **create your own private space** when handling daily problems. By all means avoid the touts and the *"good deal"* merchants; none have anything special to offer you other than getting you to pay exorbitant prices. Learn about quality goods; do comparative shopping before you go to Hong Kong so that you don't get cheated.

If you prefer not experiencing poor service, leaky plumbing, bugs, uncomfortable beds, and dimly lit rooms, then stay at the better hotels; you tend to get what you pay for—a cheap hotel can very well ruin your whole visit. If you want to avoid stomach problems, then be careful what and where you eat. If you want to experience good food, then frequent those restaurants with reputations for good food. If you hate crowds, then retreat from them whenever you feel the urge to *"get away from it all"* or be alone. If the heat, humidity, and traffic bother you, take air-conditioned taxis. Don't punish yourself by walking long distances in the heat of the day or by riding crowded buses. If smokers bother you, then avoid them. And if you don't want any surprises in restrooms, then stay close to major hotels and carry sufficient paper with you.

Our point is that Hong Kong can be a wonderful experience if you let it be by approaching it properly and by using common sense. Hong Kong is remarkably tolerant, flexible, and filled with options enabling the visitor to make adjustments and shift gears when necessary. You will need to adapt to Hong Kong by seeking alternatives which, in the end, will more than meet your needs. You should find this place exceptionally convenient, comfortable, and enjoyable. Feel free to pamper yourself in this relatively hassle-free city.

7 DISCOVERING FINE HOTELS AND RESTAURANTS

Hong Kong offers some of the world's best food and accommodations. You will find luxurious accommodations conveniently located in the central shopping areas as well as outstanding restaurants offering all varieties of international cuisines.

A GASTRONOMIC DELIGHT

Along with shopping, food is one of Hong Kong's great treats and it tends to be reasonably priced for such a cosmopolitan city. It's everywhere, with nearly 19,000 establishments ready to respond to all your gastronomic needs—one for every 300 people!

Be sure to pick up a copy of HKTA's free *Official Guide to Shopping, Eating Out, and Services in Hong Kong* for a list of member restaurants.

You won't go hungry in Hong Kong, and it's difficult to make many mistakes in choosing restaurants. Your restaurant choices are seemingly endless, ranging from such western fast-food restaurants as McDonald's, Burger King, Wendy's, and Kentucky Fried Chicken to superb French, Italian, American, Mexican, Middle Eastern, German, Indian, Southeast Asian, Korean, Japanese, and Chinese restaurants.

In general, the best restaurants are found in hotels, such as the Regent, Peninsula, Mandarin, Hilton, and Grand Hyatt. They may be expensive but by no means exorbitant. Don't overlook the hotel coffee shops where you can find good meals, familiar menus, and reasonable prices.

If you are in Hong Kong between August 14 and September 14, you can experience the annual Hong Kong Food Festival. Sixty of Hong Kong's top restaurants present special menus to celebrate this food extravaganza.

FINE CHINESE FOOD AND RESTAURANTS

The world's best Chinese food is reputed to be found in Hong Kong—not in China. If you journey into China, you will quickly learn that most of the good Chinese cooks are in Hong Kong, many of whom fled there in 1949. And your choice of regional Chinese cuisines is the most extensive of anywhere in the world: Cantonese, Chiu Chow, Hangchow, Peking, Mongolian, Shanghai, Szechuan, and Taiwanese.

Don't miss out on the *dim sum* which literally means *"to touch the heart."* These are little savory and sweet tidbits served at lunch time in many restaurants. Pick up a copy of HKTA's **Guide to Dim Sum Delights** (HK$5) for a listing of *dim sum* restaurants. *Dim sum* is unique to Cantonese-style Chinese restaurants. It's usually served from 11am until late afternoon, although some start serving as early as 7am. Tea is served throughout the meal. Plan to arrive at the restaurant early, before 12 noon, if possible, since many people in Hong Kong start lunch around 12:30. If you show up at the door after 12:30 you may have a long wait for a seat.

In the traditional *dim sum* restaurants the waiters push around serving carts loaded down with baskets and small plates of a single variety of *dim sum*. If you see an item you'd like to try, either signal the waiter or simply take a plate from the cart. There are usually two to four pieces to a plate, which you share with others at the table. Choose as many or as few plates as you want. At the end of the meal the waiter will count the number of empty dishes on the table and prepare your bill accordingly. Don't worry. *Dim sum* is quite reasonably priced and well worth the experience.

Some of the best *dim sum* meals are found at the following restaurants:

HONG KONG ISLAND:

> **Cleveland Szechuen Restaurant**
> 6 Cleveland St.
> Causeway Bay (11-4) (Szechuen style)
>
> **Flower Lounge**
> 441 Lockhart Rd. (11-5)
>
> **Jade Garden** (3 restaurants)
> 53 Paterson St., (2:30-6)
> Swire House 1/F, (2:30-6)
> 30-34 Queen's Rd. basement (11:30-6)
>
> **King Bun**
> 158 Queen's Rd., Central (7-4)
>
> **Luk Yu Tea House**
> 26 Stanley Street (7-6)
>
> **Maxim's Palace**
> World Trade Centre 1/F (8-6)
>
> **Peking Garden Restaurant**
> Excelsior Hotel (11:30-3)

KOWLOON:

> **Capital Restaurant**
> 36-44 Nathan Rd. (7-5)
>
> **Chui Heung Lau**
> Basement, Peninsula Centre,
> Tsimshatsui East (11-6)

Jade Garden Restaurant (2 restaurants)
25-31 Carnarvon Rd. (7:30-6)
4/F Star House, Star Ferry (11:30-6)

North Park Restaurant
2/F TsimShaTsui Centre,
Tsimshatsui East (11-4)

Ocean Empire Restaurant
3/F Silvercord, 30 Canton Rd. (8-6)

Peking Garden Restaurant
3/F Star House, Salisbury Rd. (11:30-2:30)
(Peking style)

South Villa Restaurant
58-60 Cameron Rd. (11-5)

Spring Deer Restaurant
42 Mody Rd. (12-2) (Peking style)

Chiuchow Garden Restaurant
2/F, Tsimshatsui Centre, (11:30-6)
(Chiu Chow Cuisine)

These restaurants are also open for dinner.

FAVORITE DINING SPOTS

Should you wish to treat yourself to some fine restaurants, complete with excellent food, good service, and nice ambience, try a few of our favorites:

NOON BUFFETS:	**La Ronda** (Hotel Furama) and **Veranda** (Peninsula Hotel).
CHINESE FOOD:	**Lai Ching Heen** (Regent Hotel), **Eagle's Nest** (Hilton Hotel), **Tai Pan** (Omni Hong Kong Hotel), **Spring**

Moon (Peninsula Hotel), **Toh Lee** (Hotel Nikko), **Shang Palace** (Shangri-La Hotel), **Hunan Garden** (Central), and **Fook Lam Moon** (Wanchai).

WESTERN FOOD: Gaddi's (Peninsula Hotel), **Plume** (Regent Hotel), **Le Restaurant de France** (Regal Meridien Hotel), **Pierrot** (Mandarin Oriental Hotel), **Margaux** (Shangri-La Hotel), **Hilton Grill** (Hilton Hotel), **La Rose Noire** (Central), and **The Bloom** (Central). **Jimmy's Kitchen** (Ashley Rd., Kowloon, and 1 Wyndham St., Central), though not as exquisite as the others listed here, is worth a stop if you like solid British cooking.

Reservations are required for many of these restaurants.

For a superb view of Hong Kong, take the tram to Victoria Peak and try the **Peak Tower Restaurant**, especially for the weekend luncheon buffet. It's best to make reservations.

Our favorite coffee shop is **Harbour Side** (Regent Hotel), offering both a great view and good food.

For afternoon tea, **The Peninsula Hotel Lobby** is a tradition. We also enjoy taking tea in the **Regent Hotel Lobby** where the view of Hong Kong Harbour is superb, and in the third floor lobby of the **Royal Garden Hotel**, where fatigue is lulled away by the sound of soothing piano music, a waterfall and pool, and a soaring 30-story atrium.

Food Street in Causeway Bay has several ethnic restaurants if you want to try something other than Chinese or Continental fare.

For fast food, McDonald's is good, but don't expect fast service or a place to sit; the crowds are incredible. You will also find Kentucky Fried Chicken, Wendy's, and Burger King along with numerous ice cream parlors such as Swensen's.

For the more adventuresome who also like cheap eats, try the *dai pai dong*, or street restaurants. The three best locations are the **Poor Man's Nightclub** (Hong Kong and Macau Ferry Terminal in Central), the **Yaumati Night Market** (Shanghai Street in Kowloon), and **Canal Road** (tram depot in Causeway Bay). Although generally safe to eat here, sanitation standards of these food stalls may not be the same as yours.

SELECTING ACCOMMODATIONS

It is always good to book hotel reservations before arriving in Hong Kong. Although occupancy levels have dropped somewhat in the past two years—a result of both Tiananmen Square and the opening of several new hotels—they can be heavily booked when a large convention is in town as well as during the pleasant weather months of October and November and the sale months of December and June. January is also a very high occupancy month since it is the month of the busy Chinese New Year.

Hotel prices tend to be high in Hong Kong compared to much of Asia—over US$140 a night for first-class and deluxe hotels. But Hong Kong also offers several inexpensive alternatives. Your best hotel value will be through a package tour to Hong Kong which includes both airfare and hotel. Most package tours use very good hotels which ordinarily cost US$90 to US$150 a night. They receive special discounts by reserving large blocks of rooms and thus pass savings on to you. Six nights in Hong Kong, including round trip airfare from the U.S. west coast and accommodation in a first-class hotel, may only cost you $1299—nearly the cost of your hotel room alone had you made your own arrangements—and this frequently includes breakfast!

Two hotels in Kowloon deserve special mention if you believe you should save your money for shopping. The recently rebuilt YMCA on Salisbury Road is surely the best housing bargain in the best location in all of Hong Kong. With views across the harbour and only two short blocks from the Star Ferry the location couldn't be better and the room rates are low for Hong Kong. There's another well-located YMCA in Wanchai on Hong Kong Island. The Kowloon Hotel is just a block away, on Nathan Road behind the Peninsula. Owned by the Peninsula, the Kowloon was built as a businessperson's headquarters. The tiny rooms are masterworks of efficiency, complete with a computer, but a bit small for avid shoppers who won't find much room to stash their purchases!

If you haven't made advance reservations, stop at the Hong Kong Hotel Association's hotel reservation desk located in the Buffer Hall at Hong Kong International Airport. Here, you should be able to identify hotels within all budgets. The moderately priced **Ritz** is a good buy as well as the **Grand**, **Astor**, **Empress**, and **Ambassador** hotels.

OUTSTANDING HOTELS

But if you wish to splurge and stay in some of the world's finest hotels, try **The Regent** (Salisbury Road, Tsimshatsui), **Mandarin Oriental** (Connaught Road, Central), **Peninsula** (Salisbury Road, Kowloon), **Marriott** (Pacific Place, Central/Wanchai), **Conrad** (Pacific Place, Central/Wanchai), **Island Shangri-La** (Pacific Place, Central/Wanchai), or the **Grand Hyatt** (Harbour Road, Wanchai). While not cheap, these hotels are quite reasonable by Toyko, London, and New York standards. Other excellent hotels which are less expensive include the **Furama Kempinski** (Connaught Road, Central), **Hong Kong Hilton** (Queen's Road, Central), **New World Harbor View** (Harbour Road, Wanchai), **Onmi The Hongkong** (Harbour City, Tsimshatsui), **Kowloon Shangri-La** (Mody Road, Tsimshatsui), **Hyatt Regency** (Nathan Road, Tsimshatsui), **Holiday Inn Golden Mile** (Nathan Road, Tsimshatsui, **Holiday Inn Harbour View** (Mody Road, Tsimshatsui), **Hong Kong** (Canton Road, Tsimshatsui, Kowloon) **Marco Polo** (Harbour City, Canton Road, Tsimshatsui, Kowloon), **New World** (Salisbury Road, Kowloon), **Prince** (Harbour City, Kowloon), **Royal Garden** (Tsimshatsui East, Kowloon), and the **Sheraton** (Nathan Road, Kowloon).

Since most of the deluxe and first-class hotels have shopping arcades and offer some of the best restaurants, you will undoubtedly visit several hotels during your stay in Hong Kong. One of the most interesting hotels with a spectacular atrium is the **Royal Garden**; for a view of the harbor, visit the **Regent**; for people watching, have tea at the **Peninsula**.

For additional information on deluxe and first-class accommodations, see Appendix C for a listing of Hong Kong hotels. The Hong Kong Tourist Association also publishes a *Hotel Guide* which provides a current list of hotels with addresses and tariffs.

PART III

SHOPPING WELL

8 CONQUERING THE STREETS OF HONG KONG

Hong Kong is a relatively easy city to navigate even though it appears crowded and confusing for many first-time visitors. Since the major shopping areas are relatively small, compact, and conveniently located in relationship to one another, you seldom need to spend more than 20 minutes going from one shopping area to another.

Nevertheless, like many other visitors, you may become overwhelmed by the number and variety of shops in Hong Kong as well as by the sea of people and the intense atmosphere of this giant city. If you prepare for the streets of Hong Kong by studying the general layout of the city and observing some basic shopping rules, you should have no problem easily navigating its streets.

DO YOUR HOMEWORK

Shopping in exotic Hong Kong is no fun if you must spend a great deal of time trying to find quality shops, learning what is a good local buy, and determining how to communicate your needs to shopkeepers. Guidebooks and maps help you navigate through the labyrinth of unfamiliar places, but these basic travel tools must be supplemented by other useful shopping tools and techniques. Above all, you need to

84 *Shopping Well*

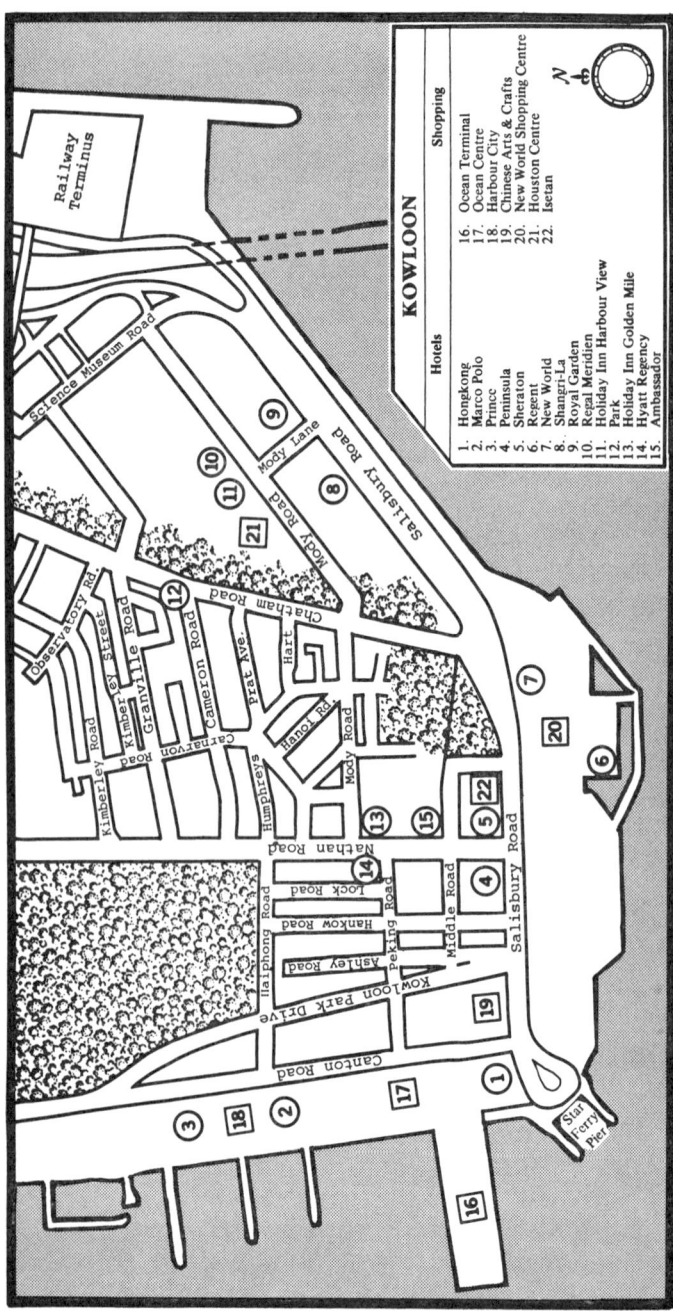

Conquering the Streets of Hong Kong 85

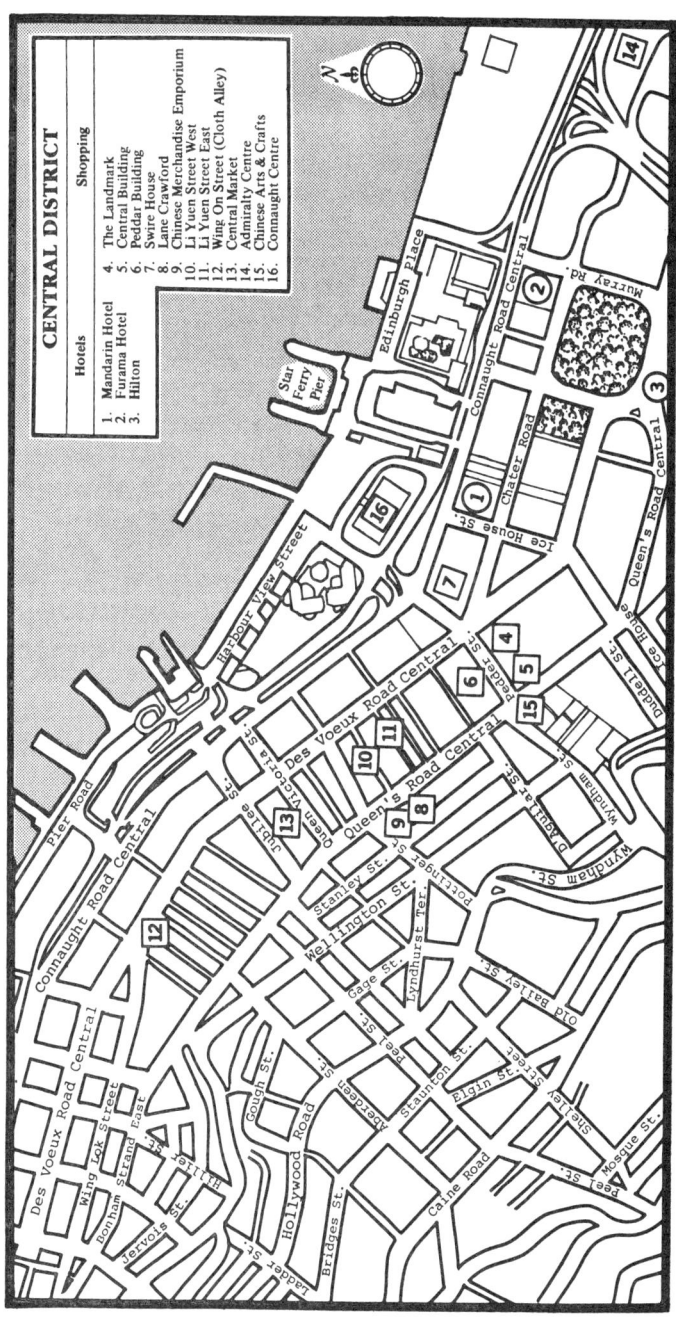

know how to identify quality and communicate your quality needs to others.
　　Preparation for quality shopping includes doing homework in three major areas: mapping the city, networking for information and advice, and shopping for comparable quality and prices. Once you have completed this homework, you will be well prepared to literally hit the ground running when you arrive in Hong Kong.

ORIENT YOURSELF TO KEY AREAS

Begin orienting yourself to Hong Kong before you leave home by studying a map of Hong Kong's 413 square miles. Start with our maps at the beginning of Chapter One on pages 84-85, but by all means pick up a more detailed map at any of the HKTA offices. One of the first things you should notice is that Hong Kong is divided and subdivided into areas, districts, sections and neighborhoods.
　　Hong Kong's major geographic division is between **peninsular** and **Island** Hong Kong. Peninsular Hong Kong consists of two major subdivisions, the **New Territories** and **Kowloon Peninsula**. The **New Territories** occupies three-fourths of peninsular Hong Kong and is located between the central commercial districts of Hong Kong and the border with China. Often called "The Land Between," this is an area of rice and vegetable farmers as well as new towns accented by industrial and high-rise housing estates. Although many locals and expatriates shop in this area, for the most part the New Territories is of little interest to short-term visitors to Hong Kong.
　　The southern tip of the peninsula is called **Kowloon**. A densely populated area housing some of Hong Kong's major commercial buildings, hotels, shops, and shopping arcades, Kowloon is further divided into two major shopping areas: **Tsimshatsui** and **Tsimshatsui East**. The major streets bounding these shopping areas are Nathan, Chatham, Salisbury, and Canton. Along Chatham Road you will find such world famous hotels as The Peninsula and Regent as well as adjacent shopping arcades. Canton Road fronts onto the mammoth Ocean Terminal shopping complex. Nathan Road is lined with numerous shops, arcades, emporiums, and hotels. The many small streets connecting Nathan Road to Chatham Road are crowded with small shops and restaurants.

Directly across the harbor to the south of Kowloon is **Hong Kong Island.** An island of beautiful mountains and beaches to the south and a striking commercial center on the northern shore, this is one of Hong Kong's major commercial, residential, shopping, and recreation centers. Subdivided into several districts, the two major commercial and shopping areas for tourists are found in **Central District** and **Causeway Bay.** The **Wanchai** area, once known for its bars and tawdry nightlife, is emerging as an area of upscale hotels and shops. Hugging the harbor directly across from Kowloon, these areas are connected to Tsimshatsui and Tsimshatsui East by ferry as well as by rail and auto tunnels. Within each of these areas street shops, shopping centers, factory outlets, and hotel shopping arcades are only short walks apart. The streets are crowded with shopping centers, department stores, small shops, and restaurants. Des Voeux Road Central, Queen's Road Central, and Hollywood Road are some of its major shopping streets. Other districts on Hong Kong Island, such as Eastern and Western are of less interest to most shoppers.

The remaining 234 **Outer Islands** are spread throughout the harbor area. Sparsely populated, these islands offer few shopping opportunities for locals and tourists alike. Some of the islands, such as Lantau and Cheung Chau, are nice places to visit for sightseeing and relaxation.

MAP THE CITY

Your preparation should include surveying a detailed map of the city. Such a map exercise should prepare you well for tackling the major shopping areas and streets of Hong Kong. Examine your map carefully with an eye toward the major shopping areas. Begin by locating Kowloon Peninsula, Hong Kong Island, the New Territories, and the Outer Islands as well as the major districts within each of these areas.

Next, locate your hotel and nearby shopping districts, streets, shopping centers, hotels, department stores, and markets. If you stay in **Tsimshatsui District** on Kowloon Peninsula, locate the shopping streets of Cameron, Canton, Chatham, Granville, Haipong, Mody, Nathan, Peking, and Salisbury Roads. If your hotel is in **Central District** or **Wanchai**, find the shopping streets of Connaught, Des Voeux, Pedder, Li Yuen, Pottinger, Wellington, Jubilee, Hollywood, and Queens Road. In **Causeway Bay**, locate Jardine's Bazaar, Jaffe,

Leighton, Lockhart, Hennessy, Harbour, Food Street, Gloucester, Great George, Patterson, and Yun Ping Roads.

Finally, refer to a list of shops you wish to visit or ones we include in Chapter Ten and Appendix B. Locate each shop on your map and note its location in relation to your hotel and the major shopping areas.

PLAN YOUR ATTACK

Each day you should work out a system for approaching different sections of Hong Kong. Each night, for example, review the day's events as well as plan your attack for tomorrow. Determine which areas you plan to visit and decide how you'll get there. Be sure to ask your hotel desk clerk to write out your destination in Chinese characters. This information will be especially useful for communicating with taxi drivers who do not speak English.

GET A GOOD OVERVIEW OF THE CITY

If you can get a good overview of Hong Kong's geography, people, and personality, you will greatly enhance the success of your shopping and travel adventure. Therefore, we highly recommend that you do three things during your first day in Hong Kong:

1. Enjoy a half-day organized tour of the city. You'll see some of the major highlights of the city as well as gain a geographical overview. HKTA offices and your hotel have information on such tours.

2. Even though this may not be on your normal first-day agenda, try to fit in a visit to the Hong Kong Museum of Art. It is conveniently located only two minutes walk from the Star Ferry, Hong Kong side. You'll see a wonderful collection of art, including rubbings, ceramics, bronzes, paintings, lacquer ware, jade, cloisonne, paper-cuts, and embroidery. This visit will better acquaint you with the best of Asian arts. If arts and crafts are one of your shopping interests, a visit here may help you better discriminate quality items.

3. If you intend to have any made-to-order work done, such as tailoring, shoes, furs, or jewelry, be sure to visit the shops immediately. You will need to make all the necessary arrangements so the process can be completed in ample time before your departure date. You will need, for example, a minimum of three days to complete any tailoring work. The sooner you start the made-to-order process, the more likely you will be able to control the final outcome.

BALANCE YOUR SCHEDULE

You need not *"shop 'til you drop,"* although this is both tempting and easy to do in Hong Kong. If you do not carefully pace your activities, three days of hard, non-stop shopping in Hong Kong may result in shoppers' burnout. To prevent this from happening to you, do what many experienced travelers do—balance your activities with complementary opposites. In Hong Kong you should work hard and play hard. Shopping is hard work, and spending all your time shopping with no touring and recreation will turn you into a dull and exhausted traveler.

We recommend that you set aside some time each day for sightseeing, people watching, strolling, entertainment, dining, exercise, and using your hotel recreational facilities. These other activities will nicely complement your shopping activities. In fact, most shops do not open until around 10am and many stay open until 9pm. If you are an early riser, why not enjoy a nice breakfast buffet and take an early morning tour or stroll? After doing a few hours of shopping, you may wish to rest for two hours in the early afternoon, resume your shopping around 2pm, and end your day with dinner in a nice restaurant with a view of the city lights or harbour. If you balance work with play, take life easy, go with some of the flow, and don't run around trying to squeeze all your plans into a tight time schedule, you will experience the unique subtleties and serendipity which make Asian travel such an enjoyable experience.

LOCATE QUALITY SHOPS

Most of the better quality shops in Hong Kong are located in the major hotels and specialty shopping arcades. The general rule is that the best shops can be found where the money is. Look for designer boutiques and high quality specialty shops, for example, in The Peninsula, Regent, Mandarin, and Grand Hyatt hotels, as well as in arcades such as The Landmark, Swire House, and Lane Crawford in Central District and Pacific Place in Central/Wanchai. Many of the world's best known designers are represented in the shops of Hong Kong.

Many more shops selling goods of moderate quality will also be found in the shopping arcades of first-class and deluxe hotels as well an in the lanes and streets near these hotels. As you travel farther away from the hotel areas you are less likely to find goods which will appeal to western tastes, and you will find fewer shopkeepers who speak any language other than Chinese. The lesser quality goods are found where rents are lower—in the lanes, alleys, markets, and upper floors of the Hong Kong skyscrapers and factories. Here you will find more bargain-priced items: factory seconds and overruns, everyday household goods, and used items.

NETWORK FOR INFORMATION

You should try to network with people in Hong Kong (shopkeepers, business associates, expatriates, your hotel concierge, and other acquaintances) who can direct you to some of Hong Kong's best shops. Ask them *"Where would be a good place to buy _____?"* If you ask several people this same question, you should quickly identify a few shops that have a reputation for good quality and reliability. But keep in mind that not everyone has the same standards of taste and quality. When meeting someone for the first time, pay particular attention to the person's clothing, accessories, furnishings, or anything that would give you non-verbal clues of the person's sense of taste and quality. We know, for example, people who locate excellent tailors by people-watching in the lobby of their hotel. When they spot someone wearing a beautiful suit, they initiate a conversation to get the name of the person's tailor. Not everyone is so brave in approaching strangers, but such an approach does get good results.

You can also network with people on the streets and in the shops of Hong Kong. As you strike up conversations ask some *"Do you know where...?"* questions. Again, watch for non-verbal clues as you listen for facts. If you ask a young clerk in a teen-oriented shop for sources, you'll get a very different answer than you would get from someone who is working or shopping in a designer boutique. But don't ask your tailor what other tailor shop you should check out! Rather, ask your tailor to recommend a leathergoods shop or a good jewelry shop. He may even own just such a place and be willing to give you better prices because you're already a customer.

GO FOR QUALITY

Unless you are a junk collector or are simply unable to discern good from inferior quality, you should concentrate on buying items of excellent quality. You may pay more, but quality products last and are things you will be pleased to own. Especially in the case of clothing and accessories, it is best to buy fewer and the finest you can afford. If you would normally spend $150 each for several woman's off-the-rack suits, instead spend $350 for one of exceptional quality. It will look better and last longer, give better service, and make you feel great every time you wear it.

While doing comparison shopping, you should become familiar with various levels of quality. At the very least, **window shop** in the better stores before you leave home to learn to recognize good quality products. The differences between quality levels may not be obvious to the undiscerning eye, but very real differences separate excellent quality from mediocre quality. To judge quality for yourself, examine the materials used, construction techniques, time-consuming details, finishing, trims, volume of materials used (the pleats in a high quality skirt will be deeper, using more fabric, than the pleats in a mediocre skirt), richness of color, and styling.

No matter what goods you seek, we strongly advise you to always buy less, but buy the best: one great sweater instead of two or three mediocre ones; one piece of truly fine art rather than several pieces of touristy trash; one magnificent sapphire rather than a dozen pieces of costume jewelry. You will be forever glad you bought the best, for you will use and enjoy the finest item so much longer than you would items of inferior quality.

You will find lots of junk in Hong Kong. But Hong Kong also offers some of the finest goods in the world. Merchants provide something for everyone, at every price and quality level. It's *"let the buyer beware.*" If you learn to recognize top quality, you will avoid being swayed by the lure of low prices for inferior goods.

It would be wonderful if we could tell you how to recognize quality in a few sentences, but that would take a miracle! Knowing quality is a skill which develops among those who expose themselves to the world of good taste. It's never too late to start to learn more, however. And the best way to learn quality is to simply expose yourself to it.

Start window-shopping and comparison shopping in the best city stores. If you live in a small town, arrange a day or two in the nearest city and spend lots of time looking in stores which handle top quality merchandise. Become familiar with the look and feel of good quality. You will buy some of these goods in Hong Kong, but you won't be paying the high prices.

When shopping for clothing, notice the fabric first. Wide ranges of quality will be apparent among each type of fabric, both natural and man-made. Look for fabrics which feel good. Handle a rough inexpensive wool jacket and then examine one in an upper price range. Differences in quality fabrics are obvious in both the feel and look. Lower quality fabrics may look rough and will probably have fewer threads woven per square inch. Examine the details: buttons, lining fabrics, buttonholes, amount and type of interfacings, the general workmanship. Is the garment lined, partially lined, or fully lined? Lining helps hold the shape of the garment, protects it from wear, and finishes the inside. A full lining of a firm rayon fabric is a sign of quality. Check the seam width to see if it is ample and that seams and hems are finished appropriately.

Avoid rushing into buying just because you have only a day or two to shop and you fear that you will never return. Maybe you won't, but your life won't be ruined just because you passed up a terrific jacket or an unusual set of brassware. Don't allow anyone to push you into buying something you are uncertain you want or need. When in doubt, don't. But if you can't live without it, you need it, want it badly, and can afford it, then by all means buy it. You will have a purchase that will give you great pleasure for many years to come.

COMMUNICATE YOUR NEEDS WITH CLARITY

English is the working language of most merchants working in the tourist areas, and many employees are chosen for their command of other languages. Indeed, most of the larger tailoring establishments have salesmen who are also fluent in Spanish, French, Japanese, German, and Portuguese. However, half of communication involves understanding the nuances, the shades of meaning. The merchant may not perceive the meaning of what you say, may think he understands but doesn't, or he may know he doesn't understand but does not want to lose face by admitting that he doesn't understand. The merchant will smile broadly, nod agreement, and assure you *"no problem,"* but then he fails to deliver what you thought he promised. Many merchants you encounter may speak English quite well, but when it comes to communicating details, they revert to their native tongue which you don't speak. So what do you do?

Yes, indeed, *"a picture is worth a thousand words"* in the shops of Hong Kong. We use pictures to communicate our desires when we shop in Asia. Take pictures or drawings with you of the items you want. If, for example, you are planning to have rattan furniture made for your sun room, be sure you take magazine photos of each piece as well as room and furniture measurements. If you want to purchase a certain style of ring, take several pictures of rings similar to what you want. If you plan to have a coat tailored, take a picture or a line drawing that shows details.

As you talk with merchants, use as few words as possible to communicate ideas. Think through how you can describe what you want in simple succinct language. Avoid slang, colloquialisms, or flowery phrases. It is doubtful that any Hong Kong tailor will understand what you mean when you say you want them to give you *"upscale styling"* or the *"latest from Vogue."* Show a picture of exactly what you mean. Think how hard it is to even begin to understand or keep up with new slang expressions back home. How much harder it is for a resident of Hong Kong to understand your terminology when he doesn't live in your culture. Plus, he's trying to make sense out of several varieties of English spoken by tourists from Australia, New Zealand, Great Britain, and Canada as well as the United States—and we have trouble understanding each others' English!

CUSTOM TAILORING—MYTHS AND REALITIES

Many shoppers make custom tailoring mistakes because they come to Hong Kong with a set of tailoring beliefs that are anything but accurate. Over the years we have discovered four recurring myths and realities about Hong Kong tailoring:

MYTH 1: **Hong Kong tailors are the best in the world.**

REALITY: While many Hong Kong tailors are as good or even better than those in the famed tailor shops of London's Savile Row, many are mediocre. Since there are literally hundreds of tailor shops from which to choose, finding an excellent tailor is simply a matter of making the right choice.

MYTH 2: **Everyone who goes to Hong Kong should have tailoring done.**

REALITY: Tailoring isn't for everyone. People who benefit the most are those who don't fit well into ready-to-wear clothing without major alterations: the very small adult; the person with major physical limitations; the very large or tall person; or the person who knows exactly what he/she wants and can find neither the ready-to-wear garments nor a good tailor at home.

MYTH 3: **Having a garment made for me will take no longer than shopping for ready-to-wear.**

REALITY: If you'll be in Hong Kong less than five days, tailoring probably should be left off your "Must Do" list. Tailoring is time consuming and a major undertaking. For the most efficient use of your time, choose the best tailor you can find in or near your hotel. Choosing fabric and placing your order will involve approximately two to three hours. Each of the three or four fittings could take two hours or more, since you may have to sit around the shop waiting for the garment to be delivered from the workroom. That can add up to several hours spent in the tailor shop—nearly a full day out of your trip. You can save some time by requesting that the tailor bring the garment to your hotel room for fittings.

MYTH 4: **Tailored garments always look better than off-the-rack merchandise.**

REALITY: The sewing of tailored garments may be technically perfect, but if the tailors cannot render a stylish version according to your instructions and if the fabrics, lining, and interfacings are not appropriate for the garment, the resulting garment may lack style. We have seen many perfectly sewn garments which do not fit well even after several fittings. On the other hand, many lower-priced, off-the-rack garments are sewn well.

HANDMADE SHOES

You used to be able to get custom-made shoes and boots in Hong Kong that were inexpensive and generally fit well. But no more. While you can find excellent cobblers in the shopping arcades of Hong Kong, getting an inexpensive and great fitting shoe is the stuff that dreams are made of. Cobblers work with standard lasts, and although they will measure the length and circumference of your foot and have you back for several fittings, most custom-made shoes don't fit any better than ready-made shoes. We've had several made which were adequate, but none that looked or fitted like the best Italian shoes for a fraction of the cost. Most shoes custom-made in Hong Kong will cost you upwards from $75, and fit and look like comparably priced shoes in your hometown. However, boots can be made for considerably less and will fit as well as, or better than, ready-made boots.

As with all custom work, be sure to take along pictures of the shoes/boots which you want to have made. Handbags can be copied by most of the cobblers.

DELIVERY ARRANGEMENTS

When you place an order for any custom-made item, and before money changes hands, be sure to make arrangements for the time and date of delivery. If the shop cannot promise delivery of the item, or you sense that they will not produce, do not complete the order and do not pay a deposit.

Arrange to accept delivery one day before you leave, if possible, to allow plenty of time to check over the merchandise and to complete any necessary alterations. Determine your options if the merchandise is unacceptable. Do you get all of your deposit back or only a portion? What happens if the garment doesn't fit and there is not enough time for alterations? What if you don't like it? Will they refund your deposit money in full or in part? Do you just take your chances?

If an item cannot be completed before you leave, you must decide whether you want to take the chance of having it shipped and then discover it still does not fit. We will not go through with tailoring unless we are certain the garments will be completed to our satisfaction and ready to go home in our suitcase.

Although you are on vacation from your work schedule, you should take along a daily calendar for the days you will be traveling. In addition to recording the times and dates for tours and dinner dates, include your fitting appointments and delivery arrangements on this calendar. Arrange fitting times at your convenience but also respect the tailors' work schedule.

Once you approve and pay for your garments, the tailor will have them delivered to your hotel.

FOLLOW THE RULES

As you navigate through the streets of Hong Kong, keep in mind a few rules for making the most of your shopping adventure:

HONG KONG SHOPPING RULES

- **Focus each shopping foray in and around specific districts, shopping centers, and hotels rather than on stores and street addresses.** Once in a particular shopping district, you can explore and discover many interesting shops near the particular ones on your "Must Visit" list.

- **Walk short distances between shops within districts, but take public transportation** when going from one shopping district to another or for distances requiring more than a 15 minute walk.

- **For the best use of your time, plan your schedule around specific districts and specialty items within each district.** Start with Kowloon where most of the shops are concentrated. Next, move on to the Western, Central, and Wanchai Districts. Plan on spending a half to a full day in each district. If you plan to visit Stanley Market, plan this cross-island trip along with a stop in Happy Valley and Causeway Bay.

- **During the cool or hot and humid seasons, plan much of your shopping around indoor shopping centers, department stores, and hotel shopping arcades.** Mixing bad weather with wonderful shopping will quickly dampen your enthusiasm!

- **Be careful when crossing the streets.** Always look to your right before stepping from the curb because vehicles drive on the left-hand side. If you are accustomed to looking left, you may be in danger of being hit by a bus or taxi. Cross with the light.

9 PLANNING, BARGAINING, AND PROCURING QUALITY PRODUCTS IN THE LOCAL SHOPPING CULTURE

Hong Kong is one of those unique cities where you should be able to get whatever you want—for a price. But where you buy and the price you pay will depend on how skilled you are in finding shops and negotiating the right prices.

BARGAIN FOR BARGAINS

Most items you buy in Hong Kong will be one-fourth to one-third less expensive than at home. Such savings are due to the absence of local taxes and duties, low transportation costs from nearby production sites, and inexpensive local labor. However, Hong Kong's best bargains are reserved for those who know how to use one of the most important shopping skills in Asia—**bargaining**.

Bargaining is both a process and a skill you can learn through knowledge and practice. For the inexperienced, the bargaining process can be a real challenge, both intimidating and frustrating. To be an effective shopper, you must sharpen your communication and interpersonal skills to tackle Hong Kong's local shopping culture. You must be sufficiently street-wise and aggressive—but always civil—if you want to get the best price on most goods and services you purchase.

Planning, Bargaining, and Procuring Quality Products 99

Once you develop effective bargaining skills, shopping in Hong Kong becomes a tremendously rewarding experience both personally and financially. Fortunately, you can easily learn and apply these skills by following a few basic rules on how to communicate with local business people.

PLAN AND COMPARE PRICES

We strongly recommend that you approach Hong Kong with a well organized **shopping plan which includes comparative pricing information**. If you followed our advice in Chapter Four, you already have comparative pricing information from shops and discount houses back home. Now you need to turn your attention to gathering comparative pricing information in Hong Kong.

Your plan should include a list of items you want to purchase as well as a list of shopping areas and specific shops you wish to visit. List the items you wish to purchase and the people for whom you are buying:

PRIORITY SHOPPING LIST

Items to Buy	Size/Brand	For Whom

Now make a list of the shopping areas, streets, or specific shops you wish to visit. Include in this list what you expect to find in each area and a price for comparable items back home.

SHOPPING TARGETS

Shopping Area	Items	Price

This well organized shopping plan will enable you to make the most of your shopping time in Hong Kong. It will help remind you where to shop, what to buy for whom, and how much money you should spend in the process of getting what you want.

TREAT STATED PRICES AS STARTING PRICES

Bargaining is a way of life in Hong Kong. While most stores display price tags on items, except for the truly "fixed price" department stores, don't take such labeling as a sign of the final price you should pay. Rather, treat stated prices as starting prices from which you begin a bargaining process to determine the final price **you** will pay.

DETERMINE FAIR LOCAL MARKET VALUES

Before you can effectively play the bargaining game, you need to have some idea of the fair local market value for various items. Since Hong Kong department stores have fixed prices, begin identifying fair market values for comparable items by visiting department stores. Keep in mind that small shops selling the same items should be 10 to 20 percent less than the department stores simply because their overhead is less. Once you have department store pricing information, begin visiting shops on your list. But before making a purchase, try to visit three shops to get comparative prices for the same items. Check these prices with your home and department store pricing information and then begin bargaining in earnest for your best deal. If the price is no different than the department store price, buy it at the department store where you will encounter few problems should you need to return the item.

PREPARE FOR PRICE UNCERTAINTY

Most North American and European tourists come from fixed-price cultures where prices are nicely displayed on items. The only price uncertainty may be a sales tax added to the total amount at the cash register. Only on very large-ticket items, such as automobiles, boats, houses, furniture, carpets, and jewelry, can you expect to negotiate the price. If you want to get the best deal, you must do comparative shopping as well as wait for special discounts and sales. Bargain shopping in such a culture centers on comparative pricing of items. Shopping becomes a relatively passive activity involving the examination of printed advertisements in newspapers and catalogs.

Expert shoppers in fixed-price cultures tend to be those skilled in carefully observing and comparing prices in the print advertising media. They clip coupons and know when the best sales are being held for particular items on certain days. They need not be concerned with cultivating personal relationships with merchants or salespeople in order to get good buys.

Like fish out of water, expert shoppers from fixed-price cultures may feel lost when shopping in Hong Kong. Few of their fixed-price shopping skills are directly transferable to the Hong Kong shopping environment. Except for department stores and a few small ads on the back page of the *South China Morning Post*, Hong Kong shops seldom advertise in the print media or on TV and radio. Special sales are rare, except for the June and December sales.

Goods in Hong Kong fall into three pricing categories: **fixed**, **negotiable**, or **discounted**. The general trend in Hong Kong is toward fixed prices on more and more goods. If you are returning to Hong Kong after an absence of more than a year, you may discover fewer shops willing to bargain or discount prices. However, you will still find plenty of opportunity to practice your bargaining skills in the smaller shops and markets.

Price uncertainty—negotiable or discounted prices—is the standard way to sell most goods and services in Asia, but in Hong Kong price uncertainty applies to only some situations. The general guideline is this: **unless you see a sign stating otherwise, you can expect prices of most goods in small shops to be negotiable.** You can safely assume that all stated prices are the starting point from which you should receive anything from a 10 to 50 percent discount, depending upon your haggling skills and level of commitment to obtain reduced prices.

Discount percentages in Hong Kong will vary for different items, but expect to receive at least a 10 to 20 percent discount on most items in stores willing to discount.

The structure of prices on certain goods and services varies. The prices on items in department stores are fixed. Prices for tailors, hairdressers, taxis, and medical personnel are fixed. Hotel prices are subject to a variety of discounts for different categories of travelers-- VIP, business, government, weekend, and tourist.

When in doubt if a price is fixed, negotiable, or subject to discounts, **always ask for a special discount**. After the salesperson indicates the price, ask one of two questions: *"What kind of discount can you give me on this?"* or *"What is your best price?"* If the person offers a discount, you can either accept it or attempt to negotiate the price through a bargaining process.

While skilled shoppers in fixed-price cultures primarily compare prices by reading ads and listening to special announcements, the skilled shopper in bargaining cultures is primarily engaged in face-to-face encounters with sellers. To be successful, the shopper must use various interpersonal skills. Once you know these and practice bargaining, you should become a very effective shopper in Hong Kong.

ESTABLISH VALUE AND PRICE

Not knowing the price of an item, many shoppers from fixed-price cultures face a problem. What is the actual value of the item? How much should I pay? At what point do I know I'm getting a fair price? These questions can be answered in several ways. First, you should have some idea of the value of the item, because you already did comparative shopping at home by examining catalogs and visiting discount houses, department stores, and specialty shops (Chapter

Planning, Bargaining, and Procuring Quality Products 103

Four). If you are interested in pearls, for example, you should know what comparable quality pearls sell for back home.

Second, you have done comparative shopping among the various shops you've encountered in Hong Kong in order to **establish a price range** for positioning yourself in the bargaining process. You've visited a department store in Hong Kong to research how much a similar item is selling for at a fixed price. You've checked with a shop in your hotel and compared prices there. In your hotel you might ask *"How much is this item?"* and then act a little surprised that it appears so expensive. Tell them that you are a hotel guest and thus you want their *"very best price."* At this point the price may decrease by 10 to 20 percent as you are told this is *"our very special price," "our first-customer-of-the-day price,"* or *"our special hotel guest price."*

Once you receive a discounted *"special price"* from your first price inquiry, expect to get another 10 to 20 percent through further negotiation. But unless this is a one of a kind item and you are certain that you want to purchase it, do not negotiate any more at this time. Take the shop's business card and record on the back the item, the original price, and the first discount price; thank the shopkeeper, and tell him or her that you may return. Repeat this same scenario in a few other shops. After doing three or four comparisons, you will establish a price range for particular items. This range will give you a fairly accurate idea of the going discount price. At this point you should be prepared to do some serious haggling, playing one shop off against another.

Effective shoppers in Hong Kong quickly learn how to comparative shop and negotiate the best deal. In learning to be effective, you don't need to be timid, aggressive, or obnoxious—extreme behaviors frequently exhibited by first-time practitioners of the Asian art of bargaining. Although you may feel bargaining is a defensive measure to avoid being ripped off by unscrupulous merchants, it is an acceptable way of doing business in many Asian cultures. Merchants merely adjust their profit margins to the customer, depending on how they feel about the situation as well as their current cash flow needs. It is up to you to adapt to such a pricing culture.

One problem you may soon discover is that every situation seems to differ somewhat, and differences between items and shops can be significant. For example, you can expect to receive larger discounts on jewelry than on shoes. Discounts on jewelry may be as great as 50 to

60 percent whereas discounts on home furnishings may only be 10 to 20 percent.

The one major exception to bargaining concerns tailors. Tailors normally quote you a fixed price subject to little or no negotiation; you merely trust that you are getting a fair price and, after all, it is not a good idea to make your tailor unhappy by bargaining when he doesn't want to. He may compensate by cheapening the quality of your clothes. Only in tailor shops do we avoid forcing the price issue by bargaining. At best ask for *"your best price,"* use a common friend's name as reference, or ask for an extra shirt, but don't risk being short-changed on quality just to save a few dollars. If you comparative shop among a few tailor shops, you will quickly identify what should be the fair market rate for tailoring services assuming the use of comparable quality materials.

Our general rule on what items to bargain for is this: **bargain on ready-made items you can carry out of the shop**. If you must have an item custom-made, be very careful how you arrive at the final price. In most cases you should not bargain other than respond to the first price by asking *"Is this your best price?"* Better still, drop a few names, agree on a mutually satisfactory price, and then insist that you want top quality for that price.

Except for custom-made items, department stores, and shops displaying a "fixed price" sign, **never accept the first price offered**. Rather, spend some time going through our bargaining scenario. Once you have accepted a price and purchased the item, be sure to **get a receipt** as well as **observe the packing process**. While few merchants will try to cheat you, some tourists have had unpleasant experiences which could have been avoided by following some simple rules of shopping in unfamiliar places. If you choose to ship the item home, read our shipping advice in Chapter Twelve.

GET THE BEST DEAL POSSIBLE

Chances are you will deal with a Chinese merchant who is a relatively seasoned businessman; he or she is a family entrepreneur who thrives on status and personal relationships. As soon as you walk through the door, most merchants will want to sell you items then and there. Sometimes shop girls in Hong Kong follow you around so closely that you may inadvertently step on them. If you occasionally back up abruptly, you can discourage this closeness and give yourself some personal space. Some shopkeepers will be aggressive and pester you, trying to sell you anything and everything in their store; this may make you feel uncomfortable and you quickly attempt to flee from the shop! Others are very low-keyed, letting visitors wander around on their own and then slowly engage them in conversation. They know that once you leave their shop, you probably will not come back. Before you leave, the merchant must convince you that you are getting the best possible deal and that you should not waste your time talking to others. In many cases you will, in fact, get the best possible deal in such a shop.

The best deal you will get is when you have a personal relationship with the merchant. Contrary to what others may tell you about bargains for tourists, you often can get as good a deal—sometimes even better—than someone from the local community. It is simply a myth that tourists can't do as well on prices as the locals. Indeed, we often do better than the locals because we have done our comparative shopping and we know well the art of bargaining—something locals are often lax in doing. In addition, some merchants may give you a better price than the locals because you are *"here today and gone tomorrow";* you won't be around to tell their regular customers about your very special price.

More often than not, the Hong Kong pricing system operates like this: **If the shopkeeper likes you, or you are a friend of a friend or relative, you can expect to get a good price.** Whenever possible, drop names of individuals who referred you to the shop; the shopkeeper may think you are a friend and thus you are entitled to a special discount. But if you do not have such a relationship and you present yourself as a typical tourist who is here today and gone tomorrow, you need to bargain hard.

PRACTICE THE 12 RULES OF BARGAINING

The art of bargaining in Hong Kong can take on several different forms. In general, you want to achieve two goals in this haggling process: **establish the value of an item and get the best possible price.** The following bargaining rules generally work well.

EFFECTIVE BARGAINING PRINCIPLES

1. **Do your research before initiating the process.** Compare prices among various shops, starting with the fixed-price items in department stores. Spot-check price ranges among shops in and around your hotel. Also, refer to your research done with catalogs and discount houses back home to determine if the discount is sufficient to warrant purchasing the item abroad rather than at home.

2. **Determine the exact item you want.** Select the particular item you want and then focus your bargaining around that one item without expressing excessive interest and commitment. Even though you may be excited by the item and want it very badly, once the merchant knows you are committed to buying this one item, you weaken your bargaining position. Express a passing interest; indicate through eye contact with other items in the shop that you are not necessarily committed to the one item. As you ask about the other items, you should get some sense concerning the willingness of the merchant to discount prices.

3. **Set a ceiling price you are willing to pay.** Before engaging in serious negotiations, set in your mind the maximum amount you are willing to pay, which may be 20 percent more than you figured the item should sell for based on your research. However, if you find something you love that is really unique, be prepared to pay whatever you must. In many situations you will find unique items not available anywhere else. Consider buying **now** since the item may be gone when you return. Bargain as hard as you can and then pay what you have to—even though it may seem painful—for the privilege of owning a unique item. Remember, it only hurts once. After you return home you will most likely enjoy your wonderful purchase and forget how painful it seemed at the time to buy it at less than your expected discount. Above all, do not pass up an item you really love just because the bargaining process does not fall in your favor. It is very easy to be *"penny wise but pound foolish"* in Hong Kong simply because the

bargaining process is such an ego-involved activity. You may return home forever regretting that you failed to buy a lovely item just because you refused to *"give"* on the last $5 of haggling. In the end, put your ego aside, give in, and buy what you really want. Only you and the merchant will know who really won, and once you return home the $5 will seem to be such an insignificant amount. Chances are you still got a good bargain compared to what you would pay elsewhere if, indeed, you could find a similar item!

4. **Play a role**. Shopping in Hong Kong involves playing the roles of buyer and seller. Asians tend to be terrific role players, moreso than Westerners. In contrast to many western societies, where being a unique individual is emphasized, high value is not placed on individualism in Hong Kong. Rather, the Chinese learn specific sets of behaviors appropriate for the role of father, son, daughter, husband, wife, blood friend, classmate, superior, subordinate, buyer, seller. They easily shift from one role to another, undergoing major personality and behavioral changes without experiencing mental conflicts. When you encounter a Chinese businessman, you are often meeting a very refined and sophisticated role player. Therefore, it is to your advantage to play complementary roles by carefully structuring your personality and behavior to play the role of buyer. If you approach sellers by just *"being yourself"*—open, honest, somewhat naive, and with your own unique personality—you may be quickly walked over by a seasoned seller. Once you enter a shop, think of yourself as an actor walking on stage to play the lead role as a shrewd buyer, bargainer, and trader.

5. **Establish good will and a personal relationship.** A shrewd buyer also is charming, polite, personable, and friendly. You should have a sense of humor, smile, and be light-hearted during the bargaining process. But be careful about eye contact which can be threatening to Asians. Keep it to a minimum. Asian sellers prefer to establish a personal relationship so that the bargaining process can take place on a friendly, face-saving basis. In the end,

both the buyer and seller should come out as winners. This can not be done if you approach the buyer in very serious and harsh terms. You should start by exchanging pleasantries concerning the weather, your trip, the city, or the nice items in the shop. After exchanging professional cards or determining your status, the shopkeeper will know what roles should be played in the coming transaction.

6. **Let the seller make the first offer.** If the merchant starts by asking you *"How much do you want to pay?"*, avoid answering; immediately turn the question around: *"How much are you asking?"* Remember, many merchants try to get you to pay as much as you are willing and able to pay—not what the value of the item is or what he or she is willing to take. You should never reveal your ability or willingness to pay a certain price. Keep the seller guessing, thinking that you may lose interest or not buy the item because it appears too expensive. Always get the merchant to initiate the bargaining process. In so doing, the merchant must take the defensive as you shift to the offensive.

7. **Take your time, being deliberately slow in order to get the merchant to invest his or her time in you.** The more you indicate that you are impatient and in a hurry, the more you are likely to pay. When negotiating a price, **time** is usually in your favor. Many shopkeepers also see time as a positive force in the bargaining process. Some try to keep you in their shop by serving you tea, coffee, soft drinks, or liquor while negotiating the price. Be careful; this nice little ritual may soften you somewhat on the bargaining process as you begin establishing a more personal relationship with the merchant. The longer you stay in control prolonging the negotiation, the better the price should be. Although some merchants may deserve it, **never** insult them. Merchants need to *"keep face"* as much as you do in the process of giving and getting the very best price.

8. **Use odd numbers in offering the merchant at least 40 percent less than what he or she initially offers.** Avoid stating round numbers, such as 60, 70, or 100. Instead, offer $62.50, $73.85, or $81.13. Such numbers impress upon others that you may be a seasoned haggler who knows value and expects to do well in this negotiation. Your offer will probably be 15 percent less than the value you determined for the item. For example, if the merchant asks $100, offer $62.50, knowing the final price should probably be $75.00. The merchant will probably counter with only a 10 percent discount—$90. At this point you will need to go back and forth with another two or three offers and counter-offers.

9. **Appear disappointed and take your time again.** Never appear upset or angry with the seller. Keep your cool at all times by slowly sitting down and carefully examining the item. Shake your head a little and say, *"Gee, that's too bad. That's much more than I had planned to spend. I like it, but I really can't go that high."* Appear to be a sympathetic listener as the seller attempts to explain why he or she cannot budge more on the price. Make sure you do not accuse the merchant of being a thief! Use a little charm, if you can, for the way you conduct the bargaining process will affect the final price. This should be a civil negotiation in which you nicely bring the price down, the seller *"saves face,"* and everyone goes away feeling good about the deal.

10. **Counter with a new offer at a 35 percent discount.** Punch several keys on your calculator, which indicates that you are doing some serious thinking. Then say something like *"This is really the best I can do. It's a lovely item, but $67.25 is really all I can pay."* At this point the merchant will probably counter with a 20 percent discount—$80.

11. **Be patient, persistent, and take your time again by carefully examining the item.** Respond by saying *"That's a little better, but it's still too much. I want to look around a little more."* Then start to get up and look toward the door.

At this point the merchant has invested some time in this exchange, and he or she is getting close to a possible sale. The merchant will either let you walk out the door or try to stop you with another counter-offer. If you walk out the door, you can always return to get the $80 price. But most likely the merchant will try to stop you, especially if there is still some bargaining room. The merchant is likely to say: *"You don't want to waste your time looking elsewhere. I'll give you the best price anywhere—just for you. Okay, $75. That's my final price."*

12. **Be creative for the final negotiation.** You could try for $70, but chances are $75 will be the final price with this merchant. Yet, there may still be some room for negotiating *extras*. At this point get up and walk around the shop and examine other items; try to appear as if you are losing interest in the item you were bargaining for. While walking around, identify a $5-10 item you like which might make a nice gift for a friend or relative, which you could possibly include in the final deal. Wander back to the $75 item and look as if your interest is waning and perhaps you need to leave. Then start to probe the possibility of including the extras while agreeing on the $75: *"Okay, I might go $75, but only if you include this with it."* The *this* would be the $5-10 item you eyed. You might also negotiate with your credit card. Chances are the merchant is expecting cash on the $75 discounted price and will add a 2-5 percent *commission* if you want to use your credit card. In this case, you might respond to the $75 by saying, *"Okay, I'll go with the $75, but only if I can use my credit card."* You may get your way, your bank will float you a loan in the interim, and in case you later learn there is a problem with your purchase—such as misrepresentation—the credit card company may even help you. Finally, you may want to negotiate packing and delivery processes. If it is a fragile item, insist that it be packed well so you can take it with you on the airplane or have it shipped. If it is a large item, insist that the shop deliver it to your hotel or to your shipper. If the shop is shipping it by air or sea, try to get them to agree to absorb some of the freight and insurance costs.

Planning, Bargaining, and Procuring Quality Products 111

This slow, civil, methodical, and sometimes charming approach to bargaining works well in most cases. However, merchants do differ in how they respond to situations. In some cases, your timing may be right: the merchant is in need of cash flow that day and thus he or she is willing to give you the price you want, with little or no bargaining. Others will not give more than a 10 to 20 percent discount unless you are a friend of a friend who is then eligible for the special *"family discount."* And others are not good businessmen, are unpredictable, lack motivation, or are just moody; they refuse to budge on their prices even though your offer is fair compared to the going prices in other shops. In these situations it is best to leave the shop and find one which is more receptive to the traditional haggling process.

Bargaining in traditional markets requires a different approach and may result in larger discounts. In contrast to the numerous polite middle-class merchants you encounter in shops, sellers in open-air markets tend to be lower-class, earthy, expressive, pushy, persistent, and often rude as they attempt to sell you many things you cannot use or have no desire to even inspect. They may joke a great deal, shout at you—*"Hey, you mister"*—push and shove, and pester you. These markets are similar to a great big carnival.

In contrast to our previous bargaining rules, successful bargaining in open-air markets should involve **little time** and a great deal of **movement**. If you are interested in an item, ask the price, counter with a price you are willing to pay, and be relatively firm with this price. Since there is a great deal of competition in these markets, it is to your advantage to spend very little time with any one vendor. State your offer and slowly move on to the next vendor. Sellers know they will probably lose you to the competition, so they need to quickly conclude a deal before someone else gets to you; they are motivated to give you large discounts. You also can be a little more aggressive and obnoxious and less charming in these places. If, for example, an item is quoted at $10, offer $4 and move on toward the next vendor. Chances are the seller will immediately drop the price to $7. If you counter with $5 and are moving while stating your offer, the seller will probably agree to your offer. But be sure you want the item. Once your offer is accepted, you are expected to carry through with the purchase. Open-air stalls are great places to accumulate junk while successfully practicing your bargaining skills!

BARGAIN FOR NEEDS, NOT GREED

One word of caution for those who are just starting to learn the fine art of Asian bargaining. **Be sure you really want an item before you initiate the bargaining process**. Many tourists learn to bargain effectively, and then get carried away with their new-found skill. Rather than use this skill to get what they want, they enjoy the process of bargaining so much that they buy many unnecessary items. After all, they got such *"a good deal"* and thus could not resist buying the item. You do not need to fill your suitcases with junk in demonstrating this ego-gratifying skill. If used properly, your new bargaining skills will lead to some excellent buys on items you really need and want.

EXAMINE YOUR GOODS CAREFULLY

Before you commence the bargaining process, carefully examine the item, being sure that you understand the quality of the item for which you are negotiating. Then, after you settle on a final price, make sure you are getting the goods you agreed upon. While most merchants are honest, some are known to switch to inferior items when doing the final packing. You should carefully observe the handling of items, including the actual packing process. If at all possible, take the items with you when you leave the shop. If you later discover you were victimized by a switch or misrepresentation, contact the HKTA as well as your credit card company if you charged your purchase. You should be able to resolve the problem through these channels. However, the responsibility is on you, the buyer, to know what you are buying.

BEWARE OF SCAMS

Although one hopes this will never happen, you may be unfortunate in encountering unscrupulous merchants who take advantage of you. This is more likely to happen if you wander away from HKTA recommended shops in discovering your own *"very special"* bargains or enter the *"Hey, you mister!"* shops. The most frequent scams to watch out for include:

POTENTIAL SCAMS

1. **Switching the goods.** You negotiate for a particular item, such as a watch, camera, or blouse, but in the process of packing it, the merchant substitutes an inferior product.

2. **Misrepresenting quality goods.** Be especially cautious in jewelry stores and antique shops. Sometimes so-called expensive watches are excellent imitations and worth no more than US$15—or have cheap mechanisms inside expensive cases. Precious stones, such as rubies, may not be as precious as they appear. Synthetic stones, garnets, or spinels are sometimes substituted for high quality rubies. Some substitutes are so good that experts even have difficulty identifying the difference. Accordingly, you may pay $2,000 for what appears to be a ruby worth $10,000 back home, but in fact you just bought a $25 red spinel. Pearls come in many different qualities, so know your pearls before negotiating a price. Real jade is beautiful, but many buyers unwittingly end up with green plastic, soapstone, or aventurine at jade prices. The antique business is relatively unregulated. Some merchants try to sell *"new antiques"* at *"old antique"* prices. Many of the fakes are outstanding reproductions, often fooling even the experts. Better still, there is a reputable business in fakes. You may want to simply shop for fakes!

3. **Goods not shipped.** The shop may agree to ship your goods home, but once you leave they conveniently forget to do so. You wait and wait, write letters of inquiry, and receive no replies. Unless you insured the item and have all proper receipts, you may never receive the goods you paid for.

Your best line of defense against these and other possible scams is to be very careful wherever you go and whatever you do in relation to handling money. A few precautions should help avoid some of these problems:

TAKE ADEQUATE PRECAUTIONS

1. **Do not trust anyone with your money** unless you have proper assurances they are giving you exactly what you agreed upon.

2. **Do your homework** so you can determine quality and value as well as anticipate certain types of scams.

3. **Examine the goods carefully**, assuming something may be or will go wrong.

4. **Watch very carefully how the merchant handles items** from the moment they leave your hands until they get wrapped and into a bag.

5. **Request receipts** that list specific items and the prices you paid. Although most shops are willing to *"give you a receipt"* specifying whatever price you want them to write for purposes of deceiving customs, avoid such pettiness because Customs officials know better, and you may need a receipt with the real price to claim your goods or a refund. If the shop is to ship, be sure you have a shipping receipt which also includes insurance against loss **and** damage.

6. **Patronize shops which are members of the Hong Kong Tourist Association.** They are more likely to treat you honestly since the parent organization does somewhat police its members.

7. **Protect against scams by using credit cards** for payment, especially for big ticket items which could present problems, even though using them may cost you more.

If you are victimized, all is not necessarily lost. You should report the problem immediately to the Hong Kong Tourist Association, the police, your credit card company, or insurance company. While inconvenient and time consuming, nonetheless, you should eventually get satisfactory results.

PART IV

DISCOVERING HONG KONG'S SHOPPING SECRETS

10 WHAT TO BUY

Hong Kong is one great emporium for shoppers. You can find just about every conceivable consumer product here at prices competitive to those in stores back home. Whether you are looking for particular products or just browsing along the high density shopping streets of Central, Tsimshatsui, or Tsimshatsui East districts, you will discover a myriad of choices. With a good pair of walking shoes, plenty of time, and dogged persistence, you will be a successful Hong Kong shopper.

Knowing what to buy is just as important to successful shopping as knowing how and where to buy. The previous chapters focused on important *"how"* questions. The next chapter examines critical *"where"* questions for navigating Hong Kong's most important shopping streets, centers, arcades, markets, department stores, and shops. While this chapter concentrates primarily on *"what"* questions, it also places these questions within the larger *"how"* and *"where"* contexts of successful Hong Kong shopping.

When we refer to place names in this and subsequent chapters, please refer to our general maps at the beginning of Chapter One and on pages 84 and 85 as well as more detailed maps provided by the Hong Kong Tourist Association. You'll need these tools to place the barrage of names and addresses in their proper spatial context.

EXPORTS AND IMPORTS

What makes this city so unique is its role as both an importer and exporter of goods from all over the world. It imports, manufactures, and re-exports an incredible variety and volume of goods. Alongside the *"Made in Hong Kong"* clothing, electronic goods, and toys you will find numerous items from China, Japan, Korea, Taiwan, France, Germany, Italy, and the United States.

Except for Japanese goods, which are often cheaper in Hong Kong than in Japan, most foreign-made imported goods are not as great a bargain as their *"duty-free"* status might suggest. Transportation costs to Hong Kong usually make these goods more expensive than in their country of origin, but they may still be less expensive than in your own country.

BEST BARGAINS

Expect to find your **best bargains** on items made from inexpensive skilled Hong Kong labor—items small enough to carry home or ship by parcel post. Many of these items carry international labels and reflect excellent quality workmanship at bargain basement prices. Additional bargains are found on items imported duty-free from neighboring China. Pearls, jade, furs, tailor-made clothing, silk, table linens, porcelain, and optical goods are especially good Hong Kong buys. The craftsmanship is both excellent and inexpensive. Ready-to-wear clothing sold at factory outlets or in retail shops during semi-annual sales can be another excellent buy.

Our general rule for getting a good bargain in Hong Kong is this: **If you can purchase an item for 30 percent less than at home and do not need to ship it, you have a Hong Kong bargain.**

But price alone should not be the only determiner of a good buy or a shopping value. Indeed, looking only for bargains can blind you to some of Hong Kong's great shopping discoveries. If you find something you really love, especially unique jewelry, arts, antiques, or home decorative items that you can't find back home, consider it a bargain, even if you have to pay shipping charges. After all, one of the real pleasures of shopping abroad is finding unique items not available elsewhere. You will cherish such items for years to come.

What to Buy

Most Hong Kong shoppers can expect to find the following items in the numerous small shops, emporiums, department stores, and markets throughout Hong Kong.

ARTS AND ANTIQUES

If you are an art and antique collector or just interested in acquiring some quality items for home decorative purposes, you may find just what you want in Hong Kong's numerous art, antique, and home decorative shops.

Collectors of fine arts and antiques must work much harder these days in finding very old, quality pieces at reasonable prices. Once a major world center for Chinese arts and antiques, today the selections and quality in Hong Kong are limited and prices can be high. However, more and more lovely antiques from Korea, Japan, Taiwan, Thailand, and Burma are appearing in Hong Kong shops. Expect to pay high prices for good quality antiques depending upon rarity, age, and condition. Beware of paying *"old"* prices for *"new"* antiques. If your art and antique interests are primarily home decorative, consider buying some excellent reproductions which are increasingly available throughout Hong Kong.

Two of the best sources for locating quality art and antique shops are the monthly issues of the Hong Kong-published **Arts of Asia** magazine and Drummond's **Hong Kong Guide to Art & Antique Dealers**. The **Arts of Asia** magazine is widely available in Hong Kong bookstores and in major libraries abroad. We subscribe to this beautifully illustrated magazine to keep abreast of new developments in the Asian art and antique scene. It's filled with informative articles as well as ads from the major art and antique dealers. If you wish to subscribe or acquire back issues of this magazine, write to: Arts of Asia Publications Ltd., 1309 Kowloon Centre, 29-39 Ashley Road, Kowloon, Hong Kong. Drummond's **Hong Kong Guide to Art & Antique Dealers** is available in Hong Kong book stores, hotel shops, Altfield shops (Lattices, Altfield Design Services, Altfield Fine Arts) on Hollywood Road, or write directly to the publisher—Drummond's Guides Series, 31 Lyndhurst Terrace, Central, Hong Kong.

Hollywood Road, spanning both Central and Western districts of Hong Kong Island, is still the major center for arts and antiques. Many shops along this road offer very nice collections. However, this street seems to transform itself every two years as many shops go out of business and new ones appear offering different types of arts, antiques, and home decorative items. Skyrocketing rents have forced many businesses to either close or relocate to less expensive quarters, such as Pacific Place in Wanchai. Several new shops with owners based in Taiwan have recently opened ceramic shops along Hollywood Road. We especially like **Schoeni, L'Extreme Orient, Hobbs and Bishops**, Honeychurch Antiques, **Gu Yue Xuan, Golden Dragon Corner, Morning Calm Gallery, Altfield Interiors, Netsuke House, Kander's, Eastern Dreams, Noble House**, and **Silk Road House**. If you have time to visit only a few shops along this road, we highly recommend **Honeychurch Antiques, Schoeni, L'Extreme Orient, Kander's, Eastern Dreams, Noble House**, and **Morning Calm Gallery**. Each shop offers its own unique mix of arts, antiques, and home decorative items.

Do browse through the shops along the adjacent **Cat Street** which is the nickname for Upper Lascar Row. To get there from Hollywood Road, turn north at the Man Mo Temple onto **Ladder Street**, and take the first left into Upper Lascar Row or Cat Street. Here you will find numerous sidewalk vendors selling watches, stones, jade, and used clothes, fans, sewing machines, and lots of other junk. A few antique shops along this street are well worth visiting—**Masterpieces of Netsuke Art** (#1) and **The Sculpture Gallery** (#8). The latter shop offers some of the best Southeast Asian ethnic art and antiques found in Hong Kong. It also has shops in Singapore and Bangkok. **Cat Street Galleries,** which is located between Cat Street and Lok Ku Road, has a few shops selling antiques, ceramics, arts, and home furnishings. Be sure to go to the third floor where **Martin Fund Antique and Furniture** displays a large range of attractive antiques, furniture, and home decorative items. Also look nearby for **Altfield Gallery** (31 Lyndhurst Terrace) for furniture, porcelain, textiles, prints, and lacquerware.

Pacific Place shopping center on the eastern edge of Central (adjacent to the Marriott Hotel) also has a few excellent art and antique shops: **C. P. Ching, Asiana, David Gallery**, and **Treasures of China**. One of Hong Kong's best art shops for contemporary paintings and sculptures is also found in Pacific Place—**Galerie du Monde**. This shop also is reputed to be the best framer in Hong Kong.

Several shops sell Oriental and Western paintings, prints, and maps. For small inexpensive paintings, browse through the small shops surrounding the top and bottom stations of The Tram to Victoria Peak. Other shops selling oils, watercolors, prints, and maps include **The Asian Collector Gallery** (Wilson House, Ground Floor, 19-27 Wyndham Street, Central), **Altfield Fine Arts** (1 Hollywood Road, Central), **Hanart Gallery** (40 Hollywood Road, Central), **Alisan Fine Arts** (615-616 Holland House, 9 Ice House Street, Central), **Tsi Ku Chai** (2nd Floor Hong Kong Diamond Exchange Building, 8-10 Duddell Street, Central), **Contemporary Art Hong Kong** (Macdonnell Road, Hong Kong), **China Resources Artland Centre** (Ground and 1st Floor, Lower Block, China Resources Building, 26 Harbour Road, Wanchai), **Koto Japanese Arts** (1st Floor, Hong Kong Arts Center, 2 Harbour Road, Wanchai), **Kowloon Masterpieces of Netsuke Art** (Shop 104, Basement Shopping Centre, Royal Garden Hotel, 69 Mody Road, Tsimshatsui East), **Man Shan Chai** (Shop 175, 1st Floor, Peninsula Centre, Tsimshatsui East), and **Oriental Arts Gallery Centre** (215 Silvercord, 2nd Floor, Tower II, 30 Canton Road, Tsimshatsui).

Numerous shops along **Hollywood Road** as well as in the upscale hotel shopping arcades at the Peninsula and Regent hotels offer excellent quality tapestries, cloisonne, carvings of jade and other semi-precious minerals, silk screens, and a variety of arts and crafts. We especially like the Chinese, Japanese, Tibetan, Thai, Burmese, and Cambodian selections at **L'Extreme Orient** (159 Hollywood Road, Central, opposite Man-Mo Temple; and Shop R-124, Lobby Shopping Arcade, Regent Hotel, Tsimshatsui).

If you are in the market for antique textiles, be sure to visit **Jenny Lewis** (Ground Floor, Swire House, Central), **Plum Blossom** (4th Floor, Fu House, 7 Ice House Street, Central), and **Altfield Gallery** (#305 Exchange Square, Central).

For top quality—and prices—in arts and antiques, *must* stops include **Charlotte Horstmann and Gerald Godfrey** (Ocean Terminal, Tsimshatsui, and the Mandarin Hotel, Central), **Eileen Kershaw** (Peninsula Hotel, Tsimshatsui), and **Ian McLean Antiques** (73 Wyndham Street, Central).

Charlotte Horstmann and Gerald Godfrey remains Hong Kong's premier antique shop for quality and selections. If you are a serious buyer, be sure to ask to visit their extensive showroom which is located on the lower level of Ocean Terminal. Few visitors to the main shop are aware of the collection downstairs. The upstairs shop only gives you a small sampling of their incredible showroom. But you will have to ask to see this showroom since it is not open to the general public—only dealers and serious collectors/buyers. What you will see here is simply breathtaking. This remains one of the world's finest art and antique shops.

HANDICRAFTS

Hong Kong offers a large variety of handicrafts from all over Asia. Chinese handicrafts such as cloisonne, silk paintings, embroidery, linens, and paper cuts are found in hundreds of shops throughout the city. The **Chinese Arts & Crafts** has the best selection of such items from the People's Republic of China. Several branches of this store are found in Tsimshatsui, Central, and Wanchai. We especially like the vast assortment of hand embroidered table linens, cloisonne vases, carved jade floral arrangements, and fans found in the various branches of two other China-owned department stores: **Yue Hwa** and **Chung Kiu**.

If you plan to buy table linens, be sure to take along measurements. The finely embroidered linens are hand and machine made in China and are among the most affordable in the world. While many patterns are classically Chinese, you may find items to suit the decor of your home. In addition to tablecloths and napkins you'll find placemats, runners, doilies, coasters, and bun warmers. Carefully examine the edges of each piece to be sure that they are properly trimmed and overstitched to prevent raveling. You'll find numerous textile shops on Wyndham Street in Central District which sell curtains and bedding.

Amazing Grace Elephant Co. (B6 Gloucester Tower, The Landmark, Central; and 3236-3242 Ocean Terminal, Harbour City, Tsimshatsui) has a good selection of handicrafts from South and Southeast Asian countries.

Visit the **Banyan Tree** shops (238 Trinity Court, Canton Road, Tsimshatsui; 3045 Ocean Galleries, Harbour City, Tsimshatsui; and 214-217 Princes Building, Chater Road, Central) for a tasteful collection of Asian arts and crafts appropriate for home decorating, including handmade furniture, lamps, and carpets.

Numerous small shops in shopping centers, hotel arcades, and department stores along the streets of Central and Tsimshatsui districts offer nice collections of arts and crafts from all over the world.

In Central District, visit **Rain Field Folkcraft** (Shop 38, 2nd Floor, Admiralty Centre, 18 Harcourt Road) and **Welfare Handicrafts Shop** (15-16 Connaught Centre). In Tsimshatsui District, stop at **Grand Arts and Linen Company** (35A1 Carnarvon Road), **Regalia Art Treasures** (L1-68, New World Shopping Centre), **Royal Arts** (19 Carnarvon Road), and **Welfare Handicrafts Shop** (Salisbury Road and 2176 Ocean Terminal, Harbour City).

CARPETS AND RUGS

Many Hong Kong carpet dealers offer excellent selections of various silk and wool Chinese, Persian, Turkish, Indian, Pakistani, and Afghan carpets and rugs. Although old rugs are still available, you will find many excellent reproductions which are now being made in the New Territories or in China. Since it is difficult to get new rugs from Afghanistan and Iran, several major carpet wholesalers in Europe and North America work with carpet factories in China to recreate the classic rug patterns of the Middle East. Many carpets which feature these venerable designs find their way onto the Hong Kong market at very affordable prices.

While rug prices are generally better in Hong Kong than in Europe and the U.S., be sure to check prices versus quality at home before buying in Hong Kong. The international rug market has been depressed with an oversupply of both hand-knotted and machine-produced Oriental carpets, and prices are down by 30 percent from five years ago. The glutted auction and sale markets in some big cities outside Hong Kong may have comparable prices which would not justify the additional shipping costs incurred by making such a purchase in Hong Kong.

Prepare to buy carpets by taking your room measurements, color swatches, and photos of the rooms in which you'll use your new carpets.

You will find numerous shops offering a large variety of carpets and runs. **Banyan Tree** (Room 238 Trinity Court, Harbour City, Tsimshatsui; and 214-217 Prince's Building, Chater Road, Central) specializes in pastel colored rugs by Indian artist Shyam Ahuja. **Altfield Gallery** (1 Hollywood Road, Central) offers a wide selection of Chinese carpets from Sinkiang, Pao Tou, and Ning Shia. **Tribal Arts and Crafts** (41 Wyndham Street, Central) specializes in hand-knotted rugs from Morocco, India, Afghanistan, Iran, Pakistan, Nepal, and India. Several shops along upper Wyndham street sell Persian rugs.

If you want your own custom-made rug, be sure to visit the famous **Tai Ping Carpets**. You will find their large showroom on the ground floor of Hutchinson House, 10 Harcourt Road, Central. Their smaller shop is located in Wing On Centre, Tsimshatsui East. They have great sales in November and April.

You will find many other carpet and rug shops in Tsimshatsui District. The **Chinese Carpet Centre** shops in Ocean Terminal, Ocean Centre, and the Hong Kong Hotel Arcade have good selections of carpets. Also look for **Carpet World** (Ocean Terminal), **Eastern Rug Co.** (3 Blenheim Avenue), **Carpet House** (Shop 24 New World Centre), **Royal Rug Co.** (49-A Carnarvon Road), **Sunny Rug Co.** (102 Austin Road), and **Aristocrat Rug Co.** (625 Star House). The **Chinese Arts & Crafts** emporiums also offer a good selection of Chinese rugs.

FURNITURE

Numerous shops make and sell nice blackwood, rosewood, teak, bamboo, rattan, and cane furniture in both traditional and modern styles as well as imported furniture from China, Korea, and Japan. Many shops will custom-make furniture and are good at reproducing copies of all types of furniture. Take photos and measurements with you if you plan to place an order. Be sure to keep copies of all documents, including purchase, shipping, and insurance receipts.

You should find good buys on handmade furniture since the cost of labor is relatively inexpensive in Hong Kong. Shipping, however, can be expensive. While it is best to see the final product before shipping, this may be impractical since the work may take four to eight weeks.

Furniture shops are found throughout Hong Kong. **Queen's Road East** and **Hollywood Road** are two major areas for custom-made and antique furniture. Several good shops are also found along **Canton Road** in Kowloon. Check out the shops along **Wong Nai Chung** (east side of Happy Valley Racetrack) for imported European furniture. Several furniture shops are located on the third floor of Ocean Terminal and Ocean Centre.

If you are in the market for Korean chests and antique Chinese and Japanese furniture, be sure to visit the numerous shops along **Hollywood Road** and **Pottinger Street** in Central District and shops in hotel shopping arcades. Collectors of Korean chests will find such shops as **Morning Calm Gallery** (225 Hollywood Road), **Kim's Gallery** (5 Hollywood Road), and **Sweet Bygones** (36 Pottinger Street). For good quality antique Chinese furniture, visit **Yellow River Furniture and Arts** (84 Hollywood Road), **Honeychurch Antiques** (29 Hollywood Road), **I-Wita Antiques** (35 Hollywood Road), **Rare Antiques** (75A Hollywood Road), and **Ian McLean Antiques** (73 Wyndham Street, Central). **Altfield Gallery** (31 Lyndhurst Terrace) also has excellent quality antique Chinese furniture, but most of it is stored in its warehouse at 42A Hollywood Road.

Further from the city center you will find two of Hong Kong's largest and most reliable furniture makers: **Luk's Furniture Co.** (25/F Gee Hang Hong Centre, 65 Wong Chuk Hand Rd., Aberdeen, Hong Kong, Tel. 5-534125/7) and **Maitland-Smith Limited** (4th Floor Wyler Centre, 210 Tai Lin Pai Road, Kwai Chung, New Territories, Tel. 0-291861). Luk's Furniture has one of Hong Kong's largest selections of teak, rosewood, and lacquered furniture along with a good selection of chests and screens. While in Aberdeen, also visit **Mercy Merit** (next to the Aberdeen Marina Club) for a good selection of carved furniture and lacquer screens.

Other shops offering various selections of furniture and related home furnishings include **Evergreen Furniture & Decoration Co.** (Shop 203-204 Casey Building 38 Lok Ku Road) in Central District. But the largest concentration of furniture stores is found in Tsimshatsui District: **Banyan Tree** (238 Trinity Court, Canton Road; **Carlton Woodcraft Manufacturing** (14 Canton Road), **Cathay Arts Co.** (305-7 Ocean Centre, Harbour City), **Chak Sam & Co.** (Shop 32, 2nd Floor, Silvercord), **Chung Tai Furniture** (5 Hanoi Road), **Dragonwood Furniture Co.** (3024 Omni The HongKong Hotel Arcade), **Dynasty Arts & Crafts Co.** (A4 & A5 Sheraton Hotel, 1st Floor; and L1-79 New World Centre), **Hong Kong Manufacturers Agency** (Flat A, 13-5 Minden Avenue, 5/F), **House Arts Beautiful Furniture Co.** (A-2 Sheraton Hotel), **Majestic Furniture Co.** (5 New World Centre Shopping Mall), and **Yin Yin Woodcrafts** (3264 Ocean Terminal, Harbour City).

And still other shops sell a large variety of home decorative items along with stylish western furniture. Most of these shops are found in the major shopping complexes.

HOME FURNISHINGS AND ACCESSORIES

Hong Kong shops offer a good selection of home furnishings and accessories from all over the world. Many shops are well stocked with small tables, lacquer baskets, screens, chests, lamps, statues, woodcarvings, and vases from China, Japan, Korea, Thailand, and the Philippines. Prices will be more expensive than in the countries of origin, because of shipping costs to Hong Kong, but will be less expensive than back home where duties may be added. If you plan to travel to these other countries, unless you find something you love, wait and buy there since selections and prices will be much better.

Most of the shops selling home furnishings and accessories will be found in the major shopping centers, department stores, and in and around Hollywood Road and Wyndham Street in Central District. **Banyan Tree** shops (238 Trinity Court, Canton Road, Tsimshatsui; and 214-217 Princes Building, Chater Road, Central) are well worth visiting. We especially like **Altfield Interiors** (38 Hollywood Road, Central) for excellent quality and beautiful imported upholstery and drapery materials; they will also custom make furniture and accessories.

Several shops carry a good selection of locally produced lamps using such unique motifs as abacus and Buddhist inspired figures. Some shops offer custom-made lamp shades. Several such shops are found in Ocean Terminal, Tsimshatsui.

CHINA, PORCELAIN, CRYSTAL, AND GLASSWARE

You will find numerous small shops and department stores offering a wide selection of good quality china, porcelain, crystal, and glassware items, from tableware to porcelain planters, vases, flower pots, jars, figurines, and animals. Most department stores and Chinese emporiums offer good selections. The **Wah Tung China Co.** in the Cat Street Galleries (38 Lok Ku Road, Central) has one of the largest such collections of porcelain in Hong Kong.

In Central and Western districts, look for **C & T Porcelain** (37 Lyndhurst Terrace), **Craig's** (Ground Floor, St. George's Building, 2 Ice House Road, and G2 Kowloon Hotel), **The Wedgwood Shop** (G7A Gloucester Tower, The Landmark, Pedder Street), **Lane Crawford** (70 Queen's Road), and **Scandinavia Arts** (Room 228 Prince's Building). Along Hollywood Road visit **Everlasting, Eastern Dreams, Silk Road, Monsoon,** and **Cheung Po Cha Antique Co.**

In Tsimshatsui East District, visit **Art Universe Co.** (B101 and Flat/Rm. 301, Royal Garden Hotel; B113 Royal Garden Hotel Arcade), and **Sheung Yu Ceramic Arts** (UG6 South Seas Centre).

If you are shopping in Tsimshatsui District, be sure to visit **Eileen Kershaw** (Peninsula Hotel Lobby), **Hunter's of Hong Kong** (Mezzanine 2 & 3, Peninsula Hotel Arcade; and Shop 2122 Ocean Terminal, Harbour City), **Craig's** (Shop 341, 3rd Floor, Ocean Centre, Harbour City; G-2, Street Level, Kowloon Hotel, Hankow Road; and G4, Lobby Shop, The Hongkong Hotel, Harbour City), **Town House** (2163A Ocean Terminal, Harbour City; 2116C Ocean Terminal, Harbour City; 337 Ocean Centre, Harbour City), **Crystal Gallery** (260 World Shipping Centre, Harbour City), **Lane Crawford** (74 Nathan Road), **Scandinavia Arts** (3201A Ocean Terminal, Harbour City), and **Stephen & Son** (G11A, 100 Nathan Road).

GEMS AND JEWELRY

You will find all types of jewelry in Hong Kong. The quality is excellent, designs and settings are outstanding, and many shops will simply dazzle you with their selections and displays. Expect to find exceptionally good buys on jade, pearls, opals, lapis, precious and semi-precious stones. It is best to frequent only the HKTA-recommended shops, shops in the top hotels, or shops which have been recommended to you by people who know their gems. In many cases you can expect to save up to 70 percent of the cost of similar jewelry back home. However, not all jewelry is a bargain. Gold and some semi-precious stones are no bargain in Hong Kong unless you are looking for the nearly pure gold jewelry sold in the Chinese gold shops. 22-24K gold, without the alloys added to the 14K gold Americans are used to, has a different color which you may or may not like. Here you pay the daily gold price plus a small mark-up for the workmanship. Consider taking advantage of Hong Kong's low labor costs and skilled designers for redesigning and mounting your own gemstones. It is extremely helpful to have a collection of pictures and drawings of jewelry designs in order to communicate your needs to the designer and to save time and lessen the chances of disappointment.

Our recommendation: **shop for unique designs, quality, and craftsmanship in the case of semi-precious stones; shop for price in the case of pearls and jade**. Don't buy diamonds and other precious gemstones unless you know what you are doing. Visit one or more of the major jewelry stores back home to sharpen your quality-recognition skills.

Be sure to pick up Joan Reid Ahrens' and Ruth Lor Malloy's *Hong Kong Gems & Jewelry*. This book details how and where to buy gems and jewelry in Hong Kong. HKTA's *The Official Guide to Shopping, Eating Out, and Services in Hong Kong* lists numerous jewelry shops throughout Hong Kong. In general, you will find some of the best quality jewelry stores in the hotel shopping arcades, especially the **Peninsula, Mandarin, Regent, Hilton, Grand Hyatt** hotels, and **The Landmark** shopping center.

In Central District, visit **Amerex International** (Takshing House, Des Voeux Road) for pearls; **Anglo Tex** (22 Des Voeux Road) for pearls and Italian gold; **Casey Boutique** (106 Gloucester Tower, The Landmark) for diamonds; **Debera** (2801 Admiralty Centre, Tower 1) for diamonds; **Golay Buchel** (Room 1504, 5 Queen's Road) for pearls; **Hsudia Jewelry** (Pacific House, 6th Floor, 5 Queen's Road) for pearls and designer jewelry; **Kai-yin Lo** (Mandarin Hotel Arcade) for uniquely designed jewelry; **Lane Crawford** (70 Queen's Road) for unique designs and Mikimoto pearls; **Manning Jewellery Co.** (44 Queen's Road) for jade, pearls, and gold; and **The Showroom** (Room 1203, Central Building, 1 Pedder Street) for diamonds, pearls, and stones.

In Tsimshatsui District, stop at **Amerex** (5-15 Hankow Road, Room 314) for pearls and Italian gold; **Chow Sang Sang Jewellery Co.** (229 Nathan Road) for Chinese gold; **Chu's Jade Gallery** (106 Royal Garden Hotel); **Falconer Jewellers** (ML9-11 Mezzaine Floor, Peninsula Hotel; Regent Hotel; and Hongkong Hotel); **Maggie's Jewellery** (1st Floor, Hyatt Regency Hotel) for designer jewelry; **Mcdonald Jewellery Manufacturer Co.** (Shop B1, 16 Salisbury Road, New World Centre); **Papillon Jewellery** (G30-31 Tsim Sha Tsui Centre, Salisbury Road); **Sunny Tsui Jewellery** (Mezzaine, Holiday Inn Golden Mile); **Trio Pearl** (Peninsula Hotel); **Kai-yin Lo** (Peninsula Hotel); and **Yuan Feng Arts & Crafts Co.** (1A Mody Road).

What to Buy   129

You will also find several gem and jewelry wholesalers as well as factory showrooms in Hong Kong. Wholesalers provide some of the best selections but not necessarily the best prices. And don't expect to receive any special savings on jewelry by shopping at the factory showrooms. Most such showrooms sell gems and jewelry at the same prices offered by retail shops in Central and Tsimshatsui districts. If you are being taken to such a showroom by a tour group or guide, the showroom will most likely pay someone a commission for any purchases you make. Our advice: shop in shops that have a reputation for providing good quality and reliable service.

WATCHES

You will find an incredible variety of time pieces, in every type, style, and quality, from all over the world in Hong Kong. However, this is one item you can easily be cheated on since some dealers are notorious for selling fakes as well as for putting inferior mechanisms into expensive cases. Watches can be excellent buys—if you know what you are doing. Look your purchase over carefully, shop in reputable shops, check the serial number, and be sure to get a receipt as well as the manufacturer's international warranty.

Look for watches in watch and jewelry shops throughout Hong Kong. In Central District, visit **Basel Watch Co.** (33 Queen's Road), **David Watch** (52 Des Voeux Road), **King's Watch Co.** (Ground Floor, 49 Queen's Road), **Rolex** (1407 Connaught Centre), and **Shui Hwa Watch Co.** (50 Des Voeux Road). In Tsimshatsui District, stop at **Albert & Co.** (45-47B Carnarvon Road), **Carol's Watch & Jewellery Centre** (2129, Ocean Terminal, Harbour City), **China Watch Co.** (1F, Mody Road), **Emperor Watch & Jewellery Co.** (81 Nathan Road), **Grand Watch & Jewellery Co.** (Room 2154, Ocean Terminal, Harbour City), **Sun Ray Watch Company** (G14 Silvercord, 30 Canton Road), and **Watches of Switzerland** (21 Mody Road).

FURS

Furs can be another good buy in Hong Kong. The quality of the skins is excellent and the tailoring can be outstanding. However, the styling of some Hong Kong furs leaves much to be desired; many off-the-rack furs look matronly and dated. Compared to prices back home, you might save as much as 50 percent by buying a fur in Hong Kong. But check prices at home first so you'll know whether you are really getting a deal. With the recent slump in U.S. fur sales, many retailers in the U.S. have drastically lowered prices to the point where it may be no advantage to purchase a fur abroad. You may find the prices in Hong Kong aren't really the great deal you expected—especially if you will have to pay duty.

One of the most popular and aggressively advertised fur stores is **Jindo Fur Salon** (World Finance Centre, Harbour City, Tsimshatsui). This South Korean company advertises that they are the largest maker of fur garments in the world, with 3,000 pieces from which to choose, and at prices that are so low you can save your airfare on a purchase. While much of this advertising hype may be true, the quality of their furs and tailoring varies greatly—from poor to excellent. Therefore, you must be **very** selective in Jindo stores. Most of their furs are mass-produced to be sold off-the-rack. You would be foolish to expect the same quality here compared to furs made for you by Hong Kong's fine craftsmen. On the other hand, if you only plan to wear your fur for two to five years of infrequent use, you may find exactly what you need at the Jindo Fur Salon.

Know your furs before you succumb to buying a fur in Hong Kong. Our advice: visit a reputable furrier in your hometown in order to learn the difference between high quality furs and inexpensive furs. Talk to people who make it their business to hand-sew lovely garments. Then when you visit Jindo or any other fur store in Hong Kong, you will know what you are seeing and can make an informed choice. If what you see is what you want, then you will probably get a good deal.

Other popular furriers include **Siberian Fur Store** (21 Chatham Road, Tsimshatsui; and 29 Des Voeux Road, Central); **Stylette Models** (L2-388 New World Shopping Centre, Tsimshatsui; and Excelsior Hotel Arcade, Causeway Bay); and **Fur Chiba** (G43-45 New World Shopping Centre; and 18-24 Salisbury Road, Tsimshatsui). We have been pleased with a small shop called **Grand Fur** (10A Humphreys Avenue, Tsimshatsui). Although their selections are limited, it does offer fine quality furs along with excellent service and moderate prices.

LEATHERGOODS

While Hong Kong is a good place to buy excellent quality leather goods at reasonable prices, it is not the place to have leather garments tailored. You will find numerous locally-produced as well as imported leather items in shops and department stores: briefcases, handbags, purses, wallets, belts, shoes, and luggage. But you also will find a great deal of inferior quality leather and imitations of designer leather goods.

Some of the best quality leather is found at **Lane Crawford**, (70 Queen's Road, Central), **Wing On** (Connaught Road, Central), **Sincere** (Connaught Road, Central), and three Japanese department stores in Causeway Bay—**Matsuzukaya, Daimaru,** and **Mitsukoshi.** Several designer boutiques sell their line of leather in the major hotels (**Peninsula** and **Mandarin**) as well in **The Landmark. Gofuku Leather Goods Centre** (Energy Plaza, 92 Granville Rd., Tsimshatsui) features a huge collection of expensive imported designer handbags. Expect only a 10 percent discount after hard bargaining.

SILKS AND OTHER FABRICS

Many fabrics are available by the meter in specialty shops all over Hong Kong. Several shops offer excellent selections of Chinese and Thai silks, Irish linens, and fabrics from India, Malaysia, and Indonesia. British woolens are available from tailor shops as well as fabric stores and in the tiny shops of Cloth Alley. You will find very few nice cotton fabrics and almost no man-made fibers. Most of the available silks are crepe de chines from neighboring China which is excellent material for making dresses and blouses. Since silk accepts dyes easily, you will find many beautiful colors. You will also find silk brocades, printed silks, raw silk, silk corduroy, washed silk, silk ribbon gauze, and jacquards with woven-in geometric and floral designs. The China products stores (especially **Chinese Arts & Crafts** in Star House and Silvercord, Tsimshatsui) all carry a very large selection of good quality silks imported from neighboring China.

In Central District treat yourself to a most unusual display of fabrics in **Cloth Alley** on Wing On Street. Tiny fabric shops line each side of the narrow alley which is the third alley west of Central Market between Queen's Road and Des Voeux. A large concentration of cloth shops are also found along Li Yuen streets.

Look for Thai silks at **The Thailand Shop** (Silvercord, Canton Road, Tsimshatsui), **Thai Design** (Peninsula Hotel, Tsimshatsui), **Altfield Interiors** (38 Hollywood Road, Central), and **Dana Boutique** (26 Wyndham Street, Central).

Hang Kong Woolen (3rd Floor, 30-32 Cameron Road, Tsimshatsui) is a great place to buy woolen yardage which is imported from Europe. While many tailors prefer that you buy their yard goods, you might do well buying your wool and cashmere from Hang Kong.

TAILOR-MADE CLOTHING

Hong Kong still offers some of the best quality fabrics and tailoring craftsmanship in the world. Tailor shops are available throughout Hong Kong, but the better shops will be located in and around the major hotels. Expect to save up to 50 percent on comparable clothes. Avoid any shops which claim they will give you excellent quality in a short time. Quality tailoring takes time. For detailed information about custom tailoring—including fabrics, styles, choosing a tailor, communicating your needs, and money matters—please refer to **Appendix A** (pages 183-198) as well as our list of tailoring myths and realities in Chapter Eight.

You may be overwhelmed by the number of shops offering tailored clothing. Some of the best Hong Kong tailors include **A-Man Hing Choeng** (Mandarin Hotel), **H. Baromon** (Swire House), **J. J. Brothers** (19 Hilton Hotel, 20 Queen's Rd.), **Jimmy Chen** (Hong Kong Hotel), **Tak-Tak Company** (RO 43, Regent Hotel Arcade), and **W. W. Chan & Sons** (Block A, 2/F, Burlington House, 94 Nathan Rd.). Some of the top tailors specializing in shirt making include **Ascot Chang Co. Ltd.** (M-6 Peninsula Hotel and 101 Regal Meridian Hotel), **David's Shirts Ltd.** (108 Royal Garden Hotel and M7 Mandarin Hotel), and **The Custom Shop** 326 Hong Kong Hotel Arcade, 22 Central Building, 13 Queen's Rd.). These and many other well-recommended tailors are listed in **Appendix B** (pages 213-215). Your time will be best spent by choosing a tailor which is in, or near, your hotel, since you will be visiting the shop for numerous fittings.

What to Buy 133

READY-TO-WEAR CLOTHING

A large variety of ready-made clothes in different fabrics and styles is available throughout Hong Kong, ranging from the latest designer clothes in chic boutiques to inexpensive clothes in factory outlets and street stalls. Such clothes are one of the great shopping bargains and delightful shopping experiences in Hong Kong. Expect to save as much as 70 percent as compared to clothing purchased back home, especially if you shop during the semi-annual sales in January and June. Most of the clothes are made in Hong Kong.

You will find famous **designer** labels, such as Hermes, Vanderbilt, Pierre Cardin, Calvin Klein, Missoni, Yves St. Laurent, Ralph Lauren, and Charlotte Ford, which are made in Hong Kong. Numerous chic boutiques in **The Landmark** shopping center and along **Wellington** and **D'Aguilar** Streets in Central as well as major department stores and shops in hotel shopping arcades carry such labels: Basile (Regent Hotel); Bally (Peninsula Hotel, Landmark, Swire House, Sogo); Charles Jourdan (New Henry House, Central); Etienne Aigner (Park Lane Shoppers' Boulevard, Tsimshatsui); Christian Dior, Emanuel Ungaro, Givenchy, Hermes, Valentino (Landmark); Issey Miyake, Matsuda (Swire House, Central); Leonard, Lancel, Loewe, Salvatore Ferragamo (Peninsula Hotel); and Nina Ricci (Regent Hotel). The creations of noted **local designers**, such as Diane Freis, Jenny Lewis, Ragence Lam, Walter Ma, and Eddie Lau, are well represented in shops at Ocean Terminal, Swire House, Kowloon Hotel, Mandarin Hotel, Pedder Building, and Pacific Place. You will also find trendy fashions in several chain boutiques: Benetton, Crocodile, Esprit, Toppy, and Bird's.

To get started shopping for ready-to-wear clothes, try the boutiques in The Landmark shopping center, Pacific Place shopping center, and in the Peninsula, Regent, and Mandarin hotels for the latest fashion clothes. Many other choice shops are located in Ocean Terminal, Ocean Centre, and Harbour City. But don't expect cheap prices in such stores. Prices may be similar to or somewhat less than you'd pay back home for similar quality, but the selections will probably be much broader. The best bargains take place during the semi-annual sales.

Less expensive clothes, produced in Hong Kong's many textile factories, are found in the factory outlet shops, department stores, lanes, and markets. Counterfeit designer clothes are found in several markets. *Factory Bargains* by Dana Goetz lists the major factory outlets as does the Hong Kong Tourist Authority's useful brochure/ guide, *Factory Outlets* (available at all HKTA offices). For inexpensive casual clothing be sure to visit **Stanley Market** (town of Stanley) and **Granville Road** (Tsimshatsui), as well as several of the lanes just east of **Nathan Road** (Tsimshatsui). There you'll find lots of cotton and silk garments for the family such as blouses and shirts, jackets, jeans, sweaters, ski clothing, sportswear, slacks, and dresses. We often run across designer labels on overruns and slightly damaged merchandise in these factory outlets. Some of the brands often seen at Stanley Market include Christian Dior, Fila, Woolrich, Nike, Adidas, Alexander Julian, Harve'Bernard, Nordstrom, Neiman-Marcus, and Banana Republic.

In Central District you will find many interesting boutiques and some of the best quality factory outlets in the **Pedder Building** (12 Pedder Street). Take the elevator to the top floor and shop your way back down. You will find, for example, **Tacpac** (3rd Floor) which has a good selection of Anne Klein II clothes at more than a 50 percent savings over retail prices in the U.S. (Tacpac's larger outlet is in Tsimshatsui, Rm. 201, Oriental Centre, 67 Chatham Road South). Many clothing shops are located on the basement levels of **Swire House** and **The Landmark**. Also browse through the tiny shops in the **Lanes**: Li Yuen East and West, and Pottinger Street.

In Tsimshatsui District, visit the many clothing shops in the **hotel arcades** and **Ocean Terminal** as well as browse through the clothing shops which line **Haipong Road, Mody Road, Carnarvon, Hanoi,** and **Hart Avenue** between Nathan Road and Chatham Road.

SHOES

Hundreds of shops sell a large variety of factory and hand-made shoes. However, quality varies considerably. Many leather shoes labeled *"Made in Italy"* are actually produced in Hong Kong and quality is often poor. Shops do not carry large sizes or extra narrow widths. While shoes may appear to be a good bargain, you will probably do just as well back home by watching sales.

The major areas on Hong Kong Island for inexpensive ready-made shoes are **Wong Nai Chung** and **Leighton Road** in Happy Valley, and **Prince Edward Road** near the Prince Edward Mass Transit

Railway station. In Kowloon you'll find many shoe shops to the east of **Nathan Road**, particularly along **Hanoi Road**.

The best quality and most expensive shoes will be found in major department stores, hotel arcades, and shopping centers where you'll find such brands as Charles Jourdan, Romano, Bruno Magli, and Ferragamo, with savings of around 25 percent.

In Central District, visit **Celine** (Shop Q, First Floor, Furama Hotel, 1 Connaught Road), **Hugo** (215 Gloucester Tower, The Landmark), **Kow Hoo Shoe Co.** (1st Floor, 27 Hilton Hotel), and **Mayer Shoes Co.** (M-23 Mandarin Hotel).

If you are in Tsimshatsui District, stop at **A Beauty Shoes Co.** (Shop 48, Ground Floor, 54-64 Nathan Road), **Asia Shoes & Luggage Co.** (81-B Nathan Road), **Italy Shoes & Handbags Co.** (B-14 Basement, Hyatt Regency Shopping Arcade, 67 Nathan Road), **Lee Kee Boots & Shoe Maker** (65 Peking Road and 19-21 Hankow Road), **Lily Shoes Manufacturing Co.** (13, West Wing, Peninsula Hotel Arcade), and **Salon Shoe Co.** (G17, 100 Nathan Road).

OPTICAL GOODS

Eyeglasses are one of Hong Kong's best buys. You will find all forms of optical goods and services, from excellent eyeglass frames to contact lenses. Many shops use the latest computerized eye examination equipment and offer a wide selection of European designer frames. These optical shops are good sources for second and third pairs of glasses, especially prescription sunglasses as well as contact lenses. Take your eye prescription with you or get an examination in a well-established shop. If you plan to get contact lenses you will need to allow from four days to a week in order to return for several fitting adjustments. The cost of a good quality eye examination, lenses, and frames is between US$60 and US$100, depending upon the correction and frame style. Bifocals will run upwards of US$110. Contact lenses will cost about US$90.

Most hotel shopping arcades feature at least one optical shop. One of the larger concentrations of optical goods shops is along the southern half of **Nathan Road** in Tsimshatsui and along the streets which branch off from Nathan Road. You will find many good optical shops, but branches of **The Optical Shop** are especially well noted for reliability; we have been pleased with their service and quality work.

Beware of the hard sell in some optical shops. Take a friend along whose opinion you trust in matters of style, one who will tell you the truth about how each frame looks on you. If you have contact lenses, be sure to wear them when you try on eyeglass frames.

COSMETICS AND PERFUMES

You will find most major international cosmetic brands in Hong Kong, especially in the **major department stores** and **duty free shops**. Local products also are well represented. Expect some savings on these items, but you'll probably do just as well shopping at discount outlets or department store sales back home. Nonetheless, Hong Kong offers a wider selection of cosmetics and perfumes from all over the world than you may be able to find at home.

STEREO, HI-FI, AND VIDEO EQUIPMENT

Thousands of shops in Hong Kong sell a wide range of stereo and hi-fi equipment. You may find good bargains on the latest innovations from Japan and Hong Kong, products which often take another two years before they enter the North American and European markets. Then again, you may find the same equipment back home for less. If you priced similar items in discount stores back home, you should know whether you are getting a bargain.

The largest concentration of shops are found along **Nathan Road** in Tsimshatsui and along **Hennessy Road** in Causeway Bay. Be very careful to check the electrical system of each item for plugs and voltage which can be used in your home. Many which are sold in Hong Kong will not work in the United States.

TELEVISIONS, CAMERAS, AND ACCESSORIES

Thousands of shops offer almost every make and model of televisions, cameras, and accessories. The largest concentration of shops is found along **Lock Road** and lower **Nathan Road** in Tsimshatsui and along **Hennessy Road** in Causeway Bay. However, very few real bargains are available on these items. If you check prices with discount houses and direct mail companies in the United States (see contact information in Chapter Four), the same televisions, cameras, and accessories usually can be purchased there for less. Nevertheless, you may find many items which are not available back home. Hong Kong also is a good place to buy discontinued and specialty lenses for your older model cameras, or to find discontinued camera models.

Be very careful when purchasing television and video equipment in Hong Kong. Many of the Hong Kong models are designed for the Asian and European PAL system; these will not work in the United States which uses the NTSC system. In fact, most of the televisions in Hong Kong will not work in the United States.

If you are in Central District, visit **Asia Photo Supply** (5 Queen Victoria Street), **Broadway Photo Supply** (3 Queen Victoria Street), **Fujimage** (Shop 3, Lower Ground Floor, Connaught Centre), **Kodak** (Ground Floor, Liu Chong Hing Bank Building, 24 Des Voeux Road), **Mark's Photo Supplies** (Ground Floor, Tak Shing House, 20 Des Voeux Road), and **Realty Audio & Video Supplies** (Shop E1, Ground Floor, Wing On House, 71 Des Vouex Road).

In Tsimshatsui District, look for **Capital Photo Supplies** (G21 Holiday Inn Golden Mile Hotel Arcade, 50 Nathan Road), **Carlton Audio & Photo Supplies** (Ground Floor, 80D Nathan Road), **Crown Photo Supplies** (Ground Floor, 27 Hankow Road), **Esquire** (Ground Floor, 8 Cameron Road), **Sunlight Photo Supplies** (Ground Floor, 208 Mody Road), and **Wood's Photo Supplies** (13th Floor, 1313A Ocean Centre).

COMPUTER HARDWARE AND SOFTWARE

You will find the latest models, peripherals, and software from the United States, Japan, Korea, Taiwan, and Hong Kong in several areas in Kowloon. Hardware purchases are no longer the bargain they used to be. In fact, you may be able to do just as well, or better, by buying through mail-order in the United States.

If you do buy hardware, make sure it is properly converted for your electrical system back home. Most computers sold in Hong Kong are wired for 220 volt systems. Most stores can put a conversion switch on the back of the computer so you can switch back and forth between 110 and 220 volts.

On the other hand, software is extremely inexpensive because much of it is pirated. Software packages selling for US$500 in the United States may be purchased for less than US$25 in Hong Kong. But be aware that you are purchasing pirated software. While ostensibly no longer available in Hong Kong, it still can be purchased if you ask for it at many computer shops. The quality cannot be assured unless you test it. If you are a U.S. citizen, you could have problems taking it through U.S. Customs. We know people who have mailed the manuals and diskettes home by parcel post and declared it as *"educational materials"* or *"printed matter"* and had no problem.

If you want to make computer software and hardware purchases, visit the unique **Golden Arcade Shopping Centre** in Sam Shui Po. You will find numerous vendors offering all kinds of computer hardware and software computer products. To get there, take the MTR to the Sam Shui Po stop; look for the Fuk Wah Street exit, and you'll find the Golden Arcade directly in front of you. Golden Arcade is packed with shops selling computers, printers, peripherals, software, and books. Many of these shops sell pirated goods. You'll also find several computer shops along **Canton Road** and in **Houston Centre** (Tsimshatsui East). The **Asia Computer Plaza**, for example, is located on the bottom two floors of the **Silvercord** shopping center which is located across the street from the Marco Polo Hotel on Canton Road.

If you are in Central District, you may want to visit the **Dodwell Computer Store** (310 Two Exchange Square, 8 Connaught Place), **The Personal Computer Centre** (805-6, 88 Queen's Road), and **System Technology** (Shops 42 and 78, 1st Floor, Admiralty Centre, 18 Harcourt Road).

In Tsimshatsui East District look for **NEC Business Systems** (910-917, Tower B, Mandarin Plaza, 14 Science Museum Road) and **Wintact Computer Co.** (Room 18, Basement 2 Houston Centre, 73 Mody Road) along with several other small and reliable computer stores throughout the Houston Centre Building.

In Tsimshatsui District, in addition to several shops along Canton Road, you will find the **East Asia Company** (1203 Tung Ying Building, 100 Nathan Road), **Quality Electronic & Computer Co.** (Shop 739, Star House, 3 Salisbury Road), and **Vincent Computer Centre** (Rm. 608 Austin Tower, 22-26 Austin Avenue).

Wherever you shop, be sure to bargain hard for all your hardware and software needs. Expect to receive discounts ranging from 10 to 40 percent—even on the already dirt cheap software programs!

TEA

If you like Chinese teas, Hong Kong is the place to pick up numerous varieties of green, black, and oolong teas. You will find excellent quality, inexpensive teas which make nice gifts for tea connoisseurs. Several tea shops are located in Western District along Queen's Road West and Des Voeux Road West and along Stanley Street in Central District. The China products stores and major supermarkets, especially Park 'n Shop, sell many varieties of tea.

MORE DISCOVERIES

Shops in Hong Kong are filled with every conceivable item you might want to buy. In addition to the items outlined so far, you will find snuff bottles, name chops, embroideries, porcelain, ceramics, crystal, brassware, silverware, pewterware, electrical appliances, toys, children's wear, luggage, musical instruments, sporting goods, coins, and stamps. Hong Kong is also famous for fakes and counterfeit items, especially watches, designer label clothing and leather goods, and computer hardware. If you are into boating and sailing, Hong Kong is also an excellent place to have both large and small boats built as well as to purchase marine and yacht supplies.

11 WHERE TO SHOP

Your shopping options are simply overwhelming in Hong Kong. You can confine yourself to hotel shopping arcades and department stores, wander into large shopping centers and emporiums, explore factory outlets, or stroll through small and congested lanes as well as colorful markets and bazaars. Wherever you go, you will observe Hong Kong's primary preoccupation—shopping.

Major place names—districts, streets, hotels, and shopping centers—appearing in this chapter are found on all Hong Kong maps. While you will want to initially refer to our general maps at the beginning of Chapter one and on pages 84 and 85 to orient yourself to our discussion, you should also consult larger and more detailed maps of Hong Kong, especially those provided free of charge by the Hong Kong Tourist Association.

SHOPPING AREAS

Hong Kong's major shopping areas are divided between the peninsula and island of Hong Kong. **Peninsular Hong Kong** borders China and is divided into two major sections: the New Territories and Kowloon. Except for a few factory outlets and local shopping centers which cater

Where To Shop 141

primarily to locals in the New Territories, most of your shopping will be confined to the shopping areas at the southern tip of Kowloon Peninsula. **Island Hong Kong** has several major commercial and residential areas, but its major shopping areas are concentrated in the Central, Western, and Wanchai districts along the north shore.

KOWLOON

Thrusting confidently into Victoria Harbour with magnificent hotels and shopping centers and blazing neon signs, Kowloon Peninsula is located directly opposite Hong Kong Island's congested north shore. Here is one of the world's greatest shopping meccas. You'll find Hong Kong's largest concentration of shops, shopping centers and arcades, and department stores in **Tsimshatsui** and **Tsimshatsui East** districts on the southern and eastern tips of Kowloon Peninsula. Bordered on the east, west, and south by Victoria Harbour and on the north by Gascoigne Street, Tsimshatsui and Tsimshatsui East districts are also choice hotel locations for visitors intent on shopping. You'll discover a large variety of shops and stalls, from department stores and chic boutiques to camera shops and factory outlets, throughout these areas.

Further north along Nathan Road, between Gascoigne Road and Boundary Street, you will come to three additional shopping districts: **Yaumati, Mongkok**, and **Sham Shui Po**. Primarily frequented by locals, these areas are especially noted for less expensive Chinese emporiums, department stores, computer shops, restaurants, and hotels.

If you head directly east of these districts—also north and east of Tsimshatsui East, and near the airport—you will discover **Hung Hom,** Hong Kong's famous factory outlet district. Many shoppers go here to get bargains on jewelry and clothing. **Man Yue Street** is especially popular for its bargains, as is the **Kaiser Estates** complex with its many factories and factory outlets.

Most shoppers, however, will concentrate on the many shopping centers, hotel shopping arcades, department stores, and small shops that line the narrow streets of Tsimshatsui and Tsimshatsui East districts. These are great areas to browse from one shop to another to discover many of Hong Kong's shopping delights. If you venture further north and east to Yaumati, Mongkok, and Sham Shui Po districts, it's best to know where to buy particular items: the Golden Arcade Shopping Centre in Sham Shui Po for computerware; Chung Kui Chinese Products Emporium in both Mongkok and Yaumati for inexpensive household goods; and Kaiser Estates in Hung Hom for factory outlets selling clothing and jewelry.

Tsimshatsui District

The central and western sections of **Tsimshatsui District** house Hong Kong's largest concentration of shops and tourist hotels. **Nathan Road**, also known as the "Golden Mile", bisects this area from north to south. At the northern end, just south of Kimberly Road, is the Park Lane Shopping Boulevard with its numerous upmarket clothing, shoe, and jewelry stores as well as the Yue Hwai Chinese Products Store and Park Lane Square. The **Ocean Terminal/Ocean Centre/Harbour City** complex comprises its western boundary, stretching northward for several blocks from the **Star Ferry** along Canton Road to the **China Hong Kong City** hotel, shopping, and terminal complex. The **New World Shopping Centre,** just off the intersection of Salisbury and Chatham roads, is in the southeast section of this area. The north-south **Chatham Road** sets the eastern boundary for Tsimshatsui District as well as the western boundary for Tsimshatsui East District. As a shopping area for locals, the northern boundary of Tsimshatsui continues to expand beyond **Jordan Road** toward the New Territories and includes the areas of Yaumati, Mongkok, and Sham Shui Po. Major hotels such as the Ambassador, Grand, Holiday Inn-Golden Mile, Hong Kong, Kowloon, Marco Polo, Miramar, New World, Park, Peninsula, Prince, Regent, and Sheraton are located within the central and southern sections of Tsimshatsui District. Many of these hotels, especially the Peninsula, Regent, New World, Kowloon, and Sheraton, are attached to quality shopping arcades or are located in the midst of many independent shops.

Most shops in the Tsimshatsui area are located south of **Kimberley Road.** This area, bounded on the west by Chatham Road and on the east by Canton Road, is a beehive of short narrow streets lined with thousands of shops at ground level and on upper floors. Browsing through these shops is a true shopper's high. You'll see shops of every kind: shoe stores, tailor shops by the dozens, jewelry stores, shops featuring products from neighboring China, factory outlets for clothing, camera and electronic shops, toy shops, and department stores. There are very few grocery stores in this area although you will find some small mom and pop grocers near the hotels as well as branches of the Park 'n Shop grocery stores. Few locals buy their food in the tourist area, but you'll find enough basics to stock your hotel room refrigerator with snacks and beverages. Ask at your hotel for the location of the nearest *"supermarket."*

Tsimshatsui East District

Tsimshatsui East District is a newly developing shopping, hotel, restaurant, and office complex. Wedged between **Chatham and Salisbury Roads** on the west and south and bordered by **Granville Road** on the north, this district consists of several centers and plazas anchored by such major hotels as the Nikko, Holiday Inn Harbour View, Regal Meridien, Royal Garden, and Shangri-La. Major shopping complexes in this area include Tsimshatsui Centre, Empire Centre, Houston Centre, Peninsula Centre, South Sea Centre, and Wing On Plaza. Most shopping, especially for electronic products, takes place in the small shops which occupy these multi-story shopping arcades.

HONG KONG ISLAND

Hong Kong Island, the city's major banking, commercial, and government center, is home for several major shopping areas. The five most popular areas border the north shore of the island: Western District, Central District, Wanchai, Causeway Bay, and Eastern District. Similar to Tsimshatsui District on Kowloon Peninsula, each of these areas is relatively compact and thus can be explored on foot. While the distances between these shopping districts are not great—perhaps a half-hour walk—the inclines are sufficiently steep to require the use of public transportation. This is especially true during the hot and humid months when a half-hour walk up and down hills will physically drain you. We recommend using taxi cabs or the tram between these shopping areas.

Western District

Located just west of the Central District and including Kennedy Town to the far northwest, **Western District** is one of the oldest and most congested yet fascinating sections of Hong Kong Island. This traditional *Chinatown* area is populated by numerous small street shops, street vendors, and craftsmen selling costumes, furniture, baby apparel, luggage, fans, traditional Chinese medicine, antiques, rattan, clothes, and an incredible variety of knickknacks, curios, and bric-a-brac along narrow streets and lanes. The area is crowded and at times appears to be an undulating sea of humanity pushing and shoving to advance from one shop to another. This is the area of the famous **Ladder Street, Hollywood Road, Chinese Merchandise Emporium, Cloth Alley, Wellington Street**, and **Night Market** near the Macau Ferry Pier. Strolling through the streets of Western District, which often zig-zag and stretch along steep inclines, is an adventure in itself. This whole area is full of surprises as a kaleidoscope of people, shops, and goods unfold at every turn of its many streets and lanes.

It is well worth beginning your shopping and sightseeing adventures at the western end of **Hollywood Road**. We recommend this approach to Central District because it starts you at the highest elevation. As you progress along Hollywood Road and adjacent side streets and lanes, you will be walking down steep inclines to the shopping areas at lower elevations. If you start at the lower elevation and walk up the hills to Hollywood Road, you may become one very exhausted shopper!

Take a taxi to the western end of Hollywood Road where it intersects with Queen's Road. Walk southeast along Hollywood Road for about one kilometer as it meanders into and becomes Wyndham Street. Occasionally venture east into side streets such as Ladder and Peel streets, and then descend into the Central District by way of **Pottinger Street**, located at a juncture where Hollywood Road becomes Wyndham Street. As you walk along this street you make a striking transition from the more traditional "Chinatown" Hong Kong to the modern western trade and commercial complexes of Central District.

Central District

Central District is Hong Kong's major financial and commercial center. Banks, hotels, department stores, shopping centers, and exclusive shops occupy some of the world's most expensive real estate. This is the most sophisticated and exclusive—as well as expensive—area of Hong Kong. It is home for the world-famous Lane

Crawford department store, The Landmark shopping center, and numerous chic boutiques. Some of the world's best restaurants and fine hotels with shopping arcades (especially the Furama, Hilton, and Mandarin) are located within this district. If you are looking for the finer things in life, such as fashionable and chic clothes, quality jewelry, and exclusive decorative items, and if money is no object, this should be your major shopping destination. Being a relatively compact area, with most shops located within one square kilometer, you can easily walk to most places within the Central District.

Central has one large and very deluxe shopping center, **The Landmark**, bounded by Des Voeux Road, Queen's Road, Pedder Street, and Ice House Street. The Landmark features three floors of exclusive high fashion shops and tea rooms. Free entertainment is provided most afternoons around the lovely fountain on the ground floor as well as special art and historical displays. Other nearby shopping centers include **Swire House** which is west across Pedder Street, **The Pedder Building** with several factory outlets, and **Central Building**. **Lane Crawford** (70 Queen's Road, Central) is Hong Kong's most luxurious department store. Other Lane Crawford branch stores are located in Tsimshatsui District at the Peninsula Hotel Arcade, Ocean Terminal (Harbour City), and 74 Nathan Road. Although Central is the financial center of Hong Kong, it houses many interesting shops along its streets and lanes. Be prepared to climb as you explore Central, for this area is built at the base of a steep hill, and some streets go straight uphill.

Central District is pushing its eastern boundaries into the adjacent Wanchai District with more upscale shopping found in and around Pacific Place and the new Marriott Hotel and Conrad Hotel. This area is most easily reached via the Admiralty station of MTR or by taking the tram from Central.

Wanchai District

Wanchai District is directly east of the Central District with Arsenal, Jaffe, Gloucester, Lockhart, and Hennessy Roads being the major shopping arteries. Attempts are being made at upgrading the area. Two recent additions to this area are likely to significantly transform the western end of Wanchai District into an upmarket shopping, hotel, and contention center. The new **Hong Kong Convention and Exhibition Center** with its neighboring hotels, the

Grand Hyatt Hong Kong and the New World Harbour View along the waterfront near the Wanchai Ferry Pier, have sparked some zealous renovation of the entire area. Very upscale shopping arcades offering selections from some of the worlds' top designers have opened in the hotel arcades, and more shopping variety is sure to come. The nearby **Pacific Place** shopping center and adjacent Marriott, Conrad, and Island Shangri-La hotels, while ostensibly at the eastern end of Central District, are completing the transformation of this area.

A mixed area for shoppers, parts of Wanchai still project a somewhat sleazy *Suzie Wong* image of tattoo shops, sailor bars, and ladies of the night crowded into an ugly, decaying, and neon blazing stretch of urban gaiety. Yes, you can still get a good tattoo here, especially along Jaffe Road, although we would not risk the possibility of encountering contaminated needles. With new commercial and shopping areas developing within Wanchai, this district offers some things for daytime shoppers. Small shops and stalls sell a large variety of cheap clothing, furniture, household goods, knickknacks, and souvenirs. Tailor, jewelry and electronic shops are found alongside restaurants, supermarkets, and banks.

Happy Valley is located a short distance south of Wanchai. Especially famous for the Happy Valley Racecourse and the garish Tiger Balm Garden, Happy Valley also is a great place for buying cheap shoes—both factory and handmade—along Leighton Road. Numerous shoe shops and several European style furniture studios are found on the eastern side of the race track. Don't expect to walk away from this area with shoes that will last very long. Shoes in this area are cheap for both price and quality.

Causeway Bay

Causeway Bay is located just east of Wanchai District and northeast of Happy Valley. From Central District, Causeway Bay is easily reached by tram, MTR, or taxi. The Cross-Harbour Tunnel connects Kowloon with Hong Kong Island at Causeway Bay. Completed in 1973, this tunnel has transformed a once traditional community into a bustling city.

Causeway Bay is a large and diverse shopping area anchored by five Japanese department stores with literally hundreds of small hi-fi, camera, electronics, shoe, tailor, clothing, souvenir, and art shops. It includes everything from large stores to street vendors. It is home for the Plaza, Lee Garden, and Excelsior Hotels, the World Trade Centre, Jardine's Bazaar, and numerous restaurants and theaters.

Eastern District

Eastern District is primarily a residential area where many locals shop. It also has some interesting shopping sections. Consisting of North Point, Quarry Bay, and Shaukeiwan, Eastern District is best noted for the huge Cityplaza at Tai Koo Shing (Quarry Bay) and several department stores, especially along King's Road. Locals like to refer to the ever expanding Cityplaza as *"Nathan Road under a roof."*

Stanley

Stanley Village is the only important shopping area outside the northern shore districts of Hong Kong Island. This small southern shore town is famous for the **Stanley Market**, a potpourri of small stalls and shops. This is a shopping mecca for inexpensive clothing, especially designer jeans, T-shirts, and jackets as well as antiques, handicrafts, baskets, art, and home furnishings. Although recently sold to a large consortium, shops refurbished, and prices raised, hunting for bargains in Stanley Market is still great fun and often very rewarding. From Central District, Stanley can be reached by bus (numbers 6 or 260) or by taxi. Stanley Market is on most island tour itineraries.

SHOPPING CENTERS

Much of your shopping will take place in the numerous air-conditioned shopping centers found throughout Hong Kong. The major ones you should know about include the following.

MAJOR SHOPPING CENTERS

Ocean Terminal/Ocean Centre/Hong Kong Hotel/Harbour City/China Hong Kong City: One of the world's largest shopping complexes. Located in Tsimshatsui District at the tip of Kowloon Peninsula adjacent to the Star Ferry and stretching several blocks north along Canton Road. Packed with hundreds of shops selling everything from the latest electronic goods and fashion clothes to elegant arts and antiques. Anchored by major hotels (Hong Kong, Marco Polo, Royal Pacific, World Pacific). The newly completed China Hong Kong City also serves as a major terminal for China and Macau. Can easily spend a full day shopping this rather crowded complex.

The Landmark: Unquestionably the most elegant shopping center in Hong Kong and most of Asia. Located in Central District and connected to Swire House shopping arcade by an overhead pedestrian walkway which, in turn, is connected to Connaught Centre. Bounded by Des Voeux Road, Queen's Road, Pedder Street, and Ice House Street. Houses chic boutiques, art galleries, jewelry stores, and cafes.

New World Centre: Across the street from the Sheraton Hotel, attached to the New World Hotel, and next to the Regent Hotel on Salisbury Road in Tsimshatsui District. This multi-level shopping center has hundreds of jewelry, leather, computer, clothing, optical, arts and crafts, tailor, and electronic shops as well as restaurants and the Japanese Tokyu Department Store.

Admiralty Centre: Located in Central District and connected to Queensway Plaza and United Centre. Filled with small boutiques, toy shops, tailors, optical shops, art galleries, and electronic shops.

Pacific Place: A new upscale shopping arcade which appeals to the more affluent. Located in Admiralty on Queensway next to the Marriott Hotel, Conrad, and Island Shangri-La hotels. A relatively new and upscale shopping arcade filled with boutiques, jewelry stores, and art and antique shops.

New World Harbour View Shopping Arcade: Located on the second floor of the new Convention and Exhibition Center and adjacent to the Grand Hyatt Hong Kong and New World Harbour View hotels in Wanchai District. Contains numerous upscale jewelry, tailor, clothing, shoes, leather, antique, and art shops. Connected to other shopping plazas, department stores, and shops in a newly developing shopping, hotel, and convention complex.

Cityplaza: A popular shopping center for local families on weekends. Located in Tai Koo Shing, Quarry Bay, east of North Point and not on most tourist maps. Includes six floors of shops, major department stores (Marks & Spencer, UNY, Wing On, Dodwell), and popular ice and roller skating rinks. The newly opened Phase II has added many new shops. A good place to buy children's clothes and toys, but not a high priority shopping center for visitors.

Other shopping centers of interest to many visitors include **Wing On Plaza, Empire Centre, Houston Centre, Tsimshatsui Centre, Auto Plaza, Energy Plaza**, and **South Seas Centre** in the Tsimshatsui East District of Kowloon; **Princess Shopping Plaza** next to the Miramar Hotel on Kowloon; and **Queensway Plaza, Swire House,** and **United Centre** in Central District.

HOTEL SHOPPING ARCADES

Some of the best shops in Hong Kong are found in the shopping arcades of major tourist hotels, which also tend to be located near the major shopping centers. These arcades are generally found on the first and second floors of the hotels. The most elegant, expensive, and best quality hotel shopping arcades in Tsimshatsui District are found in the **Peninsula Hotel** and in the **Regent Hotel**. Other popular hotel arcades in both Tsimshatsui and Tsimshatsui East districts are found at the **Sheraton, Hyatt, Miramar, Holiday Inn Golden Mile, Royal Garden**, and **Hong Kong** hotels. The most elegant hotel shopping arcade in Central District is in the **Mandarin Hotel.** Other popular hotel shopping arcades on Hong Kong Island are in the **Hilton** and **Furama** hotels in Central, the **Grand Hyatt Hong Kong** in Wanchai, and the **Excelsior Hotel** in Causeway Bay.

Hotels do not assume responsibility for the rented shops in their arcades. However, the quality of the hotel and its clientele does have an influence upon the quality of shops. If you are looking for lower prices, check the arcades in the second and third-class hotels. You'll also find poorer quality products in these arcades.

DEPARTMENT STORES

Excellent shopping can be found in many of Hong Kong's department stores. Most offer a good range and quality of goods at fixed prices. You will find most of the department stores in or around the major shopping centers. British, Japanese, and Chinese department stores are well represented in Tsimshatsui, Tsimshatsui East, Central, and Causeway Bay.

MAJOR DEPARTMENT STORES

Lane Crawford: Unquestionably Hong Kong's most elegant British department store. The main branch, with the best selections, is located at 70 Queen's Road in Central District. Smaller branches are found in Causeway Bay at Windsor House and in Tsimshatsui District at 74 Nathan Road, the Peninsula Hotel Arcade, and Ocean Terminal. Includes excellent selections of jewelry, clothing, leather goods, and home decorative items.

Dodwell's: Popular British department store offering inexpensive product lines of good quality clothing. Look for the Marks and Spencer's St. Michael label. Located in Ocean Terminal (Tsimshatsui) and the Excelsior Hotel shopping arcade (Causeway Bay).

Sincere: Chinese department store located at 83 Argyle Street (Mongkok) and 173 Des Voeux Road (Central). Offers a good selection of fashion clothing and cosmetics.

Wing On: Chinese department store with three locations: 361 Nathan Road (Yaumati), 26 Des Voeux Road (Central), and 211 Des Voeux Road (Central). Offers inexpensive clothing. A popular store for locals rather than tourists.

Sogo: An ultra-modern Japanese department store located on Lockhart Road (Causeway Bay). Filled with good quality clothes, electronic goods, cosmetics, toys and furniture. Excellent place to find Japanese designer clothing.

Daimaru: A large Japanese department store located on Paterson Street (Causeway Bay). Includes good selections of reasonably priced clothing, housewares, furniture, jewelry, watches, and electronic goods.

Isetan: Another Japanese department store located in the Sheraton Hotel shopping arcade (Tsimshatsui). Good selection of trendy clothing for young people as well as designer labels.

Matsuzukaya: A typical Japanese department store. Located on Paterson Street (Causeway Bay). Includes the usual selection of clothing, cosmetics, housewares, toys, electronic goods, and handbags.

Mitsukoshi: One of the best Japanese department stores offering good quality products and excellent selections. Located at 500 Hennessy Road (Causeway Bay). You will find a fine selection of jewelry, watches, leather goods, cosmetics, and toys here as well as many designer labels.

Other department stores found in a few shopping centers include **Marks and Spencer** (British) and **UNY** (Japanese).

CHINESE EMPORIUMS

Chinese emporiums are actually large department stores offering a wide selection of traditional products from neighboring China as well as some imported goods. Their product range tends to be limited to cloisonne, porcelain, semi-precious stone jewelry, fabrics, hand embroidered linen, arts, crafts, luggage, medicines, foods, and inexpensive clothing. A few emporiums carry limited selections of fur and leather jackets. While these stores lack the high-tech and elegant styles of the Japanese and British department stores, many of the Chinese emporiums are upgrading the quality of their merchandize in response to the quality requirements of Hong Kong's relatively sophisticated shopping clientele.

MAJOR CHINESE EMPORIUMS

Chinese Arts & Crafts: This is the best of the emporiums and a *"must"* stop for most international shoppers. Stores are located at 24 Queen's Road (Central), Star House (across from Star Ferry, Tsimshatsui), 233-37 Nathan Road (Yaumati), New World Shopping Centre (Tsimshatsui), Silvercord Building (opposite Marco Polo Hotel, Canton Road, Tsimshatsui), and the Hong Kong Convention and Exhibition Center (adjacent to the Grand Hyatt and New World Harbour View hotels in Wanchai). These stores are operated by the People's Republic of China and will give you an excellent glimpse of quality products from China as well as *capitalistic communism*. Each store offers a good selection of jewelry, cloisonne, fabrics, arts, crafts, carpets, luggage, paper-cuts, baskets, porcelain, and inexpensive clothing. Includes some name-brand clothes produced under European designer labels.

China Products Company: Located at 19-31 Yee Wo Street (Causeway Bay), 488 Hennessy Road (Central), and 73 Argyle Street (Mongkok). Includes the usual selection of Chinese goods.

Yue Hwa Chinese Products Emporium: Located at 54-64 and 301-309 Nathan Road (Tsimshatsui). Includes a large selection of products from China, especially inexpensive clothing as well as some imported designer labels such as Givenchy, Lancome, and Chanel.

Chung Kiu Chinese Products Emporium: Located at 17 Hankow Road (Tsimshatsui), 47-51 Shan Tung Street (Mongkok), and 530 Nathan Road (Yaumati). Includes the usual selection of Chinese items. The Nathan Road branch has a good selection of Chinese arts and crafts.

> **Chinese Merchandise Emporium:** Located at 92-104 Queen's Road (Central). A popular store for locals who shop here for clothes, and household goods.

FACTORY OUTLETS

Factory outlets are one of Hong Kong's great shopping adventures and bargain sources. Indeed, many people visit Hong Kong just to shop at these outlets. These places sell a large variety of goods including carpets, shoes, arts and crafts, porcelain and china, brass and bronzeware, baskets, clothing, leather goods, furniture, furs, jewelry, linen, fabric, sportswear, and umbrellas. Most outlets sell damaged seconds or purchase a line of goods, especially clothing, just for their *"factory outlet"* stores.

When factory outlets first opened approximately 12 years ago they were the source of true bargains. These original shops were connected to the factories and sold the seconds and overruns from that factory. But the Hong Kong businessman, ever on the lookout for another source of revenue, expanded the idea until today you'll find few true factory outlets among the many modern, glitzy shops where special purchase goods are the standard rather than an exception. While you can still find bargains, we don't recommend spending much time searching through all the factory outlets—especially if you are on a tight schedule. Many are disappointing and a waste of time.

Factory outlets are now found throughout Hong Kong, in the major shopping, factory, and residential areas. The best way to shop these outlets is to get copies of the Hong Kong Tourist Association's brochure, **Factory Outlets**, available at all HKTA centers, and Dana Goetz's guidebook, **The Complete Guide to Hong Kong Factory Bargains**. The Goetz book, easily found in Hong Kong, will give you all the necessary information—including maps, addresses in Chinese, telephone numbers, price ranges, and hours—to visit all the major factory outlets. The factory guide is revised and updated yearly and features quite accurate addresses and business hours. Consult Goetz's guide for specifics, but don't expect to find the listed items available at all times. The outlets sound much better than they actually are. And much of your success depends on the lucky timing of your visit. A shop that had some good buys one week may have little of note the next. To get a sampling of these outlets, begin by checking out the outlet shops along the east end of **Granville Road** in Tsimshatsui. If you like what you find, then head next for **Kaiser Estates** in the Hung Hom area.

Hung Hom District is the major factory outlet area in Hong Kong. The once-upon-a-time rock bottom prices for silks are no longer a reality in this factory area since the tour buses discovered it a few years ago. Nonetheless, good buys are still possible, and it is worth the short taxi ride if you have the time. Allow an afternoon for shopping here. Similar items can be purchased in factory outlets in Tsimshatsui and Central districts, but then you would miss the adventure of riding freight elevators and searching through dusty hallways for the shops which are connected to the factories that produce the wares.

Factory outlets along **Man Yue**, **Man Lok**, and **Hok Yuen** streets in Hung Hom District are worth exploring. Three large blocks of buildings within the confines of these three streets make up a factory complex called **Kaiser Estates**. Within each *"phase"* of the three 13-story buildings are many factory outlets, but you have to search for them. Consult the building directory which is located on the wall just inside the front door of each high-rise for the shop number. You may find a new outlet and some real bargains. No, you will not find a Liz Claiborne outlet here; the sign you see is only for the factory office, and they won't sell to you unless you just happen to hit their one-Saturday-a-year-sale. If you are a shopper looking for adventure, then you may find a taxi or ferry ride to shop Kaiser Estates for fashion treasures to be just the ticket. Most of these factory outlets sell women's clothing and jewelry.

One of Hong Kong's best factory outlets is located just across the street from The Landmark in Central District—**Pedder Building** (12 Pedder Street). Some of the better outlet shops have recently located here. Take the elevator to the third floor where you will find some of the best outlet shops in Hong Kong. We especially like **Tacpac** with its Anne Klein II selections. Expect to save at least 50 percent or more here on fashionable blouses and jackets. Also look for **Jomea Boutique**, **La Donna**, **Furvien Co.**, and **St. Resis**. The fourth and second floors also have several boutiques offering coats, dresses, knitwear, blouses, and sweaters. One of the best shops is **Boutique Tommi** (fourth floor).

Another larger **Tacpac** outlet shop representing the Anne Klein II line is found at 67 Chatham Road South in Tsimshatsui East (#201 World Corner Building).

Where To Shop 155

Factory outlet shoppers should watch for ads in the daily newspapers. In season, after shipping their orders, many factories will have unsold goods which they make available in the outlets. Watch for ads in the *South China Morning Post*.

MARKETS, BAZAARS, AND LANES

Another interesting shopping adventure in Hong Kong is a visit to the many markets, bazaars, and street lanes. These are located throughout the major shopping areas of Hong Kong. The major ones include:

MAJOR TRADITIONAL MARKETS

Jade Market: Located at the north end of Reclamation across Kansu Street in the Yaumati section of Kowloon, just north of Tsimshatsui District. Jade traders set up shop each day from 10am to 3pm to offer jade trinkets to tourists. Be prepared to bargain hard. Consider buying dozens of small pendants and *life savers* of jade as token gifts to place beside each guest's plate at dinner parties. Jade is considered good luck. Most of the jade vendors do not speak English and bargaining is done with a pencil and paper or calculator. Choose the item(s) you want, hold them out, and ask *"how much."* The vendor will write out her first price; you should counter with an alternative offer, and so on. When you strike the final bargain, just smile, nod, and say *okay*, and the deal is made. Do not expect to buy good quality jade here. Most of it is trinket quality. If you want good jade, go to a jewelry store or a China Products store. Be sure you know your jade if you are paying a hefty price. Two stones are sold as jade—nephrite and jadeite. Nephrite is less expensive than jadeite. Also beware of soapstone which may be sold as jadeite. You can test jade by its hardness. A knife will not harm real jade.

Temple Street: Also known as the *"Kowloon Night Market"* and located in the Yaumati section of Kowloon. At night this area becomes a bustling open-air market selling everything imaginable. You will see fortune tellers, street doctors, dentists who pull teeth on the spot, mahjong game centers, impromptu

Chinese operas, as well as many other interesting sights. Open between 8pm and 11pm.

Poor Man's Nightclub: Located near the Macau Ferry Terminal on Hong Kong Island. Filled with food stalls, fortune tellers, and hawkers selling jeans, T-shirts, and other clothing. Only operates at night.

Jardine's Bazaar: Located in Causeway Bay on Hong Kong Island behind the Klasse Grand Department Store. Filled with small stalls selling a good selection of sportswear and sometimes fashionable clothing as well as fresh fruits and vegetables.

Cloth Alley: Located along Wing On Street, three blocks west of the Central Market in Central District. Well stocked with good bargains on a wide range of fabrics, from upholstery weight to light Chinese silks and suit-weight woolens.

Li Yuen Street East and West: Located between Queen's Road and Des Voeux Road, three blocks west of Pedder Street in Central District. Good place to buy fashionable but inexpensive clothing, jewelry, accessories, leather goods, and sewing notions. Watch out for pickpockets.

Cat Street or Thieves Market: Nickname for Upper Lascar Row. Located one block north of Hollywood Road at the far western reaches of Central District. Second hand shops often have very interesting old things. Check out *Cat Street Market*. Probably not on your tourist map.

Stanley Market: Located in Stanley (take bus number 6 or 260 from Exchange Square at Star Ferry in Central), this is a very popular market of congested stalls selling designer jeans, T-shirts, and jackets. Nearby shops sell products from other Asian countries. Although Stanley Market was recently sold and renovated, and prices rose accordingly, it's still fun shopping here.

Where To Shop

Other popular markets you might consider visiting include **Mong Kok Market** (Ladies' Market), **Pottinger and D'Aguilar** streets, and **Man Wa Lane.**

SHOPPING ON LIMITED TIME

If you have limited time, you may wish to concentrate your shopping efforts on several of Hong Kong's largest and best noted shopping areas.

KOWLOON

Ocean Terminal-Ocean Centre-Hong Kong Hotel-Harbour City/China Hong Kong City shopping complex located on Canton Road in Tsimshatsui just adjacent to the Star Ferry. Everything you ever hoped to buy is available here, from children's toys, stylish clothing, and jewelry to Chinese antiques. While most of the shops seem to sell similar things, you will find unique and quality items by carefully exploring one store after another. Especially unique are such shops as **Amazing Grace Elephant Co.** (home decorative items), **Charlotte Horstmann and Gerald Godfrey** (arts and antiques), and **Mountain Folkcraft** (Asian arts and crafts). The largest single collection of shops are found on the three levels of this huge complex. This can be a bewildering experience, especially on weekends, as you encounter hundreds of brightly lit shops and crowds of pushing and shoving people seemingly lost in the three miles of indoor walkways.

Peninsula Hotel Shopping Arcade (Salisbury Road) will provide you with a completely different type of shopping experience and a change of pace. Two floors of shops offer some of Hong Kong's finest quality and most elegant clothing, leather goods, jewelry, arts, and antiques.

New World Shopping Centre is a five-minute walk along Salisbury Road. The Centre is next to the Regent Hotel and is attached to the New World Hotel. The best shops in this center are just adjacent to the Regent Hotel.

Streets and shops of Tsimshatsui are filled with numerous shopping discoveries. From the three major shopping areas, walk north along famous **Nathan Road.** Along the way explore the many camera, hi-fi, video, optical, jewelry, watch, and shoe stores and boutiques which line this street and small side streets. Several hotel shopping arcades (Ambassador, Sheraton, Hyatt, Holiday Inn, and Miramar) are along Nathan. Most stores in this area are within 5-10 minute walking distance from Ocean Terminal, the Peninsula Hotel, and the New World Centre.

Streets and shops of Tsimshatsui East offer additional shopping delights. From Nathan Road walk east to **Chatham Road** via **Mody Road** where boutiques, furriers, jewelers, and electronic shops offer good choices. If you take **Granville Road** from Chatham to Nathan you will pass numerous factory outlet stores crammed with all types of ready-to-wear. East of Chatham Road South you will enter the shopping and hotel area of **Tsimshatsui East.** Here, most shops are found in hotel shopping arcades and shopping centers. Visit **Houston Centre, Tsimshatsui Centre, Empire Centre**, and **Peninsula Centre** as well as the **Royal Garden, Regal Meridian, Holiday Inn-Harbour View**, and **Shangri-La** hotels.

On **Hong Kong Island** you should concentrate much of your shopping time on the department stores, shopping centers, hotel shopping arcades, and factory outlets in Central District.

CENTRAL DISTRICT, HONG KONG ISLAND

The Landmark, one of the largest and most prestigious shopping centers in all of Asia should be your first destination. This ultra-modern 20,000 square foot multi-story atrium building houses numerous exclusive boutiques, jewelry shops, shoe stores, art galleries, luggage shops, and cafes.

Swire House is connected to The Landmark by a walkway and houses several dozen exclusive shops. Within a short walking distance, especially northwest along Queen's Road and side streets, you'll find numerous small shops as well as

Where To Shop

the main branch of the exclusive **Lane Crawford Department Store.**

Nearby streets have many shops and boutiques selling all types of goods. **Stanley, Wellington, Wyndham,** and **Hollywood Road** parallel Queen's Road to the southwest. **Pedder, Aberdeen, D'Aguilar, Pottinger,** and **Peele,** as well as numerous nearby lanes are crowded with interesting small shops and stalls. Visit the boutiques and outlets in the **Pedder Building** (12 Pedder Street). The steep inclines of the many colorful side streets can be difficult and tiring at times, but the area can only be explored on foot.

Beyond these primary shopping areas of Kowloon and Hong Kong Island are numerous other areas you may wish to visit if you have time. Shopping in Tsimshatsui and Central districts alone may take you three or four days. However, you will encounter a great deal of redundancy in terms of shops, department stores, products, and prices. Factory outlets, markets, and bazaars, such as Stanley Market, offer a change of pace from these other shopping areas.

When time is short, you need to carefully consider how you want to manage and use every precious minute. Shop the areas near your hotel first. Next, expand your search to those areas which are easily reached by public transportation. Use the most efficient and handy form of transportation. If there are underground stations of the MTR near your hotel, this may be the best way to do the majority of your travel. The MTR will quickly transport you between the major shopping areas of Hong Kong. Then walk between shops within that area. If the MTR is not nearby, use a taxi to transport you between areas or between hotels. For instance, suppose you are staying at the Mandarin Hotel in Central District and you want to shop in Tsimshatsui. There are two very efficient ways to travel across the harbour: the Star Ferry or MTR. The Star Ferry is the more exotic way to make the trip, but it only travels from shore to shore. If you are traveling to or from a more interior street of Kowloon or Hong Kong Island, you may opt for the clean and efficient MTR.

160   Discovering Hong Kong's Shopping Secrets

FASTEST TRANSPORTATION BETWEEN SHOPPING AREAS

You have numerous modes of transportation to choose from as you go from one shopping area to another. If you use taxis, you will find it's much more difficult to get a taxi in Tsimshatsui District than in Central District. In many cases you will be better off walking or taking a bus, tram, ferry, or the MTR.

BEST TRANSPORTATION CHOICES

Kowloon

Tsimshatsui East to Central: Taxi to Star Ferry.

Tsimshatsui East to Ocean Terminal: Taxi.

Tsimshatsui East to Nathan Road: Taxi or walk west on Mody Road.

Regent Hotel to any area in Tsimshatsui: Walk.

Regent Hotel to Central: Walk or taxi to Star Ferry; walk to MTR entrance on Mody/Nathan Road.

Prince or Marco Polo Hotel to Tsimshatsui East: Taxi.

Within Tsimshatsui: Walk. Taxi when in a hurry.

Tsimshatsui

Tsimshatsui hotels to Central: MTR.

Tsimshatsui to Stanley Market: Star Ferry to Central then veer left to bus stops and take #6 or #260, or take a taxi.

Tsimshatsui to Jade Market: MTR to Jordan Road. Walk one block north on Nathan to Nanking, turn left, then right on Reclamation (a street market for food and clothing) and continue to Kansu. Jade Market is across the street on the left side.

Tsimshatsui to Kaiser Estates in Hung Hom: Taxi.

Causeway Bay

Causeway Bay to Kowloon: MTR.

Causeway Bay to Central: MTR or westbound tram.

Central

Central to Tsimshatsui East: Star Ferry to Kowloon, then taxi.

Central to Kowloon: MTR or Star Ferry.

Central to Ocean Terminal: Star Ferry.

Central to Regent Hotel: Star Ferry to Kowloon, then walk east.

Central to Stanley Market: Bus #6 or #260 from Star Ferry or taxi.

Central to Causeway Bay: MTR or eastbound tram.

Within Central District: Walk.

12 PACKING, SHIPPING, AND RETURNING HOME WITH EASE

One of the worst nightmares of shopping abroad is to return home after a wonderful time to find that your goods have been lost, stolen, or damaged in transit. This is most likely to happen to people who do not know how to ensure against such problems. Failing to pack property or pick the right shipper, they suffer accordingly. This should not happen to you.

On the other hand, you should not pass up buying lovely items because you feel reluctant to ship them home. For you can easily ship from Hong Kong and expect to receive your goods in excellent conduction within a few weeks. We never let shipping considerations affect our buying decisions. We know we can always get our purchases home with little difficulty. For us, shipping is one of those things that must be arranged. We have numerous alternatives from which to choose, from hiring a professional shipping company to hand carrying our goods on board the plane. Shipping may or may not be costly, depending on how much you plan to ship and by which means. Shipping need not be a hassle in Hong Kong.

Packing, Shipping, and Returning Home With Ease 163

SHIPPING MADE EASY

Shipping is Hong Kong's lifeline and lifeblood. Expect to get excellent and relatively inexpensive shipping arranged from Hong Kong. Most shops are experienced in shipping items abroad. They tend to pack well and make correct shipping arrangements. Most shops will arrange for shipping when you purchase an item. The shop will pack the item and ship it by parcel post, air freight, or container ship, whichever is most appropriate for your needs. If you make several large and heavy purchases from different shops, you should consider consolidating the items into one large shipment. Be sure to insure the item and get a shipping receipt before you leave the shop. Whenever possible, consider using your credit card to pay for the item as additional protection against potential problems.

PACKING RIGHT

If you anticipate purchasing small delicate items which you plan to carry home, be sure to take appropriate packing materials with you on your trip. We, for example, usually leave home with at least a 20-foot length of 18-inch width plastic bubble wrap as well as scissors, strapping tape, and wrapping cord packed in our suitcase. While most shops in Hong Kong will nicely wrap your purchases, we ensure against shipping damage by wrapping our delicate purchases in plastic bubble wrap. It's better to have such packing materials with you than having to shop for them in Hong Kong while also doing your last minute shopping for more treasures.

Many hotels will also assist you with your packing needs. Contact your concierge to make special packing arrangements.

If you plan to have a shop ship your goods by parcel post, insist that they pack your purchases well. Parcel post is a very convenient and inexpensive way to ship small items. Most reputable shops are experienced in shipping abroad and they will pack accordingly. We have had very good luck with parcel post shipments of lampshades, pillows, and small pieces of furniture from Hong Kong. However, the postal system always manages to give our packages rough treatment in transit. Our shops anticipate these problems and go to special lengths to ensure problem-free shipments. They custom-build special packing boxes and line them with Styrofoam materials. Be sure your shops insure parcel post shipments for both loss and damage.

If you use a professional shipper, insist that they too pack your shipment well and insure it against loss and damage. If you are shipping items that are likely to be weather-damaged at sea, such as textiles and bronzeware, consider air freighting these items or taking them with you as part of your regular baggage allowance or pay extra to send them as *"unaccompanied baggage."*

SURVEYING YOUR ALTERNATIVES

Once you are in Hong Kong, you generally have five alternatives for shipping goods home:

- Take everything with you.

- Do your own packing and shipping through the local post office (for small packages).

- Have each shop ship your purchases.

- Arrange to have one shop consolidate all of your purchases into a single shipment.

- Hire a local shipper to make all shipping arrangements.

We have tried all of these alternatives with various results. Our normal pattern is to use a combination of methods. We take some purchases with us, especially small, expensive, and delicate items that might otherwise get damaged or stolen if shipped by alternative means. We may have a shop ship some of our items by parcel post. If our volume is large enough—at least one cubic meter—we will have most purchases consolidated into a single sea freight shipment. If the volume is much less than one cubic meter, we will either air freight our goods or take them along as unaccompanied baggage. The critical variables in making these shipping decisions are the overall volume of purchases and the value of particular items.

DOING YOUR OWN SHIPPING

Doing your own packing and shipping may be cheaper than hiring a professional, but we find it a pain to do and thus no savings in the long run. We only pack those items that go into our suitcase or accompany us on our trip home. If you must take your purchases to mail through the local post office, you will waste valuable shopping and travel time waiting in lines and trying to figure out the local rules and regulations concerning permits, packing materials, sizes, and weights. And you may not pack items as well as the professional. We do not recommend that you use this shipping alternative.

ARRANGING SHIPMENTS THROUGH SHOPS

Most major shops are skilled at shipping goods for customers. They often pack the items free of charge, unless they must build a special shipping crate, and only charge you for the actual postage or freight. If you choose to have them ship, insist on a receipt specifying that they will ship the item. Also, stress the importance of packing the item well to avoid possible damage. If they cannot insure the item against breakage or loss, do not ship through them. Invariably a version of Murphy's Law operates when shipping: **If it is not insured and has the potential to break or get lost, it will surely break or get lost!** At this point, seek some alternative means of shipping. If you are shipping only one or two items, it is best to let the shop take care of the shipping arrangements.

Some shops will also help you consolidate several purchases from other shops into a single large shipment. While some shops may be reluctant to take on this extra responsibility, other shops—especially those from which you make large purchases—may be happy to assist you. They usually have their shipper collect all your goods and pack them into a single shipment. Just ask them when purchasing large items that require professional shipping services, such as furniture or carpets, if you could include additional items in the shipment: *"I have a few other items I also need to ship home. Could I bring these to your shop and have you include them with this shipment?"* In most cases the shopkeeper will accommodate such a request.

CHOOSING A LOCAL SHIPPER

If we have several large purchases, we frequently use local shippers. We find it is much cheaper and safer to consolidate many of our separate purchases into one shipment which is well packed and insured. Sea freight charges are usually figured by volume—either by the cubic meter or a container. Air freight charges are based on a combination of size and weight. For a sea shipment there is a minimum charge—usually one cubic meter—that you will pay even if your shipment is a lesser volume. There are also port fees to be paid, a broker to get the shipment through customs, and unless your hometown is a major seaport which handles freighters, you will also pay to have your shipment trucked from the port of entry to your home. On air freight you pay for the actual amount you ship—there is no minimum charge. You can usually have it flown to the international airport nearest your home and you avoid port fees altogether. However, there will be a small Customs inspection fee.

Select air freight if the package is too large to be sent parcel post, but much smaller than the minimum of one cubic meter, and does not weigh much. Air freight is also the transportation of choice if you must have your purchase arrive right away. Sea freight is the better choice if your purchase is large and heavy and you can afford to wait several weeks for its arrival. When using air freight, we contact a well established and reliable airline. It will be most cost effective if you can use one airline, i.e., the same carrier flies between Hong Kong and your hometown. We have been very satisfied with the service provided by United Airlines. Since most air freight charges will be the same, our major concern is to find a reliable company that flies to our hometown. In the case of sea freight, we choose a local company which has an excellent reputation among expatriates for shipping goods.

It is relatively easy to get information on Hong Kong shippers. Consult the Yellow Pages under the heading *"Shipping"*. You will find numerous shippers listed, many with familiar names. However, you will be taking pot luck if you randomly choose one from such a list.

Do some quick research to determine which companies have a **reputation** for shipping excellence. If you are staying at a good hotel, ask the concierge to recommend reliable shippers. He should be able to help you. In fact, you may find a shipper located near your hotel who can assist you immediately. Outside your hotel, your best source of information will be expatriates who have experience in using local

Packing, Shipping, and Returning Home With Ease 167

shippers. Personnel at the consulate or international school know which companies are best. Contact a few expatriates and ask them for their best recommendations.

The best companies may have an expatriate handling shipping arrangements for foreigners. They speak your language and understand your needs. When using these companies, be sure you insist that your items be packed well and fully insured against loss and breakage. If you do not specify this insurance, the company has limited liability in case of problems.

Good local shippers are a god-send for international shoppers. Many will assist you in conveniently coordinating all your purchases. They free you from worrying about how to get everything back home so you can concentrate on what you do best—shop. They can save you hours and days of potential hassles in arranging your shipment. They can pick everything up at your hotel or from various shops and consolidate the goods at their office. They can hold your shipment in case you have additional items, such as furniture, being made to be included in the shipment. Furthermore, they can arrange additional shipments for you once you return home. If, for example, after returning home you decide you want another piece of furniture made in Hong Kong, a shipper can handle all the details of shipping the item from the factory to your front door. You can keep in contact with the shipper by telex, telegram, fax, or telephone. He, in effect, becomes your international life-line for conveniently purchasing items from Hong Kong.

DECIDING ON UNACCOMPANIED BAGGAGE

If you have several large purchases and plan to take your items with you rather than use local international shipping services, you should consider sending some items home as *"Unaccompanied Baggage"*. This shipping classification is less expensive than paying the normal *"Excess Baggage"* charges. Since unaccompanied baggage rates are based on weight, you can call the airline to find out how much it will cost you to ship your goods this way. Compare this rate with the cost of shipping your items by air freight or as excess baggage.

MAKING ARRANGEMENTS

When you use a shipper, be sure to examine alternative shipping arrangements and prices. The type of delivery you specify at your end can make a significant difference in the overall shipping price. If you don't specify the type of delivery you want, you may be charged the all-inclusive first-class rate. For example, if you choose door-to-door delivery, you will pay a premium to have your shipment cleared by Customs, moved through the port, transported to your door, and unpacked by local movers. On the other hand, it is cheaper for you to just have the shipment arrive at your door; do your own unpacking and carting away of the trash. You may want to pick up your shipment at the designated sea port if it's near where you live and the value and size of your shipment is small. For around $100 a local customs house broker will clear Customs and move the shipment out of the port and onto a truck for you. A day of your time may be worth more than this charge, especially if it is a large shipment.

We simply cannot over-stress the importance of finding and establishing a personal relationship with a good Hong Kong shipper who will provide you with services which may go beyond your immediate shipping needs. A good shipping contact will enable you to continue shopping in Hong Kong even after you return home!

SELECTING SERVICES

Several shipping companies can arrange for a container shipment. Check the telephone book and the Hong Kong Tourist Association for a list of forwarding agents. You might try, for example, **Michelle International Transport Co., Ltd** (Tel. 5-487617), **East Asia Shipping Ltd.** (Tel. 5-257091), **Pan Pacific Services Ltd.** (Tel. 3-6015015), **LTH International Ltd.** (Tel. 3-693424), or **Unaccompanied Baggage Ltd.** (Tel. 3-7698275). Since these companies have been recommended to us and we have not used them, we cannot vouch for how any will handle your shipment. Again, make sure you insure your shipment and get all necessary receipts and documents for claiming your shipment at home.

RETURNING HOME AND FACING CUSTOMS

When preparing to return home, be sure to pack everything well, including your most valuable items in your carry-on luggage. Wrap any breakables in plastic bubble wrap and cushion them with soft items. The hotel bellman's office can arrange for boxes, tape, and twine if you need them. There will be a small charge for the service.

It's wise to pack your purchases together in the same suitcase in case you are asked to open your luggage for customs inspection as you re-enter your country. Additional pieces of very inexpensive, durable nylon luggage can be purchased at small luggage shops in Hong Kong which can be found near all the major hotels. These can be used for packing non-breakable items such as your laundry. Also buy a luggage strap to buckle around your bags.

If you are a U.S. citizen, prepare for U.S. Customs inspection by separating all of the receipts from your purchases. Record each purchase, and file each receipt in an envelope which is placed in your carry-on luggage. Once you are on the outward-bound plane, you will be given a Customs declaration form on which you are asked to declare each purchase. Itemizing is unnecessary if your purchases total less than US$400. Total the amounts spent for major categories of goods such as jewelry, furs, clothing and accessories, electronics, and so on, including a category for miscellaneous. Then register the total amount of your purchases. This declaration will be presented for Customs inspection upon arrival and you may be asked to present your receipts as well. Be absolutely certain that no receipts are stashed in your wallet, purse, or carry-on, separate from the rest of your receipts, since finding withheld receipts may cause the inspector to initiate a search of your luggage.

Exchange all your Hong Kong currency and coins at a nearby bank, keeping out only enough for airport tips, last minute purchases, and trip souvenirs. If you are using a local shipper, make sure you have all the necessary documentation, insurance forms, and contact numbers for receiving your final shipment.

You should now be prepared to pass through U.S. Customs with little difficulty. Recent improvements have relieved the long lines and frustrations attendant upon re-entry. Wandering Customs officials may spot-check your luggage before you enter the Immigration and Customs areas and thus eliminate having to wait in line for a Customs check, depending upon the amount you spent. Avoid joining lines of non-resident Asians. These lines are invariably much slower than those for returning residents. As you pass through Immigration with your passport and Customs declaration form, the official puts your documents in either a green or red folder. If you get green, you pass through customs without inspection. If you get red, you go to an inspection line where the customs officer will ask you several questions:

- Where did you travel?

- What did you purchase abroad?

- What is the value of *item X* listed on your declaration form?

- What specific dutiable or excluded items you may have purchased but did not list on your declaration form, such as *"Do you have any watches, ivory, clothes, or jewelry you purchased abroad?"*

In addition, the officer may wish to spot-check one or two pieces of your luggage to be sure that, indeed, you have told the whole story about your purchases abroad. In extreme cases, you may be subjected to a body search.

At this point, it is important that you look neat and tidy, be honest, and respond intelligently to questions, even though you may have been flying non-stop for 14 hours. For example, when asked the purpose of your trip, do not say *"I've been on a shopping tour"* nor flash a copy of this book to indicate what you have been up to! Both responses raise questions about the success of your little shopping adventure and invite all kinds of inquiries concerning what you purchased, especially if you declare less than $400 in purchases. Respond, instead, by saying *"I've been on vacation."*

You should also dress appropriately for the occasion. Customs officials are trained to spot suspicious individuals. They are particularly keen at spotting two categories of tourists: those getting in touch with themselves through drugs, and those wearing their purchases. In the first case, long hair and shabby clothing may be a signal to give you an extensive luggage search as well as a body search—a rather demeaning encounter guaranteed to finish your trip on a low note. In the second case, if you come through Customs wearing what appears

Packing, Shipping, and Returning Home With Ease

to be a new tailored suit, lots of jewelry, and an expensive watch, you also will very likely get an extensive luggage and/or body search.

Our advice is to **be honest and document your purchases, but don't be stupid** by volunteering more information than you need to. Before arriving at Customs, put all your receipts in one envelope with an item-by-item tally on the outside of the envelope or on a separate piece of paper. Complete your Customs form on the plane. If you are assigned to the red line, hand these items to the Customs officer who will probably ask you a few questions and let you go without a hand search of your luggage. If the official does search your luggage and finds other receipts or items not listed on your form, you have some explaining to do. In short, you have a problem which could lead to a body search and a great deal of explaining and legal problems. Try to be as honest as you can. It's better to pay a little duty than to have problems with Customs.

After the Customs officer completes his inspection, he will calculate what you owe in duties should you be over your limit. If he issues you a bill for duty payment, go directly to the payment window where you can pay by cash, personal check, or at some entry points by credit card. However, credit cards are not yet accepted by customs at all entry points, so if you haven't checked ahead of time it is better to plan on paying by cash or personal check. Once you have cleared customs you are on your way. Except for whatever purchases will be arriving later and requiring another Customs inspection and possible duty payment both you and your *"treasures"* are home!

13 ENJOYING GREATER HONG KONG, MACAU, AND CHINA

Hong Kong is a wonderful place to enjoy all aspects of travel. While shopping may be your primary goal, take some time to enjoy the many pleasures of Hong Kong. These include tours, trams, restaurants, entertainment, and trips to Macau and China.

FAVORITE HONG KONG PLEASURES

Our favorite non-shopping Hong Kong activities revolve around sightseeing, restaurants, and entertainment:

- Touring the New Territories, Kowloon, and Hong Kong Island.

- Riding the tram to Victoria Peak—both during the day and at night.

- Sampling the numerous international cuisines, especially the noon buffets and *dim sum* and exquisite restaurants at night.

Enjoying Greater Hong Kong, Macau, and China

- Touring the nearby islands of Lantau, Lamma, and Cheung Chau.

- Sampling evening entertainment.

- Taking a night tour of the harbor.

- Viewing the beauty of Deep Water Bay, Aberdeen.

- Visiting Ocean Park, Happy Valley Race Track, the Middle Kingdom, and the Sung Dynasty Village.

- Taking a jetfoil or hydrofoil to Macau.

- Touring the high-tech and architecturally unique Hong Kong Bank Building.

You can engage in all of these activities on your own or through a tour group. Be sure to stop at a Hong Kong Tourist Association office to pick up literature and to ask questions about what to see and do in Hong Kong. They have many excellent brochures that outline how you can best enjoy Hong Kong on your own. The HKTA also operates its own tours, such as the "Heritage Tour" and "The Land Between Tour" which explore the New Territories. Public transportation is convenient, inexpensive, and often enjoyable. Treat yourself to the train, trams, double-decker buses, subway, ferries, jetfoils, or hydrofoils. At times the means of transportation are even more interesting and memorable than the sites they take you to!

DISCOVERING MACAU

Hong Kong is the gateway city for travel to China and Macau. Once in Hong Kong you can easily arrange short one to three-day tours to either place. If you are planning a longer visit to China, you may wish to arrange your travel plans prior to arriving in Hong Kong.

If you have at least seven days for Hong Kong, you may wish to visit the Portuguese colony of Macau, the first European settlement on mainland Asia. Located on the South China coast 40 miles from Hong Kong, Macau is a 400 year old Portuguese settlement occupying an area of six square miles. Easily accessible, it is only 45 minutes from Hong Kong by **jetfoil**; one hour by **hydrofoil, Jetcats** and **hover-ferry;** and more than one hour by **high-speed ferries.** Jetfoils leave Hong Kong for Macau every half hour. The ride itself is an interesting adventure.

Macau's population of 450,000 is mostly Chinese although about 10,000 Portuguese still reside here. Most residents live above their shops where they sell a unique mix of jewelry, antiques, birds, Portuguese porcelain, beadwork, cameras, and electronics. China is just next door. Non-stop 24-hour gambling is the magnet which draws over 5 million visitors to Macau annually.

You may wish to make a one-day trip to Macau or stay over one night. By all means avoid visiting Macau on weekends or holidays, because the local Chinese travel en masse to try their luck at gambling in Macau. Since over 15,000 people visit Macau each day from Hong Kong, the transportation is efficient and convenient. Take your passport and go to the Macau wharf just off Central District. You can also book your tickets ahead of time by using your Visa, MasterCard, of American Express card over the telephone (523-2136), through hotels and travel agents, or visit one of the computerized Ticketmate outlets at MTR stations.

Before going to Macau, you may wish to visit the Macau Tourist Information Bureau (Shun Tak Centre, 200 Connaught Road, Central, Tel. 540-8180 for information). This office will answer your questions and provide you with free maps and literature. Most Travel Agencies in Hong Kong can arrange your transportation, hotel, tours, and meals in Macau, but you do pay extra for this service and it's not necessary. Book your transportation directly at the Macau Ferry Terminal Ticketing Offices in Shun Tak Centre. Jetfoils depart every half hour and make over 100 trips every day.

Most people visit Macau to gamble or see historical sites. Shopping is **not** one of Macau's great strengths, especially compared to Hong Kong. Indeed, you will be disappointed if you visit Macau solely for shopping. Macau's shopping is more laid back; shops are smaller and more casual, the people are friendlier, and prices are cheaper on many items. Like Hong Kong, Macau is a duty-free port.

Macau does offer some good shopping and plenty of opportunities to use your bargaining skills, because in Macau you bargain for everything. Search the shops along the main streets, browse souvenir stands, search the bazaars and flea markets in the narrow streets around **St. Paul's** for *"antiques"* and treasures. One popular area for clothing is **Senate Square** near San Domingos market. Be prepared for crowds as you wander Macau's crowded, narrow streets. You can expect to pay less for goods in Macau than in Hong Kong because the overhead is much lower. Although the clothing stalls along Cinco de Outubro, Palha, and Mercadores do not accept credit cards, you may use your credit card in many jewelry and antique shops.

Most major shops are concentrated in and around Macau's major street, **Avenida Almeida Ribeiro, Avenidas D. Henrique**, and along **Mercadores, Terena, Estalangens,** and **Cinco de Outubro.** The shops sell a variety of goods but not as diverse and plentiful as in Hong Kong. Macau shopping is especially noted for antiques, clothes, crafts, gold, jewelry, and Portuguese wines. Shopping here requires a great deal of browsing and poking around, especially in antique and curio shops selling Portuguese ceramics and pottery, old parchments, ginger jars, and Chinese carvings. Beware of fake antiques from the Ming Dynasty. If you are not careful, you will pay Ming prices for yesterday's *"new antiques"*! Be especially wary of *"antiques"*. Locals suggest visitors avoid buying any gold and jewelry except from government recognized stores. Most shops around St. Pauls are tourist traps. Shopping is better in the back streets of Macau, and is good grubby fun, but finding bargains and good quality takes time. Expect to find the best buys in outlet-style shops where you'll find overruns and rejects, as well as some larger sizes.

Getting around Macau is easy since the city is so small. If you don't want to walk into town, you can catch a taxi at the ferry pier or hire a self-drive Moke. Allow the better part of the day to visit Macau. Macau is a great walking town. The streets are disorderly but you won't be lost for long. You'll find an almost living museum situation in some areas with open-fronted shops in the old style. The town is alive and real on a human scale. It's comfortable, safe, and generally friendly. Starting at the ruins of St. Paul's is a good idea since the rest of Macau is downhill from here. Wear comfortable low-heeled shoes, for many of the streets are cobblestone and the rest are rough.

Since shopping should not be your main focus in Macau, leave time to experience Macau's other attractions—historical sites, museums, gambling casinos, and restaurants. You may easily arrange a guided tour of Macau by car or van as soon as you step off the ferry. These tours will take you to the major historical sites and a few shopping areas. This is a good way to start your visit to Macau. Then at the end of your tour, ask to be dropped at one of the casinos, restaurants, or near a shopping area.

If you have been to Monte Carlo, Las Vegas, or Atlantic City, Macau's casinos may disappoint you. Nonetheless, they are the only ones around. We don't recommend throwing your money at these casinos since you probably won't get lucky. Instead, have a look around and then take your money and spend it on Macau's fine restaurants which serve excellent Portuguese food. One recommendation: **A Galera Restaurant** in the Lisboa Hotel, near the hotel's large casino. Excellent Portuguese food can be found in a very small out-of-the-way cafe called **Aluccha** (#289 Rue Do Almirante Sergio). **Fernando**, on South Island; it's excellent for Portuguese family-style dining. The Macau Tourist Bureau can provide you with lists of other restaurants.

The food in Macau is interesting and varied, with a preponderance of Chinese, Portuguese, and Macanese dishes. We think the breads of Macau are the best we've had in Asia. Lots of little restaurants provide good food for little money.

Hotels

While it is easy to see all of the most interesting sights in Macau in one day, you may want to stay one night in Macau in order to get some respite from the faster pace of Hong Kong.

Accommodations and food can cost 50 percent less than in Hong Kong. Hotel selection is limited in Macau and since each offers such bargains we recommend that you choose one of the better ones. The alternatives aren't very appealing to Western tastes. We like the **Mandarin Oriental** (H.K. Tel. 548-7676) because of its location, luxury, and wonderful service. Situated on the beach only a short 5 minute walk from the ferry pier its rooms overlook either the South China Sea or the town. Macau's most unusual hotel is the small but deluxe **Pousada De Sao Tiago** (HK Tel. 521-7413) on the site of the historic fortress of St. James. **The Hyatt Regency** (HK Tel. 559-0168) offers resort-like accommodations on Taipa island just south of downtown Macau.

JOURNEYING INTO CHINA

Trips into China from Hong Kong are more involved and less convenient than arranging a day or overnight trip to Macau. While more mysterious, China is not as much fun as Hong Kong or Macau, especially if you enjoy shopping, gambling, night life, and good restaurants—the usual decadent capitalist habits China normally frowns on! Most quality shopping in China is confined to Friendship Stores, factory shops, or hotel shopping arcades. Each are designed primarily for tourists and diplomats and emphasize Chinese arts and crafts which are produced for export. These shops are full of interesting Chinese goods which may or may not appeal to your particular tastes. Indeed, if you visit the Chinese Arts & Crafts stores in Hong Kong, you will get an excellent sampling of what you can expect to see in China.

Shopping in **Friendship Stores** may be convenient, but after visiting a few of these places, you quickly lose your interest in shopping. The same goods are repeated; it is difficult to find unique items; many items are overpriced; and there is little adventure in the shopping process.

We do not recommend going into China, especially the nearby city of Guangzhou (Canton), primarily to shop. If you are seeking quality, China will disappoint you. Go to China to see the country and its people. The food is at best mediocre, service is shoddy and often rude, entertainment is either nonexistent or uninteresting with few exceptions, and much of China is overpriced for foreigners. Unfortunately, as China modernizes, it produces a great deal of cheap junk for the export and tourist markets—similar in quality to what Japan and Hong Kong produced in the 1950s. Most items produced for internal consumption will not interest you except for their novelty and as examples of 1950s items produced today! In another 10 years China may be of greater interest, comfort, and convenience for travel and shopping.

You will probably have no interest in buying **clothes** since they are not stylish for most other cultures. Chinese clothes are primarily functional; they have a decided drab and baggy look. Buy them only if you want a *"China look"* or find yourself without sufficient warm clothes in cold weather. They may make good work or hunting clothes back home.

If you are interested in silk blouses, do keep your eyes open for Chinese silk fabric. The Chinese **silk** is ideal for blouses, and it is very inexpensive in China. In Guangzhou, for example, you can buy silk from as little as US$4 per meter. If you can find nice designs and appropriate colors, buy the silk to have your blouses made in Hong Kong or back home. Consider hand washing your light and medium colored silk yardage with a mild shampoo and hanging it to dry before taking it to your Hong Kong tailor so that the resulting garment can be hand-washed rather than dry-cleaned.

Chinese **arts and crafts** also are good buys in China. You may acquire a taste for the beautiful Chinese cloisonne items which are in all Chinese Friendship Stores. Chinese scrolls, fans, paintings, prints, silk and wool carpets, lapis figures, cinnabar boxes and bracelets, stone carvings, jewelry, calligraphy and artist supplies, cut-paper ornaments, chops and red ink, and embroidery also are excellent buys. Embroidered linen and cotton table linens are much less expensive than in Hong Kong. Be sure to take your table measurements with you. Medium and large hand-painted paper fans with lacquered wood struts are inexpensive and make elegant home decorations.

The first class hotels in Guangzhou have shipping offices conveniently located in the shopping arcades and will arrange shipping of your wrapped purchases or will wrap and crate your purchases for you. Some of the shops which cater to foreigners will also crate and ship. We have successfully shipped items from 4-foot fans to large rugs which took six to eight weeks to reach the U.S. west coast; an east coast shipment might have taken another week or two. Shops welcome credit cards, even when used for a bargained price.

Getting into China from Hong Kong is relatively easy. While it is possible to travel on your own, we recommend taking a tour from Hong Kong because of the inevitable language and bureaucratic problems you will encounter in China. In most cases tourists travel to China with an organized tour which is coordinated through the official **China Travel Service Ltd. (CTS).** CTS has two locations in Hong Kong: 77 Queens Road (2nd floor), Central (Tel 525-2284) and 27 Nathan Road (1st floor), Tsimshatsui (Tel. 721-1331). If you did not make reservations through your hometown travel agency and decide to visit China after arrival in Hong Kong, you should visit these offices for information on various tour options. They have brochures listing different tours to a variety of Chinese cities. You can book your tour directly through this office. The tours are all inclusive—transportation, accommodations, food, transfers, and tour guide. All you need is your passport and luggage; CTS more or less arranges everything else with its counterpart organization in China—the China International Travel Service. Visas are required to visit China and can be arranged before you leave home. Temporary visas may be issued in Hong Kong for short visits into China. You will need two 2x2" passport photos.

Several Hong Kong travel agents also offer tours into China. However, these tours are more expensive than booking directly through CTS. The quality of the tour will probably be the same since the travel agencies in Hong Kong also arrange their tours through CTS. The major difference is that the travel agent sends its own guide along with the group. CTS still organizes the tour and coordinates the group with local guides. You may be able to save a significant amount on a tour by booking it directly through CTS. Be sure to ask for a tour with an English-speaking guide.

The best China shopping is in **Shanghai**, especially at the Shanghai Industrial Exhibition (Sino-Soviet People's Friendship building), the Shanghai Friendship Store (on the Bund), and among the numerous shops lining both sides of the incredibly crowded Nanjiing Road (just off the Bund west of the Peace Hotel). The best Friendship Store is in **Beijing**. But you need more than a few days to visit these cities.

For further information about shops, get a copy of Roberta Stalberg's *Shopping in China: Arts, Crafts & The Unusual* (China Books & Periodicals, Inc.). The book is available in the United States and Hong Kong.

If you'd like to visit China and have limited time, you may choose a one to three-day trip to **Guangzhou** (Canton). This is one of China's largest cities (5.5 million people) located only 75 miles from Hong Kong in the Pearl River estuary. A drab and somewhat ugly city, it is a good introduction to a highly westernized Chinese city. If your primary aim is to shop, visit the Friendship Store and the shopping arcades in the White Swan Hotel and a few other first-class hotels. If you are in Guangzhou during the spring and autumn Chinese Export Commodities Fair (April 15 to May 5 and October 15 to November 5), be sure to visit the retail shops at the fairgrounds. You will also find a few department stores, factories, and antique shops in Guangzhou.

Although you will be shown what the Chinese want you to see in Guangzhou, it is possible to walk around the city to explore the old shops, markets, and neighborhoods. Unless you speak Cantonese, the language barrier prevents most people from exploring as freely as in Hong Kong. Nevertheless, the people are very interested in foreigners and will try to communicate through various means. A big smile, a hearty laugh, and a talent for mime are very helpful. The Chinese children love receiving gifts from tourists; the favorite is a ballpoint pen, so we carry a pocketful of pens when we visit.

There are several nice western style hotels in Guangzhou. Your tour guide has many options of unusual sights for your group, such as a commune; a jade, embroidery, or porcelain factory; a school or kindergarten; government buildings and memorials; various mosques, temples, and pagodas; markets; the zoo; and the most interesting countryside. Here you will see water buffalo pulling the farmer's simple plow, and village after village of picturesque farm communities.

The Friendship Store in Guangzhou stocks the usual tourist souvenirs including calligraphy supplies, cut-paper ornaments, silk robes and pajamas, cashmere sweaters in slightly old-fashioned styles, chops and red ink, and Panda T-shirts. Shopping in the hotel arcades can yield some interesting items such as table linens, fabrics, and scrolls. Shopping in other areas of the city can be tough since officially you must pay with tourist currency which can be used only in the factory shops, Friendship Stores, and hotels. The government discourages tourists from getting access to their official national currency.

RETURNING TO PARADISE

When you return to Hong Kong from Macau or China, you will be returning to one of the world's greatest shopping paradises. Macau and China have some things to offer international shoppers, but they have little to compare to the shopping diversity, volume, styles, and excitement of Hong Kong.

Hong Kong is a unique city where you can literally *"shop 'til you drop."* You can buy stylish clothes, acquire the latest technology, marvel at the amazing commercial architecture, and pamper yourself in deluxe and first-class hotels and restaurants. Few other cities in the world can offer you such opportunities. What it lacks is a well preserved history for tourists who enjoy seeing relics of the past. For exotic, commercial Hong Kong rushes you into the future at an exciting pace to confirm that it may, indeed, be a *"borrowed place living on borrowed time!"*

PART V

APPENDICES

A CUSTOM TAILORING

Tailoring can be one of the great shopping rewards of Hong Kong—if you know what you are doing. As we noted in Chapter Eight, there are many myths about tailoring that first-time visitors bring with them to Hong Kong. It's only after making tailoring mistakes they begin to recognize the realities of tailoring. This need not happen to you. You should be prepared to make the best tailoring choices possible.

CHOICES GALORE

Tailor shops in Hong Kong are truly exotic places. Whether a tiny hole in the wall on the 9th floor or a large modern establishment in a deluxe hotel, the tailor shop will be lined with dozens of shelves displaying hundreds of bolts of beautiful wool, cashmere, silk, and blends. And if this selection isn't enough, the salesman will bring out swatch books from which to choose. You first select a fabric from all these options. Your fabric choices will be greater for business suits and trousers than for sports jackets. You won't find a large stock of tweeds and herringbone jacket fabrics or heavyweight coating fabrics.

PLAN YOUR TAILORING NEEDS

Before choosing a fabric, you need to decide what type of garment you want made. If you don't know, you may be overwhelmed by the sheer profusion of choices which await you in the shop, and you probably will make poor decisions.

Avoid impulsively purchasing tailoring services just because it seems to be *"the thing to do"* when shopping in Hong Kong. Many men and women get carried away in these shops and end up ordering more garments than planned. It's better to plan your purchases by first surveying your closet at home and then go into a tailor shop knowing exactly what you need. Time spent planning your tailor order will save you valuable time and frustration.

MEN'S TAILORING CONCERNS

If you wear a tuxedo even once or twice a year, consider having one custom-made in Hong Kong. A tuxedo complete with cummerbund and shirt can be tailor-made for around US$250 and up. Two and three-piece suits will range upwards from US$250, depending upon the price of the fabric, your size, and the quality of the tailoring. Perfectly fitting trousers will cost from US$75.

Adding several extra inside jacket pockets which suit your personal needs is one of the real advantages of custom tailoring. You may have a breast pocket on each side, a pencil pocket, even an inside pocket for business cards.

Order two pairs of trousers for each jacket. Once your tailor has one pair of trousers finished and properly fit, it's easy to order additional pairs to be ready in a few days. If you have trousers made from a variety of fabric types be sure to try on each pair since the fabric can influence the fit.

WOMEN'S TAILORING ISSUES

Custom-tailoring for women is another matter. We have never been entirely satisfied with the styling of women's tailoring except for classic business suits. The fabric selection is essentially the same as for

Appendix A: Custom Tailoring

men—mostly menswear woolens or Ultrasuede. Since most customers are men, Hong Kong tailors are very good in making menswear.

Women's tailored garments are also beautifully made but not always stylish, especially today when we are more concerned with semi-fitted and unstructured garments. Women's suits usually fit snugly and lack the flair and styling which is available in the beautiful and fashionable garments done in ready-to-wear. However, if you need a classic business suit which is rather formal, and if you will take the time and effort to communicate your style preferences to your tailor, then you may be pleased with the tailoring process. You are most likely to get the styling you want if you can take an actual example of the garment you want with you and show it to the shopkeeper—indicating what it is you like about the garment's style or fit. It may also be a good idea to leave the garment for the salesperson to show to the person who will be actually tailoring your clothing. Most tailor shops will have several racks of sample garments in standard styles but will make whatever style you want.

We expect that the shortcomings in producing wonderful stylish suits for women in Hong Kong will soon be corrected. Fashionable women are making their needs known and astute tailors are working to accommodate them. Several tailor shops now focus on women's fashions and stock many beautiful and feminine fabrics. More will appear in the near future.

Lack of good communication is the major culprit in failing to receive a fabulous woman's garment. The tailor shop which you visit is only the salesroom. Either the salesman or a fitter, whose English may not be adequate, will take your measurements and style instructions. Then he will take the fabric to the workroom which is usually in a separate location. He will translate what you said, in Chinese, to the cutter who will, in turn, tell the men who sew the garment what to do. You will never have direct contact with a tailor.

Women's garments usually will have self-covered buttons which you can replace when you return home if you don't care for them. But don't ask for fancy buttons because Asian tailors do not have them. Better still, if you know the items and colors you want, take buttons with you.

BEWARE OF ULTRASUEDE

Tailors in Hong Kong have cornered the Asian market on Ultrasuede, which is a registered trademark for a polyester pseudo-suede fabric made in Japan for Skinner Fabrics. There is a great deal of fake *"Ultrasuede"* in Hong Kong which seems like the real thing until you wash it or have it dry cleaned. The fakes get stiff and do not look nearly as good. Visit fabric shops back home to acquaint yourself with Ultrasuede fabrics. When in a Hong Kong tailor shop, ask to see the Skinner Ultrasuede label on the bolt.

TAILORING SKILLS AND CUSTOMER SATISFACTION

Like any skills, you will find a large range of tailoring skills in Hong Kong. U.S. tailors tend to be critical of Asian tailors because they are often asked to remake garments which were butchered by inept and careless workers. Since the U.S. tailor seldom sees the truly superb workmanship and fit which comes out of the best tailor shops in Hong Kong, they have an understandably biased opinion. We will also find poor tailors at home. Overall, you can expect to find several tailor shops that will produce garments which surpass the best of the off-the-rack suits, garments which rival the best of Savile Row in London.

Some customer dissatisfaction of this inferior work is caused not by lack of tailoring skill, but by the customer putting unreasonable demands on the tailor. Many customers, for example, want their garments completed within 48 hours. Since it takes time to produce quality tailored garments, please allow your tailor plenty of time. If you don't have the time, don't have tailoring done. We recommend giving a tailor no less than five days to complete a suit, and longer if you have the time. But insist upon at least three fittings. Stress the importance of having the garment completed no later than the day before you leave town so that any adjustments can be made without being forced into a frantic 6am fitting before you catch a 9am flight!

If the tailor's workshop crew is pressed for time by several big orders while they are working on yours, your salesman may try to convince you to allow them to mail your garments to you. If at all possible avoid doing this because:

Appendix A: Custom Tailoring

- The tailor may include an inadequate amount for shipping charges. In the United States, you will probably be billed through UPS or the Postal Service for additional shipping or postal charges to deliver the goods from the U.S. port of entry to your home.

- You may be required to pay more duty to your Customs service for tailoring shipped home than you would if the garments accompanied you in your luggage. U.S. duty on clothing may be as high as 35% of the purchase price!

- You will not have a final fitting in the presence of your tailor once the garment is finished. If it still does not fit correctly, you will have to pay for alterations at home.

These problems can usually be avoided by following our advice: allow five days for the tailoring and refuse to pay for a garment which isn't completed and properly fitted before you leave Hong Kong.

CHOOSING A TAILOR SHOP

Identifying the right tailor shop for you requires essentially the same procedure as choosing any other shop whether at home or in an exotic locale. Start collecting the recommendations of friends and then visit the shop.

Since tailoring will take the longest amount of time, finding a good tailor shop should be your first priority. Take your collection of shop names and addresses gathered from contacts at home and abroad, map out your route, and shop for your tailor. You will save considerable time if you choose a tailor shop in or near your hotel.

Each tailor shop will have racks of completed sample garments. Carefully examine these garments to determine the quality of materials used and the level of tailoring expertise. Begin by checking the general appearance of each garment including topstitching, buttonholes and button quality, smoothness of darts, and pocket application. Hand sewing is one mark of quality custom tailoring. Turn up the collar and examine the underside for the slightly uneven hand stitches which indicate that it was partly hand sewn. Check the lining to see that good quality materials were used which match the color of the fashion fabric.

Bemberg rayon is the fabric of choice for lining; do not accept nylon. The sleeve lining should be secured in the armseye with small stitches to assure its durability. A nice extra is a patch of fashion fabric sewn to the lining at the underarm of the jacket, inside the hem in the back of the trousers, and inside the crotch area to reduce wear. Check the way hems are finished. Check women's jackets and coats to see that the chest area is not excessively form fitted with darts which create an *"iron maiden"* bosom. Asian tailors usually fit such garments to women with the buttons buttoned. When we wear them unbuttoned and loose, a couple of extra unflattering bumps are created across the chest.

Next, go to the rack where other customers' unfinished garments are waiting for first or second fittings. Take this opportunity to examine the inside construction of several tailored garments to see how well each garment is constructed. Firm interfacing should be used inside the upper part of jackets and coats and inside the lapels and collar to give support and shape to the garment. Many tailors now use fusible interfacing to save time instead of using the more supple woven interfacing which must be hand-sewn into place. Fusible interfacing is fine when used in a limited way, but the exclusive use of fusible rather than woven interfacing results in stiff garments. More supple garments are created when the tailor takes the time to hand stitch woven interfacing into the lapel, collar, chest, and shoulder areas of a garment. If you squeeze the lapel of a suit interfaced with a fusible, you can feel the stiffness. Fusible interfacing should never be used with cashmere or other very soft woolens.

Check the pattern match of the fabric at the center back seam, center front, hemline, at the side seams of trousers, and at the forward edge of the collar. The pattern should never be off even a bit at these points.

Most Hong Kong tailors put a full lining in suit jackets. This has an advantage over the half-lining of some ready-made. It extends the wear of the garment, helps it shed wrinkles better, and makes it easier to slip on and off. Consider lining your trousers to just below the knee to prevent the fashion fabric from bagging in the seat and knees. A good tailor will sew in a patch of the fashion fabric over the crotch seam of trousers to prevent wear.

Appendix A: Custom Tailoring

FINDING APPROPRIATE FABRICS

When choosing the most appropriate fabric for your tailored garment, you should consider:

- **Style of garment.** Firm fabrics for suits, trousers, blazers, straight skirts. Soft and supple fabrics for gathered skirts, unstructured jackets, and dresses.

- **Climate and season of the year.** Heavy woolens for winter and cooler weather; light tropical weight woolens for year-round wear except in very hot climates.

- **Occasion.** Rough tweeds for sportswear; smooth woolens for business suits; satin lapel for formal occasions.

Select the best quality of fabric you can afford. The best suits are usually made of natural fabrics.

As you select fabrics, keep in mind what each fabric is made of and how it will wear. The major fabrics consist of:

TYPES OF FABRICS

- **Wool.** A fabric made from the fleece of sheep, goats, and llama. A major characteristic of wool fabrics is its tendency to shed wrinkles. It can be woven into many different textures and can be blended with other fibers such as silk, cotton, cashmere, or polyester. Wool has excellent insulating properties and sheds dirt. It must be dry cleaned and requires pressing to set creases and is resilient, that is, it springs back into shape. Woolen fabrics have a somewhat fuzzy soft surface and do not shine from wear. Woolens are good for jackets and coats but rarely chosen for trousers.

- **Worsted wool.** This is made from wool yarns which are combed to remove the short fibers. The resulting fabric has a smooth, compact, hard surface which wears well and resists felting at points of wear. It is usually chosen for suits and trousers.

- **Cashmere.** The wool of the cashmere goat is noted for its softness. One of the luxury fibers, it is usually blended with sheep wool to reduce the cost of the finished fabric and to improve its wearing ability. Cashmere is used for jackets and coats.

- **Gabardine.** This is a strong fabric with a twill weave which creates a recognizable diagonal rib. It can be made of any fiber (wool, cotton, rayon, etc.) and is most often used for trousers and skirts.

- **Herringbone.** This type of twill weave forms "V"s in the weave pattern. Suits and jackets are made of this fabric.

- **Flannel.** A soft fabric of wool or cotton with a brushed surface and usually used for sports jackets and casual slacks.

- **Knits.** These fabrics are not appropriate for tailoring and are unavailable in tailor shops. We see very few knits in Hong Kong except those used in sweaters.

- **Silk.** This luxury fiber is made into many types of fabric. It is an absorbent, luxurious, and lustrous fabric which resists mildew and moths. It will stain and watermark and is weakened by perspiration. Hence, silk is generally unsuitable for linings and inappropriate for wearing in extremely hot and humid climates. Some silk fabrics are appropriate for tailored jackets and suits, but it is more frequently blended with wool or cotton to add luster to these fabrics.

- **Cotton.** This is a fabric made by spinning and weaving the fibers of the cotton plant to produce a cool, comfortable, and strong garment. Cotton will wrinkle easily unless treated and therefore is not used much in tailoring. Cotton and polyester blends may sometimes be found which will make highly satisfactory summer suits. Look for a blend of 65% cotton and 35% polyester.

Appendix A: Custom Tailoring

Consult your local library or fabric store for more detailed information about fabrics. Spend some time reading clothing labels to become familiar with the fabrics which designers choose for various types of garments. If you are planning to have tailored garments made in Hong Kong, spend time familiarizing yourself with the best of the off-the-rack suits back home.

SPECIFYING THE RIGHT STYLE

The particular lines and features of a garment form its style or type. Menswear has three basic silhouettes for suits:

- **The American Silhouette** is derived from the Brooks Brothers *"sack"* suit of the '50s. Cut straight and full with lightly padded natural shoulders, a center rear vent, and medium armholes, it is body concealing and conservative.

- **The European Cut Silhouette** is sleeker and features a more dramatic fit around the chest and hips with padded shoulders, high armholes, narrow lapels, and a generally slim line which looks best on smaller men.

- **The British Silhouette**, often call the Updated American model, has slightly padded shoulders, nipped in the waist, two deep rear side vents, and cuffed and pleated trousers. The jacket pockets are angled and flapped.

Any silhouette can be double or single breasted or have two or three buttons, and details can be changed to suit your taste. Since there are presently many variations in styles of men's suits, it would be wise to spend time browsing and trying on a variety of suit styles back home, before you travel, in order to familiarize yourself with current styles and what looks best on you.

Women's styles change so frequently that we won't attempt to give much advice beyond a few cautions and recommendations. Our major cautions are:

1. **Be prepared with photos of what you want.** The sample garments in tailor shops are frequently behind current

fashion trends at home, and if you are not prepared to resist, you may settle for less than what's best for you.

2. **Don't let yourself be swayed by fashion advice from a salesman in a tailor shop.** He doesn't know your lifestyle, tastes, and needs. Look upon him as the person who takes your order for what you want and who acts as your representative in the shop. He can show you fabrics, explain what the workshop can and cannot do, determine the price, and set up appointments. He is not an image consultant!

Follow these cautions with a few recommendations on improving your sensitivity to styles and image:

1. **Spend several hours in a store** trying on various styles, taking length measurements, and making notes on what looks good on you.

2. **Buy an Image Map and work through it.** Trace the *"best bets"*, cut photo examples of each best bet from pattern catalogs, and take the resulting collection with you when you place your tailor order. You can get this map—***Styles to Flatter Your Figure***—by writing to Jan Larkey, 126 Hawthorne St., Pittsburgh, PA 15218 (send $9.95, which includes postage and handling) or call 412/731-8558 (Visa or MasterCard orders).

3. **Seek the advice of a local image consultant** who can help you choose appropriate style lines for your body. Our favorite is Color 1. Call their toll-free number to get the name and address of the consultant nearest you: 1-800/523-8496. Alternatively, read the Color 1 book, ***Color Wonderful*** (Bantam).

4. **Study current fashion magazines to learn what's new.** Try *Vogue, Glamour,* and *W*.

5. Read *Clothes Sense* by Barbara Weiland and Leslie Wood, (a Palmer, Pletsch publication available in fabric

Appendix A: Custom Tailoring 193

stores). It's a no-nonsense approach to clothing selection and wardrobe management.

COMMUNICATING WITH TAILORS

Since you will be communicating with the salesman who uses English as a second language, your verbal descriptions may not be understood accurately. As a result, you may become frustrated when you discover at the first fitting that the garment is not what you envisioned.

One of the best ways to clarify your ideas is to take a picture of the garment with you to the tailor. If you also can tell him some styling specifics, that would help, too. Rather than just say *"I want a business suit,"* tell the salesman all the styling details you want—the silhouette, lapel width and style, snugness of fit, number and placement of vents, size of trouser pleats, cuffs, leg width, and number of buttons. He will also be able to show you sample and line drawings of the shops' standard styles from which to choose. Many people take a favorite garment to be copied. We have been quite satisfied with men's sports coats copied from an old favorite. However, let the tailor make trousers to fit rather than copying old ones. You will find these fit better through the seat and thighs.

Women should go to Hong Kong tailors with photographs and measurements to clearly communicate their preferences. Search fashion magazines and pattern books for the styles you want to have made up and take these photos with you. Don't bother taking a pattern because they probably won't use it anyway. You can buy slightly outdated pattern books from your local fabric stores for $2 and up. Use these sources for design photos. Do some pre-shopping at home. Set aside half a day to do some *"dressing room research"* into which current styles look best on you. Actually try on garments such as you might want to have made and record the details. Take a retractable tape measure to the store with you to measure the length of the jackets and skirts which are flattering as well as the width around the hem. This accurate information will be extremely helpful in the tailor shop as you place orders for garments which you will actually enjoy wearing. Without specific pre-planning, it is so easy to be swayed by an aggressive salesperson. Know what you want and be specific.

You will not be expected to give the tailor your body measurements. Once you have placed your order the fitter will be called in to take your measurements. Women should wear slacks when ordering slacks since measurements will be taken with your clothes on. The fitter will give your measurements and the fabric you have selected to his tailoring workroom where the garment will be cut and temporarily sewn together. It should be ready for your first fitting the following day. At the first fitting, the fitter will have you try on the garment, will mark the adjustments needed, and will return the garment to the workroom for sewing. This is your opportunity to make any style changes. At your second fitting a day or two later, your garment will have the look of the final garment, although it may still have chalk marks and basting threads. Final adjustments are indicated and the final work takes place. If the garment is satisfactory, you may be able to make full payment and take it with you. If not, it will go back to the workroom once more.

At each fitting you should focus all your attention upon this garment and indicate any changes early in the construction. As construction progresses, it becomes more and more difficult to make changes. Take control; don't keep quiet but voice your opinion in order to have the best chance of success.

AVOID HASTE

Tailoring is seldom completed overnight. Be sure to allow four to five days for your tailoring to be completed—longer if possible. When you place your order the salesman will ask when you are leaving town because he wants all the time possible for his tailors to complete their work. Arrange to have the suit completed the day before you leave in order to allow time for last-minute alterations. We have had some bad experiences with taking delivery of garments late the night before our flight home and having a poorly fitting suit which must be reworked overnight. Haste nearly always results in dissatisfaction. If you do not have at least four days for tailoring, then you are better off having your tailoring done at home.

EXPECTED COSTS

Yes, you can save money on tailoring done in Hong Kong. While you can get garments tailored cheaply in Hong Kong, remember that good

Appendix A: Custom Tailoring

quality costs money. Better still, quality tailored garments will last a long time and you will enjoy them more than cheap ones. Our advice: pay extra to have good quality tailoring done. Expect, for example, a good custom-tailored suit (women's or men's) in Hong Kong, using quality materials and expert tailoring skills, to start at US$350-400, compared to US$700 and up back home. Expect to get an outstanding quality suit in the $400 to $500 range from our recommended tailors. Yes, there are tailor shops that charge less, but don't expect top quality fabrics or tailoring. Even in Hong Kong you get what you pay for.

Dresses costing $400 or more back home can be designed and cut in Hong Kong for around $250. Blouses going for $250 or more back home can be designed and cut in Hong Kong for $125.

Among the advantages of custom-tailoring are the many choices of fabric, color, style, and good fit. The disadvantages are that you won't know exactly what the garment will look like until it is finished, and the ordering and fitting process eats up a lot of your vacation time.

Tailors aren't dressmakers. The skills mastered by the tailor are different from those of a dressmaker. While we have seen some satisfactory dresses and blouses which were made by a tailor shop, they tend to cost about the same as those made by dressmakers at home.

Why should you go to the trouble of having tailoring done in Hong Kong when you can buy ready-to-wear? Clothing which is custom-tailored by careful craftsmen may yield the first garment you have ever worn which actually fits properly. And although you can achieve the same results at home, you will pay more and spend much more time if you are having several garments made. The work done overseas can be finished in a few days and save you hundreds of dollars while you are enjoying a wonderful vacation in one of the world's most interesting places.

GETTING A GOOD FIT

Ready-to-wear garments are made to fit a standard size body. Unfortunately, most bodies are not standard, whatever that is. We have asymmetrical bodies which don't always fit into those off-the-rack clothes. One hip may be higher than another or one shoulder lower than the other. Each of these figure irregularities will alter the fit of clothing. The results are unsightly folds and creases, fabric straining across a too-tight area or bunching where there's too much fabric, hems which hike up, collars too tight, slacks which are baggy—all signs of a poor-fitting garment. Minor alterations can compensate for figure irregularities for some people, but others will be much more satisfied with custom-made garments.

Most people get dressed and then view themselves from the waist up, neglecting to check the full-length and rear view. *"Just okay"* seems to be the standard. Mediocrity reigns, especially regarding fit in clothing. But a good fit is critical when one desires to be well dressed. For many people this is the main reason to have garments custom-tailored.

While it isn't your job to create the perfect fit, it is your responsibility to recognize a good fit and to see that the tailor attends to the fitting. When you try on your garment, the tailor will pull and pat it into place as you stand erect (and somewhat stiffly self-conscious) in front of the mirror. Examine your full-length reflection front and rear. Starting at the neckline, look for these tailoring points:

FITTING CONSIDERATIONS

- Does the collar hug your neck, fitting snugly against the base of your shirt? A common ready-to-wear problem is a collar which rides away from the neck, sitting too low or standing away from the collar.

- The jacket should hang comfortably from your shoulders with the top of the sleeve seam crossing your shoulder over the end of your shoulder bone. The should seam should bisect your shoulder, lying neither too far back nor too far forward, nor should the seam be crooked.

- Think of your shoulders as a hanger. Your garments should fit through the shoulders and hang from them, skimming your body but not hugging it.

- Accept no garment which hikes up in front, back or on the side.

Appendix A: Custom Tailoring

- If you have a low shoulder, ask the tailor to put in extra padding to level out the shoulder line. This will also create a straighter hemline. In fact, most major fitting adjustments will be made in the shoulders of a jacket, coat or dress, and at the waist and hips of slacks.

- Watch for gaping or pulling at the neckline.

- Watch for horizontal ridges of fabric across the shoulder blade indicating a too-tight upper sleeve or diagonal folds across the shoulder blades which indicate that adjustments need to be made for sloping shoulders.

- See that the jacket hem does not hike up and out at center back. Corrections for this problem are made at the neck/shoulder line, not at the hemline.

- Your jacket should button comfortably without causing the fabric to pull around the waistline.

- Insist on a trouser waistband which is comfortable when you sit as well as when you stand. If the fabric bunches into a roll just below the waistband, the hips are too tight.

- Slacks for men and women should skim the body, not hug it, for a perfect fit.

- The crotch fit is critical and causes the main problems in fitting trousers. When improperly fit, the fabric across the back of the legs will hang, creating big U-shaped drapes of material. When the fit is correct, the fabric of trousers will fall straight from the buttocks without causing unsightly wrinkles down the leg.

Before you travel make it a point to become familiar with these fitting points by checking the fit of several of your own garments and also by observing the tailored garments worn by people around you. Once you are in a tailor shop, check the fit by using a three-way mirror or ask the tailor to hold up a mirror so you can see your rear view without twisting your body and craning your neck.

CUSTOM-MADE SHIRTS

The price for custom-made shirts in Hong Kong is just about the same as you would pay for ready-made shirts at home and about one-third of the cost of custom-made. You'll pay around US$40-50 in Hong Kong for a custom-made shirt as opposed to US$85 and up back home. The difference between custom-made and ready-made is that they will fit you better, you can choose your color and fabrics, and you can add all the styling details you want. If your body is at all unusual (extra long arms or torso, quite heavy, smaller than standard sizing) or you desire unusual styling, then custom-made shirts are for you. If it's easy for you to find ready-made shirts with an acceptable fit at home, don't bother with custom-made because of the tailoring time and the room they take in your suitcase.

Custom-tailored shirts are made to your measurements. Your body measurements are taken and the shirt is contoured to fit your body without gaping or binding. You select the collar style and width, shirt style, pocket type, and fabric.

Semi-custom fitted shirts are like buying ready-made ones except you have more options. You may choose the collar and pocket style, body shaping and the color. The shirt is then made up according to your neck and arm measurements. They won't cost as much as custom-tailored shirts, nor will they fit as well.

With either type of tailoring, you can have your pocket or cuff monogrammed.

B THE SHOPS

Because of the rapidly changing economy in Hong Kong with its escalating rental tariffs, shops are relocating and closing too fast for us to provide you with an accurate address list. This list serves only as a starting point. Take a few minutes each day to phone the more important shops (refer to your hotel phone book) which you plan to visit the next day to verify their existence and their current address. Making an appointment may ensure that you receive better service.

ARTS AND ANTIQUES

Hong Kong Island

Altfield Fine Arts
1 Hollywood Rd. (Central)
Maps and prints, furniture, carpets, books.

Altfield Gallery
38 Hollywood Rd. (Central)
Carpets, 18th-19th c. Chinese furniture, Jim Thompson upholstery fabric.

Amparo Antique Co.
2/F Union Commercial Bldg.
12-16 Lyndhurst Terrace
(Central)
Porcelain, jade, furniture.

Antique Mart
11 Hollywood Rd. (Central)
Japanese kimonos.

Asian Collector Gallery
19-27 Wyndham St. (Central)
Prints, maps, engravings, and lithographs.

Banyan Tree Ltd.
214/F Prince's Bldg. (Central)
Carpets, furniture, home
decor, rattan, bamboo,
fossilized coral & stone,
carved doors.

Brian Seed Antiques
48 Stanley Village Rd.
(Stanley)
Unusual items, old brass,
nautical antiques.

C.P. Ching
21 Hollywood Rd. (Central)
Japanese textiles, lacquer,
decorative pieces.

Cheung Po Chai Antique
87 Hollywood Rd. (Central)
Furniture and works of art.

Gallery 69 Ltd.
1/F Landmark (Central)
Chinese and Korean furniture,
art, decor.

Hanart Gallery
40 Hollywood Rd. (Central)
Chinese paintings.

Honeychurch Antiques
29 Hollywood Rd. (Central)
Furniture, antique English
silver, folk art, books, prints,
maps, other decorative items.

I-Wita Antiques
35 Hollywood Rd. (Central)
Chinese furniture and scrolls.

Ian McLean Antiques
73 Wyndham St. (Central)
Chinese furniture, paintings.

Kander's Arts & Antiques
56A-58 Hollywood Rd.
(Central)
Ceramics, porcelain,
paintings, calligraphy

L'Extreme Orient
159 Hollywood Rd. (Central)
Antiques & decorative items.

**Martin Fung Antiques &
Furniture Co.**
Cat Street Galleries 1/F
38 Lok Ku Rd. (Central)
Blackwood chairs, pottery.

Monsoon
37 Hollywood Rd. (Central)
Porcelain, Japanese and
Chinese textiles.

Nin Fung Curios
31-33 Hollywood Rd. (Central)
Lacquerware, furniture,
porcelain.

Noble House Antiques
32 Hollywood Rd. (Central)
Furniture, panels.

P.C. Lu & Sons Ltd.
Mandarin Hotel, M9-11
(Central)
Jade, bronze, ivory, porcelain,
cloisonne works of art.

Appendix B: The Shops

Silk Road
20 Hollywood Rd. (Central)
Japanese antiques.

Schoeni
27 Hollywood Rd. (Central)
Furniture, porcelain, cloisonne, screens, carvings, pottery.

T. Y. King & Sons Ltd.
Room 8, Central Arcade, Swire House (Central)
Ceramics, bronzes.

Tai Sing Co.
22 Wyndham St. and 122 Hollywood Rd. (Central)
Porcelain, furniture.

Teresa Coleman Fine Arts.
7/F SeaBird House, 22-28 Wyndham St. (Central)
Textiles, robes, paintings.

Tribal Arts & Crafts
41 Wyndham St. and
66 Admiralty Centre (Central)
Tribal rugs, crafts.

Tsi Ku Chai Co., Ltd.
1/F South China Building, 1-3 Wyndham St. (Central)
Old books, paintings, calligraphy.

Yue Po Chai Antique Co.
132-36 Hollywood Rd. (Central)
Folding screens & porcelains.

Kowloon

Arts of China
106 Hong Kong Hotel Arcade (Tsimshatsui)
Snuff bottles, works of art.

Charlotte Horstmann & Gerald Godfrey Ltd.
104 Ocean Terminal (Tsimshatsui)
Porcelain, jade, ceramics, sculpture, furniture, art.

Eileen Kershaw
W-5, Peninsula Hotel Arcade (Tsimshatsui)
Fine arts, ceramics, porcelain.

Gallery 69 Ltd.
Shop 031 Ocean Terminal
Korean chests, art, decorative items.

Jade House
1-D Mody Rd. (Tsimshatsui)
Snuff bottles, jade.

L'Extreme Orient
R124 Regent Hotel Arcade (Tsimshatsui)
Jade, silver, decorative items.

P.C. Lu & Sons Ltd.
G/F Peninsula Hotel Arcade (Tsimshatsui)
Jade, bronze, porcelain, cloisonne, works of art.

Robert Chang
124 Waglan Gallery, Deck 1,
Ocean Terminal (Tsimshatsui)
Porcelain, bronzes, jewelry.

Wing Hing Co.
L1-71 New World Centre, 18
Salisbury Rd. (Tsimshatsui)
Bamboo and wood carvings,
snuff bottles, glass, jade,
scholars articles.

Yung Feng Arts
Mirador Mansion, 1A Mody
Rd. (Tsimshatsui)
Embroidery, beads.

CAMERAS

Brilliant Photo & Audio
17 Carnarvon Rd.
(Tsimshatsui)

Francisco Camera Company
53 Nathan Rd. (Tsimshatsui)

Mark's Photo Supplies
20 Des Voeux Rd. (Central)

Nelson Audio & Photo Sup.
1 Humphrey's Ave.
(Tsimshatsui)

CARPETS AND RUGS

Banyan Tree Ltd. (dhurries)
223 Edinburgh Tower
The Landmark (Central)

Chinese Carpet Centre
3016 Hong Kong Hotel
Arcade (Tsimshatsui)
2164 & 2178 Ocean Terminal

Carpet House
Shop 24 & Shop 1, Level 1
New World Centre
(Tsimshatsui)

Chinese Rugs Co.
L1-77 New World Centre
(Tsimshatsui)

Eastern Rug Co.
3 Blenheim Ave.
(Tsimshatsui)

Haiking Rug Co.
22 Hanoi Rd. (Tsimshatsui)

Oriental Carpets Gallery
34 Wyndham St. (Central)

Oriental Carpet Trading House
31B Wyndham St. (Central)

Persian Carpets Centre
30 Wyndham St. (Central)

Royal Rug Co.
49A Carnarvon Rd.
(Tsimshatsui)

Tai Ping Carpet Salon
Hutchison House
10 Harcourt Rd. (Central)

Tai Ping Carpets Factory
Lot 1637 Ting Kok Rd.
Tai Po (New Territories)
Tel. 0-6565161, Miss Cindy Ho. Call ahead to arrange an appointment. Sales in November and April.

CHINA & PORCELAIN

Craig's
St. George's Building
2 Ice House St. (Central); and
G21 Kowloon Hotel

Eileen Kershaw
Peninsula Hotel Arcade
(Tsimshatsui)

Hunter's
122 Ocean Terminal and
Peninsula Hotel Arcade
(Tsimshatsui)

Overjoy Porcelain Factory
10-18 Chun Pin St., 1/F.
Block A-B
Kwai Hing Industrial Bldg.
Kwai Chung (New Territories)

Town House
116C Ocean Terminal
(Tsimshatsui)

COMPUTERWARE

Look for computer related products in several major centers around Hong Kong. The extensive selection and competitive prices in Hong Kong's computer stores should satisfy everyone.

Computer Center: Several computer shops are located on the lower ground floor of **Silvercord**, 30 Canton Road (Tsimshatsui). Among them are:

- **Dodwell Computer Store**
- **Jardine Marketing Services Ltd.**

Golden Arcade Shopping Centre
146-152 Fuk Wah St.
(Sham Sui Po, Kowloon)

Peninsula Centre Basement Computer Centre
67 Mody Rd.
(Tsimshatsui East)

Vincent Computer Centre
8/F, Kee Shing Centre
(Tsimshatsui) and
22-26 Austin Ave.
(Tsimshatsui)

Dodwell Computer Store
The Landmark
Des Voeux Rd. (Central)

FABRIC, YARN, AND SEWING NOTIONS

Cloth Alley (Wing On Street)
West of Central Market
between Des Voeux and
Queen's Rd. (Central)

Crown's Department Store
Central Building #15 (Central)
B117 Holiday Inn Arcade
50 Nathan Rd. (Tsimshatsui)

Design Thai
Peninsula Hotel Arcade
(Tsimshatsui)

Fantasia Yarn Co.
Man Yee Building UG/24
Queen's Rd. (Central)

Four Seasons
Kaiser Estates Phase III, 6/F
10 Man Lok Street
(Hung Hom, Kowloon)
Hung Hom

Hang Kong Woolen
3/F, 30-32 Cameron Rd.
(Tsimshatsui)

Kayamally Ltd.
22 Queen's Road, Mezz.
(Central)

Maiwo, Yang & Co.
1 Duddell St.
(Central)

Old Peking Silk Co. Ltd.
Rm. 505-506
Heng Ngai Jewellery Centre
4 Hok Yuen St. (Tsimshatsui)

Tung Ying (yarn)
100 Nathan Road, G/21
(Tsimshatsui)

FURNITURE

Banyan Tree
238 Trinity Ct., Canton Rd.
304-5 Ocean Galleries
(Tsimshatsui)

Carlton Woodcraft Manufacturing
2/F Kelford Mansion
168 Hollywood Rd. (Central)

Chak Sam & Co.
Shop 32, 2nd Floor
Silvercord (Tsimshatsui)

Chung Tai Furniture
5 Hanoi Road (Tsimshatsui)

Dragonwood Furniture Co.
3024 Omni The HongKong Hotel Arcade

Dynasty Arts & Crafts Co.
AA & A5 Sheraton Hotel
(Tsimshatsui)

Appendix B: The Shops

**Evergreen Furniture
& Decoration Co.**
25/F Gee Hang Hong Centre,
65 Wong Chuk Hand Rd.
(Central)

Harrison Furniture Co.
68 Canton Rd. (Tsimshatsui)

**House Arts Beautiful
Furniture Co.**
A-2 Sheraton Hotel
(Tsimshatsui)

Luk's Furniture Co.
G/F-3/F
Aberdeen Harbour Mansion
(Aberdeen)

Maitland-Smith Ltd.
4th Floor Wyler Centre
200 Tai Lin Pai Rd.
Kwai Chung (New Territories)

Majestic Furniture Co.
5, New World Centre
Shopping Mall (Tsimshatsui)

Yin Yin Woodcrafts
3264 Ocean Terminal
Harbour City (Tsimshatsui)

FURS

Canada Fur Store
150 Ocean Terminal
(Tsimshatsui)

Deep Winter Fur Co.
37 Chatham Rd.
(Tsimshatsui)

Grand Fur Trading Co. Ltd
10A Humphreys Ave. 1/F
(Tsimshatsui)
(entrance in back of tiny
watch shop)

Jindo
308, 3/F World Finance
Centre, Harbour City
(Tsimshatsui)

Ottawa Fur
1A Carnarvon Rd.
(Tsimshatsui)

Siberian Fur Store
21 Chatham Rd. South
(Tsimshatsui) and
29 Des Voeux Rd. (Central)

Universal Furs
45 Chatham Rd.
(Tsimshatsui)

GEMS AND JEWELLRY

(also see JADE and PEARL
categories)

Hong Kong Island

Golay Buchel & Co.
1503 Hang Chong Building
5 Queen's Rd. (Central)

Jade Creations
G/F Land Crawford House
(Central)

Kai-yin Lo
M6, Mandarin Oriental Hotel
(Central)
Pacific Place (Central)

Kevin
22 Hilton Hotel Arcade
(Central)

K. S. Sze & Sons Ltd.
Mandarin Hotel Arcade
(Central)

**Lane Crawford
Department Store**
70 Queen's Rd. (Central)

Larry Jewellry
G49-50 Edinburgh Tower
The Landmark
Des Voeux Rd. (Central)

Les Must de Cartier
Prince's Building
14 Chater Rd. (Central)

Kowloon

Albert Jewellry
Room 148 Ocean Terminal
(Tsimshatsui)

Amos Jewelry Co.
1/F, Royal Garden Hotel
69 Mody Rd.
(Tsimshatsui East)

Anju
41 Man Yue Street
(Hung Hom)
Factory and salesroom.

Cartier Boutique
Empire Centre
(Tsimshatsui East) and
Peninsula Hotel (Tsimshatsui)

China Handicraft Co.
21 Lock Rd., 1/F.
(Tsimshatsui)

China Watch Co.
1G Mody Rd. (Tsimshatsui)

Crown Jade Factory
Houston Centre Room 1311
63 Mody Rd.
(Tsimshatsui East)

Falconer Jewellry
Peninsula Hotel (Tsimshatsui)

Frank & Co.
M-3 Holiday Inn Golden
Mile Arcade
50 Nathan Rd. (Tsimshatsui)

House of Shen
Peninsula Hotel (Tsimshatsui)

Kai-yin Lo
BE 11, The Peninsula Hotel
(Tsimshatsui)

Kevin Jewellry
G5-6 Holiday Inn Golden Mile
50 Nathan Rd. (Tsimshatsui)

Appendix B: The Shops

King Fook Gold & Jewellry Co., Ltd.
Miramar Hotel Arcade
118-130 Nathan Rd.
(Tsimshatsui)

Larry Jewellry
33 Nathan Rd.
(Tsimshatsui)

Marco Jewellry
GF Shop 39 Hyatt Regency Hotel Arcade (Tsimshatsui)

Om-International (pearls)
6 Carnarvon Rd., 1/F
(Tsimshatsui)

Opal Creations
Burlington House
Block B4, 6/F
92 Nathan Rd. (Tsimshatsui)

Peter Jewellery Co.
41 Peking Rd.
(Tsimshatsui)

Rio Pearls
3/F, 39 Mody Rd.
(Tsimshatsui)

Shing On Ivory Factory
G58-60 Tsimshatsui Centre
66 Mody Rd.
(Tsimshatsui East)

Tse Sui Leun Jewellry Co.
30 Man Yue St. (Hung Hom)
Factory and salesroom.

Whittle Jewellry & Watch
18A Star House, G/F
Salisbury Rd. at Star Ferry

Yung Feng Arts
Mirador Mansion
1A Mody Rd. (Tsimshatsui)

HANDICRAFTS

Amazing Grace Elephant Company
Excelsior Hotel Lobby
(Central)

Amazing Grace Elephant Company
238 Lamma Gallery
Ocean Terminal (Tsimshatsui)

Amazing Grace Elephant Company Warehouse
Yeu Shing Industrial Bldg. 2/F
4 Kin Fung St.
Tuen Mun (New Territories)
Telephone 0-838156 for free shuttle bus.

Banyan Tree
Prince's Building
14 Chater Rd. (Central)

Chinese Arts and Crafts (H.K.) Ltd. (China Products)
Silvercord (Tsimshatsui),
Star House (Tsimshatsui),
233 Nathan Rd. (Tsimshatsui), New World Centre (Tsimshatsui East), Hong Kong

Convention and Exhibition
Center (Wanchai)

Chung Kiu (China products)
528 Nathan Rd. (Tsimshatsui)

Mountain Folkcraft
239B Lantao Gallery
Ocean Terminal (Tsimshatsui)
and 12 Wo On Lane (Central)

Ria
255 Lantao Gallery
Ocean Terminal (Tsimshatsui)

Yue Hwa (China products)
54 Nathan Rd. (Tsimshatsui)
301 Nathan Rd. (main store)

JADE

China Handicraft Co.
21 Lock Rd., 1/F
(Tsimshatsui)

Crown Jade Factory
Room 1311 Houston Centre
63 Mody Rd.
(Tsimshatsui East)

Hong Kong Jade Centre
AR 328
Miramar Hotel (Tsimshatsui)

Hong Kong Jade Traders
6B Carnarvon Rd.
(Tsimshatsui)

Imperial Jade Co.
15 Carnarvon Rd. G/F
(Tsimshatsui)

Jade Market.
Kansu & Reclamation Streets
(Tsimshatsui)
Near MTR Jordan Rd. exit.
10-3 daily. Open air market
for trinket jade.

Lane Crawford Ltd.
64-70 Queen's Rd. (Central)

New Asia Co.
8 E. Humphrey's Ave.
(Tsimshatsui)

LEATHERGOODS

Hong Kong Island

Cassini
G/24, The Landmark
Des Voeux Rd. (Central)

Cellni
The Landmark
Des Voeux Rd. (Central)

Dickson & Co.
128-131 Melbourne Plaza
(Central)

Etienne Aigner
Matsuzakaya Department
Store (Causeway Bay)

Appendix B: The Shops

Fendi
G/1 Hankow Centre (Central)

Great Wall Leather Goods Co.
G/F 16 Lyndhurst Rd.
(Central)

Gucci
G/1, Gloucester Tower
The Landmark (Central)

Hermes Boutique
G14A, Gloucester Tower
The Landmark (Central)

Loewe
Gloucester Tower
The Landmark (Central)
Matsuzakaya Department
Store (Causeway Bay)

Louis Vuitton
G/14, The Landmark
Des Voeux Rd. (Central)

Man Yee Building
Queen's Rd. and
Des Voeux Rd. (Central)

Kowloon

Celine
56 Nathan Rd. (Tsimshatsui)

Chanel
E-11, Peninsula Hotel Arcade
(Tsimshatsui)

Eelskin House
Room 313, Hankow Centre
5-15 Hankow Rd.
(Tsimshatsui)

Etienne Aigner
Regent Hotel (Tsimshatsui)

Gofuku Leather Goods Centre
UG/1-2, Energy Plaza
92 Granville Rd.
(Tsimshatsui East)

Lee Kee
Ocean Terminal (Tsimshatsui)

Peninsula Hotel Shopping Arcade
34 Kimberley Rd.
(Tsimshatsui)
- **Chanel**
- **Gucci**
- **Hermes**
- **Lancel**
- **Leonard**
- **Loewe**
- **Louis Vuitton**
- **Salvatore Ferragammo**
- **Bruno Magli**

OPTICAL GOODS

Chinese Optical Co.
209 World Wide Plaza
19 Des Voeux Rd. (Central)

Cony Optical
4D Carnarvon Rd.
(Tsimshatsui)

Mandarin Optical Co., Ltd.
51 Queen's Rd. (Central)

The Optical Shop
12 Star House (Tsimshatsui)
112 Ocean Terminal
(Tsimshatsui)
Edinburgh Tower (Central)
And many other locations
around Hong Kong

Victoria Optical Co.
M/F, Peninsula Hotel
West Wing (Tsimshatsui)

PEARLS

Hong Kong Island

Amerex
Tak Shing House #702
20 Des Voeux Rd. (Central)

Concorde Pearls & Gems
48 Des Voeux Rd. 11/F
(Central)

Golay Buchel & Co.
Hang Chong Building
Room 1503
5 Queen's Rd. (Central)

Herald International
Wing On Life Building, #800
22 Des Voeux Rd. (Central)

South Sea Pearl
Trading Ltd.
Prince's Building, Chater Rd.
(Central)

Kowloon

China Handicrafts
21 Lock Road, (Tsimshatsui)

Harry's
34 Cameron Rd., 7/F
(Tsimshatsui)

Om-International
6 Carnarvon Rd., 1/F
(Tsimshatsui)

Rio Pearl
39 Mody Rd., 3/F
(Tsimshatsui)

Trio Pearl Co. Ltd.
Peninsula Hotel Arcade
(Tsimshatsui)

READY-TO-WEAR CLOTHING

Hong Kong Island

Alfred Dunhill
Regal Meridien Hotel
(Tsimshatsui East)
Peninsula Hotel (Tsimshatsui)

Boutique Bazaar
Peninsula Hotel (Tsimshatsui)

Appendix B: The Shops

Caradeuc
Crocodile House, 14/F
50 Connaught Rd. (Central)

Catherine Boutique
Regent Hotel (Tsimshatsui)

CaVa (outlet)
1726 Star House
Salisbury Rd. (Tsimshatsui)

Chanel
EII, Peninsula Hotel Arcade
(Tsimshatsui)

Charles Jourdan
New Henry House, 8C Des Voeux Rd. (Central)

China Wall
309 Heng Mgai Jewelry Bldg.
4 Hok Yuen Road
Hung Hom

Christian Dior
Peninsula Hotel Arcade
(Tsimshatsui)
Kowloon Hotel (Tsimshatsui)

Daks
Prince's Building, Chater Rd.
(Central)

D'Urban
New World Centre, Ocean Centre, Ocean Terminal, Harbour City, Intercontinental Plaza (Tsimshatsui)

Diane Freis
Shop 223, L2, Phase 1,
Pacific Place, 88 Queensway
(Central)
Shop 56 Tsimshatsui Centre
(Tsimshatsui East)
Shop 271, Ocean Galleries,
Harbour City (Tsimshatsui)
Shop 259D Ocean Terminal
(Tsimshatsui)
Shop UG25, Prince's Bldg.
(Central)
Shop 109-110 Lobby, The Regent Hotel Arcade
(Tsimshatsui)
Unit G20, The Hyatt Regency Hotel Shopping Arcade,
(Tsimshatsui)
Factory Outlet:
A1, 10/F, Phase 1, Kaiser Estates (Hung Hom)

Dorfit (sweater outlet)
Rm. 1101, 11/F.
Sands Building
17 Hankow Rd. (Tsimshatsui)

Dragonseed (menswear)
2-6 Granville Rd.
(Tsimshatsui)

Esprit
Auto Plaza, 65 Mody Rd.
(Tsimshatsui East)
88 Hing Fat St.
(Causeway Bay)

Esti Tahina
G/F Star House (Tsimshatsui)

Geis & Tijan International (outlet)
12/F, Taurus Building, 21A-B Granville Rd. (Tsimshatsui)

Giorgio Armani
Mandarin Hotel Arcade (Central)

Image Creation
259 Ocean Terminal (Tsimshatsui)

Isetan of Japan
Sheraton Hotel Arcade
Salisbury Rd. (Tsimshatsui)

Italtrade (outlet)
915 Star House (Tsimshatsui)

Jennie/Nova Monde (outlet)
503 Cheony Sun Building, 52 Wellington St. (Tsimshatsui)

Jenny Lewis
ME2, Peninsula Hotel Arcade (Tsimshatsui)

Joseph Ho
Hong Kong Hotel, 3 Canton Rd. (Tsimshatsui)

The Landmark
Des Voeux Rd. (Central)
- **Boutique Bazaar**
- **Christian Dior**
- **Claude Montana**
- **Catherine Boutique**
- **Hugo**
- **Jaeger**
- **Joyce Boutique**
- **Krizia**
- **Romano**
- **Yves Saint Laurent**
- **Ungaro Boutique**

Lane Crawford Ltd.
64-70 Queen's Rd. (Central)

Lim Ying Ying (outlet)
11/F, Hang Tung Industrial Bldg. (Central)

Michel Rene (menswear)
86 Nathan Rd. (Tsimshatsui)
Ocean Centre (Tsimshatsui)
New World Centre (Tsimshatsui)

Mosaic
203 Silvercord, 30 Canton Rd. (Tsimshatsui)

Nina Ricci Boutique
Regent Hotel (Tsimshatsui)

Oriental Pacific
(sweater outlet)
602 Sands Building
17 Hankow Rd. (Tsimshatsui)

Oriental Pacific
614 Star House, Canton Rd. (Tsimshatsui)

Pace
New World Centre (Tsimshatsui)

Appendix B: The Shops

Pedder Building
Pedder St. (Central)
- **Betu** (outlet)
- **CaVa** (outlet)
- **David Sheekwan**
- **PIE Boutique**
- **Safari** (outlet)
- **Shirt Stop** (outlet)
- **Takpac Retail** (outlet)
- **Wear House** (outlet)
- **Wintex** (outlet)

Phoebian
Room 1409, Austin Tower
22-26 Austin Ave.
(Tsimshatsui)

Promadonna
Central Building, Pedder St.
(Central)

Romea
Regent Hotel (Tsimshatsui)

Shirt Stop (outlet)
Excelsior Hotel Arcade, 518
Lockhart Rd. (Causeway Bay)

Swank Shop
Peninsula Hotel (Tsimshatsui)
Regent Hotel (Tsimshatsui)
Ocean Terminal (Tsimshatsui)

Swire House (Central)
- **Bigi Boutique**
- **Boutique Bazaar**
- **Camberley**
- **Issey Miyake**
- **Jenny Lewis**
- **Matsuda**
- **Ragence Lam Ltd**
- **Yukiko Hanai**

Takpac Retail
301 Pedder Bldg. (Central)
201 Oriental Centre at
67 Chatham Rd. South
(Tsimshatsui)

Top Knitters Ltd.
1006 Sands Building
17 Hankow Rd. (Tsimshatsui)

Trussardi Boutique
In all Japanese department
stores (Causeway Bay)

Valentino Boutique
Regent Hotel Arcade
(Tsimshatsui)

Xavier Danaud Boutique
Princes Building
Des Voeux Rd. (Central)

SHIRT-MAKERS (tailor shops also take shirt orders)

Ascot Chang Co. Ltd.
M-6 Peninsula Hotel
(Tsimshatsui)
101 Regal Meridian Hotel
(Tsimshatsui East)

David's Shirts Ltd.
108 Royal Garden Hotel
(Tsimshatsui East)
M7 Mandarin Hotel (Central)

The Custom Shop
B67 The Landmark (Central)
210 Omni The HongKong Hotel

SILVER

Craig's
St. George's Building
2 Ice House St. (Central)
341 Ocean Center (Tsimshatsui)

J.A. Windson
Prince's Building
5 Ice House Rd. (Central)
26 Lock Rd. (Tsimshatsui)

Jubilee Silver Shop
N-14, Man Yee Building
60-70 Des Voeux Rd (Central)

Langard
52 Wellington St. (Central)

S.P.H. DeSilva
K226-7 Pacific Place (Central)

Sammy Arts
9 Swire House, Charter Rd. (Central)

Town & Country
31 Queens Rd. (Central)

Wai Kee Jewellers Ltd.
G/F, Central Building
3 Pedder St. (Central)

Wang Hing Silversmith Co.
288A Harbour City (Tsimshatsui)

TAILORED CLOTHING

Hong Kong Island

A-Man Hing Cheong
Mandarin Hotel (Central)

British Textile
Hilton Hotel
20 Queen's Rd. (Central)

H. Baromon
Swire House (Central)

Ideal Tailor
137 Prince's Building (Central)

J.J. Brothers
19 Hilton Hotel
20 Queen's Rd. (Central)

Jimmy Chen & Co.
B-62 Edinburgh Tower
The Landmark (Central)

King's Fabrics
G/F D'Aguilar St. (Central)

Loa Hai Shing Co. Ltd.
(ladies only)
201 Tak Shing House
20 Des Voeux Rd. (Central)

Appendix B: The Shops

Kowloon

**Beautiful Company/
Benny Lai**
UG/38, Wing On Plaza, 62
Mody Rd. (Tsimshatsui East)

Chinese Custom Tailor
2/F, 23 Chatham Rd. South
(Tsimshatsui)

Clemo
ME8, Peninsula Hotel Arcade
(Tsimshatsui)

Fat Tai Custom Tailors
2 Hanoi Rd., 1/F
(Tsimshatsui)

Henry, the Tailor
17 Cameron Rd., 1/F
(Tsimshatsui)

Houston Custom Tailors
G10 Tsimshatsui Centre
(Tsimshatsui East)

Jimmy Chen
Hong Kong Hotel, 208 & 331
(Tsimshatsui)

Mansfields Tailoring
627A Star House
Canton Road (Tsimshatsui)

Poon Keung Workshop
#11, Haiphong Mansion, 3/F
101 Nathan Rd. (Tsimshatsui)

Princeton Custom Tailors
Mary Building, 4/F, 71-77
Peking Rd. (Tsimshatsui)

Rico & Co.
115 Royal Garden Hotel
(Tsimshatsui East)

Salon Style Ltd.
Peninsula Hotel, M10
(Tsimshatsui)

Sam's Tailor (men only)
92 Nathan Rd. (Tsimshatsui)

Soong Salon de Mode
25B Mody Rd. (Tsimshatsui)

Tak-Tak Company
RO 43, Regent Hotel Arcade
(Tsimshatsui)

Ying Tai Ltd.
MW 1-2 Peninsula Hotel
Arcade (Tsimshatsui)

W. W. Chan & Sons
Block A, 2/F
Burlington House
94 Nathan Rd. (Tsimshatsui)

SHOES AND BOOTS

Beauty Leather Goods
483 Castle Peak Rd., 1/F
(Tsimshatsui)

Bruno Magli
Peninsula Hotel Arcade
(Tsimshatsui)

Charles Jourdan
New Henry House
8C Des Voeux Rd. (Central)

Jingle Boutique
The Landmark
Des Voeux Rd. (Central)

Lane Crawford Ltd.
70 Queen's Rd. (Central)

Lee Kee Boots & Shoe Maker Ltd. (custom)
19-21 Hankow Rd.
(Tsimshatsui) and
65 Peking Rd. (Tsimshatsui)

Mak's Co. (custom)
Shop 332 Hong Kong
Hotel Arcade
3 Canton Rd. (Tsimshatsui)

Maylin Shoe Co. (custom)
ME3 Peninsula Hotel Arcade
(Tsimshatsui)

Salvatore Ferragamo
Mezzanine
Peninsula Hotel Arcade
(Tsimshatsui)

WATCHES

Benny Lau Jewelry and Watch Co.
18 Carnarvon Rd.
(Tsimshatsui)

China Watch Co.
1/F, Mody Rd. (Tsimshatsui)

Emperor Watch & Jewelry Co.
81 Nathan Rd. (Tsimshatsui)

Geneva Watch Co.
64B Nathan Rd. (Tsimshatsui)

Geneve Watch Centre
G-4, Holiday Inn Golden Mile
39C Carnarvon Rd.
(Tsimshatsui)

King Fook Gold & Jewelry Co., Ltd.
Miramar Hotel Shopping
Arcade, 118-130 Nathan Rd.
(Tsimshatsui)

Kowloon Watch Centre
Basement Arcade
Hyatt Regency Hotel,
Nathan Rd. (Tsimshatsui)

Les Must de Cartier
Peninsula Hotel Lobby
Salisbury Rd. (Tsimshatsui)

C HOTELS

The following list includes the best deluxe and first-class hotels in Hong Kong. Most are conveniently located near the major shopping centers, and many include shopping arcades. Hotels with the largest and best quality shopping arcades include the Peninsula, Regent, Marco Polo, Omni the HongKong, Omni Prince, and New World hotels in Tsimshatsui District, the Mandarin and Hilton hotels in Central District, and the Grand Hyatt Hong Kong and New World Harbour View hotels in Wanchai District. Reservations for these hotels can be made through your local travel agent or by contacting the hotel directly by mail, phone, or fax. If you arrive in Hong Kong without hotel reservations, contact the Hong Kong Hotel Association service desk in the departure hall of the Hong Kong International Airport. HKHA personnel can check to see if a vacancy is available. We recommend making reservations well in advance since many of Hong Kong's best hotels are fully booked during much of the year.

Less expensive hotels, ranging in price from $30 to $100 a night, such as the YMCA and Ritz Hotel, are also available in Hong Kong. The HKHA desk will have information on these places and can help you with reservations. However, many of these hotels are fully booked weeks in advance, so consider making your reservations prior to departure.

KEY TO RATINGS:

(M) Medium: Room tariff US$100-$180
(MH)Medium high: Room tariff US$130-$225
(H) High: Room tariff US$190-$350

KOWLOON

Tsimshatsui

Ambassador Hotel (M)
Nathan/Middle Rd.
Tel. 366-6321 or
Tel. 800/227-5663
Fax 369-0663

Empress (M)
17-19 Chatham Rd.
Tel. 366-0211 or
Tel. 800/223-9868
Fax 721-8168

Grand Hotel (M)
14 Carnarvon Rd.
Tel. 366-9331
Fax 372-37840

Holiday Inn Golden Mile (M)
46 Nathan Rd.
Tel. 3699-3111 or
Tel. 800/HOLIDAY
Fax 369-8016

Hyatt Regency (M)
67 Nathan Rd.
Tel. 311/1234 or
Tel. 800/228-9000
Fax 739-7601

Imperial Hotel (M)
30 Nathan Rd.
Tel. 366-2201
Fax 311-2360

Kowloon Hotel (M)
19 Nathan Rd.
Tel. 369-8698
Fax 369-8698

Miramar (M)
134 Nathan Rd.
Tel. 368-111
Fax 369-1788

New World Hotel (M)
22 Salisbury Rd.
Tel. 369-4111 or
Tel. 800/227-5663
Fax 369-9387

Omni The Hong Kong (M)
3 Canton Rd., Harbour City
Tel. 736-0088 or
Tel. 800/THE OMNI
Fax 736-0011

Omni Marco Polo (MH)
Canton Rd., Harbour City
Tel. 736-0888 or
Tel. 800/THE OMNI
Fax 736-0022

Appendix C: Hotels

Omni Prince (M)
Harbour City, Canton Rd.
Tel. 736-1888
Fax 736-0066

Park Hotel (M)
61-65 Chatham Rd.
Tel. 366-1371
Fax 373-97259

The Peninsula (H)
Salisbury Rd.
Tel. 366-6251
Fax 722-4170

The Regent (H)
Salisbury Rd.
Tel. 721-1211 or
Tel. 800/545-4000
Fax 739-4546

Ramada Inn Kowloon (M)
73-75 Chatham Road South
Tel. 311-1100 or
Tel. 800/262-6232
Fax 311-6000

Royal Pacific (M)
China Hong Kong City
33 Canton Rd.
Tel. 363-61188
Fax 373-61212

Tsimshatsui East

Holiday Inn Harbour View
(MH), 70 Mody Rd.
Tel. 721-5161 or
Tel. 800/HOLIDAY
Fax 369-5672

Kowloon Shangri-La (H)
64 Mody Rd.
Tel. 721-2111 or
Tel. 800/228-3000
Fax 723-8686

Nikko (H)
72 Mody Rd.
Tel. 739-111 or
Tel. 800/645-5687
Fax 311-3122

Regal Meridien (M)
71 Mody Rd.
Tel. 722/1818 or
Tel. 800/543-4300
Fax 723-6413

The Royal Garden (M)
69 Mody Rd.
Tel. 721-5215
Fax 369-9976

HONG KONG ISLAND

Central

The Mandarin Oriental (H)
5 Connaught Rd.
Tel. 522-0111 or
Tel. 800/526-6566
Fax 529-7978

Furama Kempinski (MH)
1 Connaught Rd.
Tel. 525-5111
Fax 845-9339

Hong Kong Marriott (MH)
Pacific Place
88 Queensway
Tel. 810-8366 or
Tel. 800/228-9290
Fax 845-0737

Hong Kong Hilton (H)
2 Queen's Rd.
Tel. 523-3111
Fax 845-2590

Hotel Conrad (MH)
Pacific Place
88 Queensway
Tel. 521-3838
Fax 521-3888

Island Shangri-La (H)
Pacific Place 2
88 Queensway
Tel. 877-3838
Fax 821-8742

Victoria (MH)
Shun Tak Centre
200 Connaught Rd.
Tel. 540-7228 or
Tel. 800/227-5663
Fax 858-3398

Causeway Bay

The Excelsior (M)
281 Gloucester Rd.
Tel. 894-888
Fax 895-6459

Lee Gardens (M)
33 Hysan Ave.
Tel. 895-331 or
Tel. 800/223-9868
Fax 576-9775

Park Lane Radisson (M)
310 Gloucester Rd.
Tel. 890-335 or
Tel. 800/333-3333
Fax 576-7853

Wanchai

Grand Hyatt (H)
1 Harbour Rd.
Tel. 861-1234
Fax 861-1677

New World Harbour View (MH)
1 Harbour Rd.
Tel. 866-2288
Fax 866-3388

INDEX

A

Accommodations, 79-80
Admiralty Centre, 148
Airfares, 20
Airport, 19-20, 53-57
Altfield Enterprises, 23
Altfield Gallery, 123, 125
Altfield Interiors, 126
A-Man Hing Choeng, **132**
Amazing Grace Elephant Co., 122, 157
Antiques, 119-122, 199-202
Architecture, 13
Area, 17-18, 83-87
Art, 119-122, 199-202
Arrival, 19-20, 53-58
Ascot Chang Co. Ltd., 132
Asia Computer Plaza, 138
Asian Cajun, 25-26
Associations, 27-28

B

Baggage:
    excess, 167
    retrieval, 54-55
    unaccompanied, 167
Banyan Tree, 122-123, 126
Bargaining, 98-112
Bargains, 15, 118
Bazaars, 155-156
Buses, 62
Business:
    cards, 49-50
    hours, 60

C

Calculator, 49
Cameras, 136-137, 202
Carpets, 123-124, 202-203
Cash, 36
Cat Street, 120, 156
Causeway Bay, 87, 146-147
Central District, 87, 144-145, 158-159
Charlotte Horstmann and Gerald Godfrey, 121-122, 157
Chatham Road, 142
Cheating, 70-71
Checks:
    personal, 36
    traveler's, 36
China:
    1997, 2
    tours, 12
    visiting, 177-180
China Hong Kong City, 142, 147-148, 157
China Products Company, 152
China Travel Service Ltd., 178
Chinese Arts & Crafts, 122, 131, 152
Chinese Merchandise Emporium, 153
Chung Kiu Chinese Products Emporium, 152
City character, 1-3, 11-15
Cityplaza, 149
Climate, 18-19, 45
Cloth Alley, 131-132, 156

Clothes:
    factory outlet, 133-134
    packing, 45-48
    ready-made, 133, 210-213
    styles, 191-193
    tailor-made, 132, 183-198, 214-215
Commissions, 37, 59, 70-71
Communications, 92-93
Computerware, 136-138, 203
Convenience, 68-69
Cosmetics, 136
Costs:
    accommodations, 79
    air, 20
    shopping tour, 25-27
Craig's, 127
Credit cards, 36-38
Crowds, 58, 69-70
Crystal, 126-127
Currency, 38, 58
Custom Shop, 132
Customs:
    handling, 169-171
    Hong Kong, 55
    U.S., 35, 169-171

D

Daimaru, 151
David's Shirts Ltd., 132
Delivery, 96
Department stores, 150-151
Departure tax, 55
Designers, 133
Dim sum, 75
Discounts, 102-104
Documents, 20-21
Dodwell's, 150
Duty-free, 15, 118

E

Eastern District, 147
Economy, 1, 12
Electricity, 59-60
Eileen Kershaw, 121, 127

Emporiums, 151-153
Exchange rates, 38, 56, 58-59
Exercise, 66-67
Exports, 15

F

Fabrics, 131-132, 189-191, 204
Factory outlets, 133-134, 141, 153-155
Film, 66
Food, 74-79
Food Street, 78
Friendship Stores, 177
Fur Chiba, 130
Furniture, 124-126, 204-205
Furs, 129-130, 205

G

Galerie du Monde, 120
Gambling, 174
Garments, 15
Gems, 127-129, 205-207
Glassware, 126-127
Gold, 126
Golden Arcade Shopping Centre, 138
Grand Fur, 130
Granville Road, 143, 154
GSP, 35
Guangzhou, 177-178, 179-180

H

H. Baromon, 132
Handicrafts, 207-208
Hang Kong Woolen, 132
Happy Valley, 146
Harbor, 13
Hollywood Road, 119-121, 144
Home decorative items, 119-122
Home furnishings, 126
Honeychurch Artiques, 120, 125
Hong Kong Convention and Exhibition Center, 145-146
Hong Kong Island, 18, 87, 143-147, 158-159

Index 223

Hong Kong Hotel Association, 56, 79
Hong Kong Museum of Art, 88
Hong Kong Tourist Association, 10, 23-25, 56, 114
Hotels:
    Hong Kong, 79-80, 149-150, 217-220
    Macau, 176
Hung Hom District, 154
Hunter's of Hong Kong, 127

I
Ian McLean Antiques, 121
Immigration, 54
Isetan, 151
I-Wita Antiques, 125

J
J. J. Brothers, 132
Jade, 208
Jade Market, 155
Jardine's Bazaar, 156
Jewelry, 127-129, 205-207
Jimmy Chen, 132
Jindo Fur Salon, 130
Jordan Road, 142

K
Kai-yin Lo, 128
Kaiser Estates, 141, 154
Kimberley Road, 142
Kim's Gallery, 125
Kowloon, 18, 86, 141-143, 157-158

L
Ladder Street, 120
The Landmark, 133, 145, 148, 158
Lane Crawford, 145, 150
Lanes, 155-156
Language, 64-65
Leathergoods, 131, 208-209
L'Extreme Orient, 121
Li Yuen Street, 156
Location, 17-18

Luk's Furniture Co., 125

M
Macau:
    transportation, 64
    visiting, 173-176
Maitland-Smith Limited, 125
Man Yue Street, 141
Markets:
    bargaining in, 111
    traditional, 155-156
Matsuzukaya, 151
Maxicabs, 62
Mercy Merit, 125
Minibuses, 62
Mitsukoshi, 151
Money, 35-38
Money-changers, 58-60
Mongkok, 141
Morning Calm Gallery, 125
Mountain Folkcraft, 157
MTR, 61-62

N
Nathan Road, 142, 158
Networking, 32-34, 90-91
New Territories, 18, 86
New World Harbour View Shopping Arcade, 148-149
New World Shopping Centre, 142, 148, 157
Newspapers, 28

O
Ocean Terminal/Ocean Centre/ Harbour City, 142, 147-148, 157
Optical goods, 135-136, 209-210
Outlying islands, 18, 87

P
Pacific Place, 146, 148
Packing:
    checklist, 50-52
    plan, 43-44

purchases, 163-164
Peak Tram, 63
Pearls, 210
Pedder Building, 134, 145, 154
Peninsula Hotel, 149, 157
Perfumes, 136
Personal relationships, 9
Photography, 66
Planning, 31-32
Poor Man's Nightclub, 156
Porcelain, 126-127, 203
Pottinger Street, 144
Preparation, 31-52
Pricing, 100-104
Products, 117-139

Q

Quality:
    products, 91-92
    shopping, 5-6
    shops, 89-90

R

Receipts, 41-42, 114
Regent Hotel, 149
Resources, 21-23
Restaurants, 74-79
Restrooms, 71-72
Rickshaws, 63
Rugs, 202-203

S

Safety, 66
Sales, 15, 19
Scams, 112-113
Scheduling, 33-34, 89
Seasons, 18-19
Security:
    airport, 55-56
    Hong Kong, 38-39, 66
Service:
    charges, 65-66
    quality of, 70
Sewing notions, 204
Sham Shui Po, 141

Shanghai, 179
Shippers, 164, 166-167
Shipping, 162-168
Shirts, 198, 213-214
Shoes:
    handmade, 95, 215-216
    ready-made, 134-135, 215-216
Shopkeepers, 49
Shopping:
    arcades, 149-150
    areas, 140-141
    centers, 147-149
    comparative, 40-41, 99
    culture, 2
    hotel, 149-150
    information, 39
    quality, 5-6
    rules, 96-97
    services, 25-27
    skills, 5-6
    strengths, 7
Shops:
    recommended, 9-10
    shipping, 165
Siberian Fur Store, 130
Sightseeing, 172-173
Silk, 131-132, 178
Silver, 214
Silvercord, 138
Sincere, 150
Smoking, 72-73
Sogo, 151
Stanley Market, 134, 147, 156
Stanley Village, 147
Star Ferry, 61, 142
Stereos, 136
Stylette Models, 130
Subway, 61
Swire House, 145, 158-159

T

Tacpac, 134, 154
Tai Ping Carpets, 124
Tailoring:
    costs, 184, 194-195

Index 225

    decisions, 183-198
    myths/realities, 93-95
    prices, 104
    problems, 8
Tailors, 132, 214-215
Tak-Tak Company, 132
Taxis, 56, 62-63, 64-65
Tea, 139
Televisions, 28, 136-137
Temple Street, 155-156
Temptations Asia, 26-27
Thieves Market, 156
Tipping, 65-66
Tourist services, 56-57
Tours, 8, 64, 88, 172-173
Touts, 70-71
Transportation:
    best, 160-161
    airport, 57-58
    city, 60-61
    Macau, 174
Travel:
    agents, 64
    experience, 4
Traveler's checks, 36
Tribal Arts and Crafts, 123-124
Tsimshatsui, 86, 141-143, 158
Tsimshatsui East, 86, 141, 143

U
Ultrasuede, 186

V
Victoria Peak, 13, 63
Victoria Treasures, 27
Video equipment, 136
Visas, 21

W
W. W. Chan & Sons, 132
Wah Tung China Co., 126
Wanchai, 87, 145-146
Watches, 129, 216
Water, 59
Western District, 143-144

Window-shopping, 91-92
Wing On, 150

Y
Yarn, 204
Yaumati, 141
Yellow River Furniture and Arts, 125
Yue Hwa Chinese Products Emporium, 152

IMPACT GUIDES

If not available at your local bookstore, the following "Impact Guides" can be ordered directly from the publisher. Complete the following form (or list the titles), include your name and mailing address, enclose payment, and send your order to:

IMPACT PUBLICATIONS
4580 Sunshine Court
Woodbridge, VA 22192 (USA)
Tel. 703/361-7300
FAX 703/335-9486

All prices are in U.S. dollars. Orders from individuals should be prepaid by check, moneyorder, or Visa or MasterCard number. If your order must be shipped outside the U.S., please include an additional US$1.50 per title for surface mail or the appropriate air mail rate for books weighting 20 ounces each. We accept telephone and FAX orders (credit cards), and orders are shipped within 48 hours.

Qty.	TITLES	Price	TOTAL
___	*Shopping and Traveling in Exotic Asia: Hong Kong, Thailand, Malaysia, Indonesia, & Singapore*	$16.95	_____
___	*Shopping and Traveling in Exotic Hong Kong*	$12.95	_____
___	*Shopping and Traveling in Exotic Indonesia*	$12.95	_____
___	*Shopping and Traveling in Exotic Thailand*	$12.95	_____
___	*Shopping and Traveling the Exotic Caribbean*	$13.95	_____

___ *Shopping and Traveling the Exotic Philippines*	$12.95	_____
___ *Shopping and Traveling the Exotic South Pacific: Australia, New Zealand, Papua New Guinea, Fiji, and Tahiti*	$16.95	_____
___ *Shopping in Exotic Places: Hong Kong, Korea, Thailand, Indonesia, and Singapore*	$14.95	_____
___ *Shopping in Exotic Singapore and Malaysia*	$12.95	_____
___ *Shopping in Exciting Australia and Papua New Guinea*	$13.95	_____

SUBTOTAL	$ _____
Virginia residents add 4.5% sales tax	$ _____
Shipping/handling ($3.00 for first book and $.50 for each additional book)	$ _____
TOTAL ENCLOSED ⎯⎯⎯	$ _____